302.11

COMMUNITY
DEVELOPMENT
IN SOUTH WALES

Edited by
Steve Clarke, Antonina Mendola Byatt,
Martin Hoban, Derith Powell

UNIVERSITY OF WALES PRESS / GWASG PRIFYSGOL CYMRU
CAERDYDD / CARDIFF • 2002

British Library Cataloguing-in-Publication Data.
A catalogue record for this book is available from the British Library.

ISBN 0–7083–1734–0

Cover design by Acrobat
Cover photograph by Patricia Aithie, ffotograff
Typeset at University of Wales Press
Printed in Great Britain by Dinefwr Press, Llandybïe

Contents

The Contributors

The Editors

Steve Clarke has been a lecturer in community development at the University of Wales Swansea since 1982. He is an international consultant to educational and governmental institutions, and has recently been seconded to the Secretariat for Health and Social Services, National Assembly for Wales. Prior to 1982, he worked as a community development worker in south Wales, London and South Africa.

Antonina Mendola Byatt is currently regional manager of Tai Trothwy, Gwalia Housing Group. She was previously a community development worker for Swansea Council for Voluntary Service and for the City and Council of Swansea Urban Regeneration Team in Townhill, and has worked extensively in the south Wales valleys in community arts, housing and environmental posts. She is an executive member of Community Development Cymru.

Martin Hoban is a freelance community development advisor and trainer with extensive experience in community development in Ireland, the north-east of England and the south Wales valleys. He has worked for Save the Children Fund and has played a key role in major regeneration strategies in the West End of Newcastle upon Tyne and in the Cynon valley. He is currently researching new approaches to local development in the central Valleys.

Derith Powell has a track record of community development work having been a practitioner in various settings since 1979. She became a training officer for Swansea Council for Voluntary Service before her current post as principal officer for Amman Valley Enterprise. She is also chairperson of Community Development Cymru.

Other contributors

Phil Cope is a freelance community development advisor.

Maria Finnemore is a GP-practice-based community development worker in the Gwendraeth valley.

Lyz Jones is education and training manager for Bryncynon Community Revival Strategy.

Jill Owen is a local activist and chairperson of Perthcelyn Tenants' and Residents' Association.

Hayley Thomas is a health promotion development worker for the Pembrokeshire Health Promotion Centre.

Jenny Turner is a development worker in the south Wales valleys and has a long involvement in educational and development work through her work with the Valleys' Initiative for Adult Education.

Acknowledgements

You cannot produce a book like this without imposing on many other people – exploiting their patience, talents and wisdom. In addition to those people who have had this thing put upon them as a matter of course, such as Terrie, Jethro, Rose, Richard, Mared, Ffion, Stefan, there is another list of special contributors whose insight and knowledge provided back-up and impetus to the whole project.

A special thanks, therefore, to Richard Evans, Mike Fleetwood, Ken Barker, Rachel Edwards, Jas Singh, Sue Thomas, Sarah Davies, Jan Howell, Richard Penn, Rob Bevan, Jeremy Alden, Dave Smith, Clive Grace, Kieron Hatton, Maxine Woolgar, Joanne Gossage, Combat Poverty Agency Dublin, Groundwork Merthyr and Cynon, Dave McKenna, Regional Employment Centre, Swansea Miners' Library, Testun, Menter Aman Tawe, Carol Jones, and to Terrie McCarthy, without whom there would not have been an index.

We are very grateful.

Steve Clarke, Antonina Mendola Byatt,
Martin Hoban, Derith Powell

Preface

This book is an attempt to provide a context for today's community development work. It arose out of the need to find a reference on the heritage of community development in south Wales, and the desire to compare examples of practice with other examples, as we knew that there was great diversity in the field. The terms in use are vague and confusing: community work; community development; social action; social planning; locality work; adult education and so on. We were all aware, differently, of parts of the history, and we were all in contact with current work in projects, centres and agencies across the country. There was evidence of the considerable range of activities, and the many ways in which the expression of the community manifested itself through organization, participation and protest in almost universal settings and for an unlimited number of causes.

We were very conscious that there had been nothing written about the specifically Welsh experience, and that nothing had been written in the Welsh language. We felt that it was important to rectify both of these situations, and this is what we set out to try to do. Perhaps we were too ambitious, and our original expectations and intentions have not been fully realized. We made as full an audit of the extent of community development activities in the area as we could, and trawled the field for contributions. Initial responses were very encouraging, but many on the original list of potential contributors were not, in the end, able to provide articles for inclusion. The editorial board made themselves available to activists and other grassroots workers to act as ghost writers if required, as we knew that many lacked the experience of writing, particularly an analytical account of their work. We hope that this volume will inspire others to consider entering the discussion about community development through the medium of writing, and making public the experiences of the wide variety of project and programme work that is going on.

Rhagair

Ymgais i roi cyd-destun i waith datblygu cymunedol heddiw yw'r llyfr hwn. Cododd o'r angen i ddod o hyd i gyfeirlyfr ar gynhysgaeth datblygu cymunedol yn ne Cymru, a'r awydd i gymharu ymarferiad ag enghreifftiau eraill. Gwyddem fod amrywiaeth mawr yn y maes. Mae'r termau a ddefnyddir yn amwys ac yn ddryslyd: gwaith cymunedol; datblygu cymunedol; gweithredu cymdeithasol; cynllunio cymdeithasol; gwaith cymdogaeth; addysg i oedolion, ac yn y blaen. Roeddem i gyd yn ymwybodol, mewn gwahanol ffyrdd, o rannau o'r hanes, ac roeddem mewn cysylltiad â phrosiectau, canolfannau ac asiantaethau trwy'r wlad. Roedd tystiolaeth am gryn amrywiaeth o weithgareddau ac am y ffyrdd niferus y mynegodd y gymuned ei hun trwy drefnu, cyfranogi a gwrthdystio bron ym mhob man a thros achosion di-rif.

Roeddem yn ymwybodol iawn nad ysgrifennwyd unrhyw beth ynghylch y profiad a oedd yn arbennig i Gymru nac yn y Gymraeg. Credem ei bod yn bwysig gwneud iawn am y ddwy sefyllfa hyn, a dyna oedd ein bwriad. Efallai i ni fod yn rhy uchelgeisiol, ac ni chyflawnwyd yn llawn ein disgwyliadau a'n bwriadau gwreiddiol. Gwnaethom archwiliad mor llawn â phosibl o'r gweithgareddau datblygu cymunedol yng Nghymru, a chwilio'n eang am gyfraniadau. Bu'r ymatebion ar y dechrau'n galonogol iawn ond, yn y diwedd, nid oedd sawl un ar y rhestr wreiddiol o ddarpar gyfranwyr yn gallu cyflwyno erthygl. Cynigiodd aelodau'r bwrdd golygu eu hunain i ymgyrchwyr a gweithwyr cymunedol eraill i weithredu fel rhith-awduron, pe bai angen, gan i ni wybod nad oedd gan lawer brofiad ysgrifennu, yn enwedig ysgrifennu adroddiad dadansoddol o'u gwaith. Gobeithiwn y bydd y gyfrol hon yn ysbrydoliaeth i eraill ystyried ymuno yn y drafodaeth ynghylch datblygu cymunedol trwy gyfrwng ysgrifennu, gan wneud yn hysbys brofiadau'r amrywiaeth eang o waith prosiect a rhaglen sy'n mynd ymlaen.

Gwnaethom ymdrech arbennig i ddenu cyfraniadau yn Gymraeg, ond syrthiwyd yn fyr o'n gobeithion. Mae'n edifar gennym mai'r

We made a special effort to attract writing in Welsh, but we fell far short of our hopes. We regret that the result has produced uneven representation between Welsh and English articles (four out of thirteen). We had always intended to translate summaries of all the case studies to assist immediate access to the material. We now realize that our summaries go only a small way to redress the balance. The shortage of Welsh articles reflects, we believe, two main issues, which are of concern to us. Firstly, those who work for community change – professional practitioners, activists, tenants, community leaders – are far better represented through English-language schemes, both geographically and in quantity. Secondly, many practitioners, and people generally, are inexperienced and even reluctant to express themselves in Welsh on matters of this kind. Now that we have forced the issue and exposed our own shortcomings in this department, we are sure that other worthy examples will be forthcoming and that the impetus better to record our own experiences can gather force. Despite the under-representation, this book still has something positive to say about Welsh-language documentation of community development. We hope that it may serve to widen the discussion about values, ethics, development methods and outcomes across the fullest possible range of activity within Wales. If there is a Welsh model of community development, then we hope that this may start the process of defining what it is.

Having said that, we acknowledge that this volume is not a definitive record of community development in south Wales. Nevertheless, it comes at a time when this approach to social change may be on the threshold of a new era. The establishment of the National Assembly for Wales, and the lead-in to that process, has elicited a raft of new policies and programmes, all of which, if they are to be successful, require a high-profile community development input. There is an air of great expectancy around the impact of Objective One (Structural Fund for economic development) funding from the European Union. In addition, the focus on inclusive government, the search for preventive approaches to ill health and poverty, and the desire to build collaborative mechanisms for solving the enduring problems in our society will give a huge boost to developmental approaches at all levels. We draw attention to some of these initiatives in chapter 3 below, particularly *Communities First* (National Assembly, 2000a). Here, canlyniad yw cynrychiolaeth anwastad rhwng y Gymraeg a'r Saesneg (4 allan o 13). Bu'n fwriad gennym o'r dechrau gyfieithu crynodebau o'r astudiaethau achos i gyd er mwyn cynorthwyo mynediad disyfyd i'r deunydd. Rydym yn sylweddoli erbyn hyn nad yw'n crynodebau ond yn mynd ychydig o'r ffordd i unioni'r fantol. Fe gredwn ni fod y prinder o erthyglau Cymraeg yn adlewyrchu dau brif beth sydd o bryder i ni. Yn gyntaf, mae'r rhai sy'n gweithio dros newid yn y gymuned – ymarferwyr proffesiynol, ymgyrchwyr, tenantiaid, arweinwyr cymunedau – yn cael eu cynrychioli'n fwy o lawer trwy gynlluniau Saesneg, yn ddaearyddol ac o ran nifer. Yn ail, mae llawer o ymarferwyr, a phobl yn gyffredinol, yn ddibrofiad wrth fynegi eu hunain yn Gymraeg ar faterion o'r math hwn a hyd yn oed yn anfodlon ei wneud. Nawr ein bod wedi gwthio'r mater i'r golwg a dangos ein diffygion yno, rydym yn sicr y daw enghreifftiau teilwng i'r amlwg a bydd yr ysgogiad i gofnodi ein profiadau'n well yn cael ei gryfhau. Er gwaetha'r gynrychiolaeth annigonol, mae gan y llyfr hwn o hyd rywbeth cadarnhaol i'w ddweud ynghylch cofnodi datblygu cymunedol yn Gymraeg. Gobeithiwn y bydd yn agor y drafodaeth am werthoedd, moeseg, dulliau datblygu a chanlyniadau ar draws yr ystod ehangaf posibl o weithgareddau y tu mewn i Gymru. Os oes model Cymreig o ddatblygu cymunedol, yna gobeithiwn y bydd hyn efallai'n dechrau'r broses o'i ddiffinio.

Ar ôl dweud hyn, rydym yn cydnabod nad cofnod diffiniol o ddatblygu cymunedol yn ne Cymru yw'r gyfrol hon. Serch hynny, mae'n dod ar adeg pan allai'r ymagwedd hon at newid cymdeithasol fod ar drothwy oes newydd. Mae sefydlu Cynulliad Cenedlaethol Cymru, a'r cyfnod yn arwain at hynny, wedi ysgogi peth wmbredd o bolisïau a rhaglenni newydd, y maent i gyd, os ydynt i lwyddo, yn gofyn am fewnddodiant amlwg o ran datblygu cymunedol. Mae disgwyliadau mawr ynghylch dylanwad arian Amcan Un (y Gronfa Strwythurol ar gyfer datblygu economaidd) o'r Undeb Ewropeaidd. Yn ogystal, rhoddir hwb mawr i ymagweddau datblygu ar bob lefel gan y ffocws ar lywodraeth gynhwysol, y chwilio am agweddau ataliol o ran afiechyd a thlodi, a'r awydd i adeiladu ffyrdd cydweith-rediadol o ddatrys problemau parhaus yn ein cymdeithas. Tynnir sylw at rai o'r mentrau hyn ym mhennod 3 isod, yn enwedig *Communities First* (National Assembly, 2000a). Yma, mae'r Cynulliad Cenedlaethol yn trefnu bod arian 'newydd' ar gael er mwyn hybu agwedd 'o'r gwaelod i fyny' tuag at gynllunio newid cymdeithasol, ar y cyd â'r anghenion lleol. Dim ond trwy ddefnyddio

the National Assembly is making 'new' moneys available for the generation of a 'bottom-up' approach to planning social change, in concert with local needs. This can only be achieved through using community development methods, so local government is now seeking to become competent in this approach. It might be said that, if community development ever finds itself to be 'mainstream', then we have got it all wrong. This would certainly have been the message of the 1970s and 1980s, when the struggle appeared to be mainly against the forces of the state, but now our circumstances have changed – or we hope that they have. We feel strongly that, if it is possible to test the intentions of the National Assembly, then it will be through their success in designing their strategy for community development, and realizing its benefits.

The contrast between the 'old' and the new approaches by government to planning social change is one of the more important aspects of this book. From the beginnings of state-aided community development in Wales (chapters 1 and 15), there was no coherent lead taken from the centre. Development workers were untrained, and learned by experience. This is still largely the case and this is an issue that needs to be addressed quickly. But the main point was that, whereas government funded most of what community development there was, it had no strategy for its place or purpose. This state of affairs has continued until recently, and the experiences of the grassroots workers grappling with scarce resources, isolation and lack of a consistent framework for their work are evident (chapters 5, 6, 7 and 8). Our history of community development in south Wales, even if incomplete (chapter 1), demonstrates how many opportunities emerged from situations of potential conflict, rather than being planned, anticipated and well thought-through. The policies of the National Assembly can do much to redress this negative pattern.

Another issue we address is the role and status of professional community workers and the methods employed by them. We set the scene in the first three chapters, but the ensuing collection of case material demonstrates how little consensus there is. Firstly, there is the tradition of class struggle, and the question of whether or not community development is a necessary reaction to the failure of the state to provide universal services. Despite the changes in industrial and social life, the tone of some of our contributors reflects an enduring attachment to this analysis

dulliau datblygu cymunedol y gellir cyflawni hyn, felly mae llywodraeth leol yn anelu at ddod yn alluog yn yr agwedd hon. Gellid dweud ein bod wedi cael popeth yn anghywir os ceir bod datblygu cymunedol ei hun yn rhan o'r 'brif-ffrwd'. Yn sicr dyma fuasai'r neges yn y 1970au a'r 1980au, pan oedd yn ymddangos mai yn erbyn grymoedd y wladwriaeth yr oedd y frwydr, ond erbyn hyn mae'n hamgylchiadau wedi newid – neu gobeithiwn felly. Rydym yn teimlo'n gryf, os bydd yn bosibl profi bwriadau'r Cynulliad Cenedlaethol, mai trwy ei lwyddiant mewn llunio ei strategaeth ar gyfer datblygu cymunedol y bydd hyn, a thrwy sylweddoli buddion honno.

Mae'r cyferbyniad rhwng ymagweddau 'hen' a newydd y llywodraeth at gynllunio newid cymdeithasol yn un o agweddau pwysicaf y llyfr hwn. Ers i ddatblygu cymunedol â chymorth gwladol ddechrau yng Nghymru (penodau 1 a 15), ni fu arweiniad cyson o'r canol. Roedd gweithwyr datblygu heb eu hyfforddi, ac yn gorfod dysgu trwy brofiad. I raddau helaeth mae hyn yn dal yn wir, a dyma fater y mae angen ymdrin ag ef yn gyflym. Ond y prif bwynt oedd nad oedd gan y llywodraeth, er iddi ariannu'r hyn o ddatblygu cymunedol a fu, strategaeth yn ymwneud â'i le na'i bwrpas. Ni fu newid tan yn ddiweddar, ac mae profiadau'r gweithwyr yn y gymuned yn amlwg, wrth iddynt ymgodymu ag adnoddau prin, unigedd a diffyg fframwaith cyson ar gyfer eu gwaith (penodau 5, 6, 7 a 8). Dengys ein hanes o ddatblygu cymunedol yn ne Cymru, hyd yn oed os nad yw'n gyflawn (pennod 1), faint o gyfleoedd a gododd o sefyllfaoedd o wrthdaro posibl, yn hytrach na chael eu cynllunio, eu rhag-weld a'u llawn ystyried. Gall polisïau'r Cynulliad Cenedlaethol wneud llawer i unioni'r patrwm negyddol hwn.

Pwnc arall a drafodir yw rôl a statws gweithwyr datblygu cymunedol proffesiynol a'r dulliau a ddefnyddir ganddynt. Fe'i cyflwynir yn y tair pennod cyntaf, ond dengys y casgliad canlynol o ddeunydd achos gyn lleied o gytundeb sydd. Yn gyntaf, y mae traddodiad brwydr y dosbarthiadau, a'r cwestiwn a ydyw datblygu cymunedol yn ymateb angenrheidiol i fethiant y wladwriaeth i ddarparu gwasanaethau i bawb neu beidio. Er gwaethaf y newidiadau i fywyd diwydiannol a chymdeithasol, mae cywair rhai o'n cyfranwyr yn adlewyrchu ymlyniad parhaol wrth y dadansodd-iad hwn (penodau 4, 5, 6 a 8). Tybed a fydd mewnddodiant o gymorth gwladol ar draws rhychwant eang o fywyd cymdeithasol

(chapters 4, 5, 6 and 8). Could it be that an infusion of state funding across a wide swathe of social and economic life will inspire a more American, competitive response from the communities of Wales? Instead of class struggle, the perceived need of newly developed citizens might place them in conflict with the intentions (capabilities) of government. The question of whether community development is the function of 'professionals' or is better left to activists, is discussed in chapter 2. This is challenged for a variety of reasons – from a class perspective, anxieties about manipulation and hidden agendas and so on – in the case studies (chapters 4, 5, 7 and 8). We also find that there are many gaps between the expectation of government to achieve certain pre-set objectives, and the ability of the process to achieve them (chapter 11). What we need now is more evidence to assist us in moving forward together.

Now that there are government policies on so many aspects of development in the community, some areas of coverage require much more attention than we could give them here. One of them is health and well-being (chapters 12 and 13), which will be a vehicle for many developmental initiatives under the umbrella of the new Local Health Alliances (National Assembly for Wales, 1999). Education, especially through life-long learning programmes, is another (chapter 7). The most-used rationale for community development stems from regeneration schemes. There is now a range of approaches to this question, as a number of ministries and sections of government have overlapping responsibilities in this area, including health, housing and local government, and our discussion highlights some of the important issues that will shortly emerge from these policies (chapters 4, 8, 10, 11, 12 and 13). There is an imperative in government to set targets and achieve outcomes within the short time-scale of budgeting cycles and political vision. The results and benefits of community development may take longer, and it follows that those responsible for implementing programmes that are bounded in this way will seek to impose limitations on practice that ensure compliance. We do not see this tension being resolved (see chapters 8, 15 and 17).

Planned social change is one of the expected outcomes of community development (chapters 1, 8, 10–12), and yet there are still some unresolved tensions around self-determination, the right to be different and the cause of doing things for their own sake,

ac economaidd yn ysbrydoli ymateb mwy Americanaidd a chystadleuol gan y cymunedau yng Nghymru? Yn lle brwydr y dosbarthiadau, efallai bydd angen cydnabyddedig y dinasyddion newydd ddatblygedig yn eu tynnu'n groes i fwriadau (galluoedd) y llywodraeth. Trafodir ym mhennod 2 y cwestiwn a yw datblygu cymunedol yn rhywbeth i'r rhai 'proffesiynol' neu a ddylid ei adael i ymgyrchwyr. Heriwyd hyn yn yr astudiaethau achos am nifer o resymau – o safbwynt dosbarth, gofidiau ynghylch ystrywiau ac agendâu cudd ac ati (penodau 4, 5, 7 a 8). Ceir hefyd fod llawer o fylchau rhwng disgwyliadau'r llywodraeth o ran cyflawni amcanion penodol rhagosodedig a gallu'r broses i'w cyflawni (pennod 11). Yr hyn y mae ei angen yn awr yw mwy o dystiolaeth i'n cynorthwyo i symud ymlaen gyda'n gilydd.

Gan fod polisïau'r llywodraeth erbyn hyn yn ymwneud â chymaint o agweddau ar ddatblygu yn y gymuned, mae rhai meysydd yn galw am fwy o sylw nag y gellid ei roi iddynt yma. Un o'r rheini yw iechyd a lles (penodau 12 a 13), a fydd yn faes i lawer o fentrau datblygu o dan ddylanwad y Cynghreiriau Iechyd Lleol newydd (National Assembly for Wales, 1999). Un arall yw addysg, yn enwedig trwy raglenni dysgu gydol oes (pennod 7). Mae'r sail resymegol a ddefnyddir fwyaf ar gyfer datblygu cymunedol yn deillio o gynlluniau adfywio. Mae amryw ddulliau o ymwneud â'r mater hwn erbyn hyn, oherwydd mae gan sawl gweinidogaeth a rhannau o'r llywodraeth gyfrifoldebau gorgyffyrddol yn y maes hwn, gan gynnwys iechyd, tai a llywodraeth leol, a phwysleisir gan ein trafodaeth rai o'r materion pwysig a ddaw cyn bo hir o'r polisïau hyn (penodau 4, 8, 10, 11, 12 a 13). Mewn llywodraeth, mae rheidrwydd i osod targedau a chyflawni canlyniadau o fewn graddfa amser fer y cylchdroadau cyllidebol a gweledigaeth wleidyddol. Gall canlyniadau a buddion datblygu cymunedol gymryd mwy o amser, ac felly bydd y rhai sydd â'r cyfrifoldeb dros weithredu rhaglenni o fewn terfynau o'r fath am osod cyfyngiadau ar ymarferiad sy'n sicrhau ufudd-dod. Ni welwn ni mo'r tensiwn hwn yn cael ei ddatrys (penodau 8, 15 a 17).

Mae newid cymdeithasol cynlluniedig yn un o ganlyniadau disgwyliedig datblygu cymunedol (penodau 1, 8, 10–12), ac eto y mae o hyd rai densiynau'n ymwneud â hunanbenderfyniad, yr hawl i fod yn wahanol a'r achos o wneud pethau er eu mwyn eu hun, dim ond i weld lle y gallant arwain (pennod 14). Mae datrys y tyndra rhwng 'datrys problemau' a 'datblygu bro' yn broses a gaiff ei

just to see where they lead (chapter 14). Solving the tension between 'problem-solving' and 'locality development' is a process that the new army of 'social inclusion', 'regeneration', 'tenant manager', 'anti-poverty', 'community health development' workers are going to tackle. Many of these lessons have been tested earlier and some of them are here to provide the benefit of hindsight (chapters 6, 10 and 15).

When four people, who have never worked together before and who come from completely different backgrounds, try and get their minds focused on a complex subject like community development, few would predict a successful outcome. We are pleased with the result. This volume reflects the way in which we have been able to identify our differences, manage the exchange of ideas and agree on a process for presenting the south Wales experience of community development – past and present. We initially thought that it would be easy to persuade co-workers in south Wales that it would be worthwhile and rewarding to put down their thoughts on paper for inclusion here. It proved more difficult than we had anticipated, and we would like to express our gratitude to those who persevered through our barrage of exhortations and scarcely veiled threats. Having achieved that, the heavy work then took place in gathering and, in particular, in interpreting the historical and theoretical material that went into the early chapters and the conclusion. We regret that we have not been able to cover the entire field here, but we hope that this offering will act as a spur to others. There is a need to recover the past before we lose it altogether. There is also a need to be mindful of what we are currently involved in, so that we can record and analyse it all to help future generations understand what was going on.

We initially wanted the focus of this work to be on those who are working in the field today, but their work does not exist in a vacuum. We have explored some of the most accessible aspects of the history of community development in south Wales. There have been the flagship projects and programmes – the Community Development Project and the Community Development Foundation schemes. The culture of the Valleys dominated the thinking in the early days, and the philosophy of the industrialized workers gave the lead to community development. Today, things are different: the language is new – entrepreneurial even – and expectations from the state and from the people have changed. We

thaclo gan y fyddin newydd o weithwyr 'cynhwysiad cymdeithasol', 'adfywio', 'rheoli tenantiaid', 'gwrth-dlodi', 'datblygu iechyd cymuned'. Profwyd llawer o'r gwersi hyn o'r blaen a thrafodir rhai ohonynt yma er mwyn cael budd ôl-olwg (penodau 6, 10 a 15).

Wrth i bedwar o bobl nad ydynt erioed wedi gweithio gyda'i gilydd o'r blaen ac sy'n dod o gefndiroedd cwbl wahanol geisio canolbwyntio ar bwnc cymhleth fel datblygu cymunedol, ni fyddai llawer yn rhag-weld canlyniad llwyddiannus. Rydym ni'n ymfalchïo yn y canlyniad. Mae'r gyfrol hon yn adlewyrchu'r ffordd yr ydym wedi medru adnabod ein gwahaniaethau, rheoli cyfnewid syniadau a chytuno ar broses ar gyfer cyflwyno profiad de Cymru o ddatblygu cymunedol – ddoe a heddiw. Ar y cychwyn roeddem yn meddwl y byddai'n hawdd perswadio'n cyd-weithwyr yn ne Cymru y byddai'n werth chweil ac yn fuddiol i daro eu syniadau ar bapur er mwyn eu cynnwys yma. Bu'n anos na'r disgwyl, a hoffem ddatgan ein diolchgarwch i'r rheini a ddaliodd ati er gwaethaf popeth. Ar ôl llwyddo yn hyn o beth, daeth y gwaith trwm wrth gasglu ac yn arbennig wrth ddehongli'r deunydd hanesyddol a damcaniaethol ar gyfer y penodau cynnar a'r bennod olaf. Yn anffodus nid oedd yn bosibl i ni ymdrin â'r holl faes yma, ond gobeithiwn y bydd y cynnig hwn yn gweithredu fel hwb i eraill. Mae angen adennill y gorffennol cyn i ni ei golli'n gyfan gwbl. Mae angen hefyd i ni fod yn ymwybodol o'r hyn yr ydym yn ymwneud ag ef yn y presennol, fel y gallwn ei gofnodi a'i ddadansoddi i gyd er mwyn cynorthwyo cenedlaethau'r dyfodol i ddeall yr hyn a fu.

Wrth ddechrau roeddem am i'r gwaith hwn ganolbwyntio ar y rheini sy'n gweithio yn y maes heddiw, ond ni fodola eu gwaith mewn gwagle. Rydym wedi trafod rhai o'r agweddau mwyaf hygyrch ar hanes datblygu cymunedol yn ne Cymru. Cafwyd y prosiectau a rhaglenni blaenllaw – y Prosiect Datblygu Cymunedol a'r cynlluniau Sail Datblygu Cymunedol. Diwylliant y Cymoedd a fu flaenaf yn y meddwl yn ystod y dyddiau cynnar, ac athrawiaeth y gweithwyr diwydiannol fu'r prif ddylanwad cynnar ar ddatblygu cymunedol. Heddiw mae pethau'n wahanol: mae'r iaith yn newydd – entrepreneuraidd hyd yn oed – ac mae disgwyliadau gan y wladwriaeth a chan y bobl wedi newid. Rydym wedi ceisio rhoi at ei gilydd y modd y bu i'r dylanwadau cynnar siapio gwaith heddiw. Gwelwn fod y Gymraeg yn ffactor newydd yn y maes, ac rydym yn sicr y gall y llyfr hwn roi hwb i eraill trwy dynnu sylw at arwyddocâd y gwaith hwn. Sicrhawyd bod pob disgrifiad a

have tried to piece together how these early influences have shaped today's work. We see that the Welsh language is a new factor in this arena, and we are sure that this book can give encouragement to others by drawing attention to the significance of this work. We have ensured that all the descriptions and discussions in this volume are accessible, in part, to all our readers. As a tentative experiment in bilingual presentation and design, we hope that it will encourage more interest both in the format, and in the content.

We have resolved some of our differences over questions of values, ethics, models for intervention and the measurement of outcomes (and there were many) by trying to draw attention to all the dilemmas that we encountered. This does not mean that we do not have our own ideas about what is 'true' community development, but we have left you guessing to some extent. Some of the issues remain as stubborn as before: whether 'top-down' work can ever be justified in the face of the needs of participation and empowerment; is community development a paid or an activist occupation; who makes the plans; what is the limit to 'citizen participation'; and does the piper call the tune? This conflict over values, desired outcomes, theoretical models and so on is reflected in the variety of material that our case studies include. What is obvious is that workers on the ground may aspire to values and other preconditions for their work, but they are often swept up in the pressures placed upon them by their employers, by the culture of the people that they confront in the job, and by their own frailties. In chapters 2 and 3 we show how difficult it is to tie these pressures down. We hope that our readers will make a better job of it, and that this collection and analysis will mark the beginning of a thorough debate on these issues.

We apologise for any inaccuracies, omissions or distortions of historical fact. We have attempted to keep comments about individuals to a minimum, and we hope that any such comments that remain will be viewed as necessary to the argument. There is still a history to be written about community work in south Wales, and we hope that this volume will stimulate some thinking on the subject. In fact, the more personalities that come forward, perhaps with their own versions of events and the virtues of their own methods, the easier it will be to have a proper debate.

Community development, however conditioned by local circumstances, is nevertheless heavily influenced by a worldwide pool of

thrafodaeth yn y gyfrol hon yn hygyrch, yn rhannol, i bob un o'n darllenwyr. Fel arbrawf petrus mewn cyflwyno a chynllunio dwyieithog, gobeithiwn y bydd yn ennyn mwy o ddiddordeb yn y fformat yn ogystal â'r cynnwys.

Rydym wedi datrys rhai o'n gwahaniaethau'n ymwneud â gwerthoedd, moeseg, modelau ar gyfer ymyriad a mesur canlyniadau (a bu llawer) trwy geisio tynnu sylw at yr holl ddilemâu y daethom ar eu traws. Ni olyga hyn nad oes gennym ni'n syniadau ein hun ynghylch beth yw 'gwir' ddatblygu cymunedol, ond i ryw raddau rydym wedi'ch gadael heb ateb pendant. Mae rhai o'r materion yn aros mor styfnig ag o'r blaen: a ellir byth gyfiawnhau gwaith 'o'r top i lawr' yn wyneb anghenion cyfranogi a galluogi; ai rhywbeth i ymgyrchwyr neu i rai cyflogedig yw datblygu cymunedol; pwy sy'n gwneud cynlluniau; beth yw terfyn 'cyfranogi dinasyddion'; ac ai'r pibydd sy'n dewis y dôn? Adlewyrchir y gwrthdaro hwn dros werthoedd, canlyniadau dewisol, modelau damcaniaethol ac ati yn yr amrywiaeth o ddeunydd a gynhwysir yn ein hastudiaethau achos. Yr hyn sy'n amlwg yw fod gan y gweithwyr yn y gymuned werthoedd a rhagamodau y maent am eu dwyn i'w gwaith, ond yn aml cânt eu hatal gan y pwysau a roddir arnynt gan eu cyflogwyr, gan ddiwylliant y bobl maent yn eu cyfarfod wrth eu gwaith, a chan eu gwendidau eu hun. Ym mhenodau 2 a 3 dangosir mor anodd yw diffinio'r pwysau hyn. Gobeithiwn y bydd ein darllenwyr yn gwneud yn well, ac y bydd y casgliad a'r dadansoddiad hwn yn nodi cychwyn trafodaeth drylwyr ar y materion hyn.

Ymddiheurwn am unrhyw anghywirdebau, bylchau neu wyrdroi ffeithiau hanesyddol. Ceisiwyd osgoi sylwadau am unigolion cymaint â phosibl, a gobeithiwn y gwelir bod unrhyw sylwadau o'r fath sydd ar ôl yn angenrheidiol i'r drafodaeth. Mae yna hanes i'w ysgrifennu o hyd am waith cymunedol yn ne Cymru, a gobeithiwn y bydd y gyfrol hon yn ysgogi meddwl am y pwnc. Yn wir, po fwyaf o bersonoliaethau a ddaw i'r amlwg, efallai gyda'u fersiynau eu hun o ddigwyddiadau a rhagoriaethau eu dulliau, hawsaf yn y byd fydd cael gwir drafodaeth.

Faint bynnag yr effeithir arno gan amgylchiadau lleol, dylanwedir yn drwm ar ddatblygu cymunedol gan gronfa byd-eang o brofiad, gwerthoedd a gobeithion ar gyfer y dyfodol. I gydnabod hyn, rydym yn tynnu sylw at ddulliau a syniadau sy'n ein hysbrydoli a'n cyfiawnhau wrth fabwysiadu dulliau nad ydynt bob amser

experience, values and hopes for the future. In acknowledgement of this, we are able to highlight methods and insights that inform and justify our adoption of approaches that are not necessarily home-grown. One such is an import from Africa: consciousness-raising, which is an interesting study in the migration of ideas. It was feminism, a firmly northern inspiration, that first spread the ideas of the 'personal and the political' being unified. But it was in Zimbabwe that the teachings of Paulo Freire (a Brazilian), who put consciousness-raising into a formal educational methodology, were brought together in a manual for community intervention. Now the ideas return to inform community development workers in south Wales. They form the theoretical model for Derith Powell (chapter 4); also Jenny Turner's chapter on the Valleys Initiative (chapter 5), and Lyz Jones's description of work in the Cynon valley (chapter 6) and how her ideas on community development came together.

Health and the environment feature in the chapters by Maria Finnemore (12) and Antonina Mendola Byatt (11). Maria's brief is to build community around health issues within the Healthy Communities Project based in a GP's practice. This links with Hayley Thomas's contribution (chapter 13) on the 'New Public Health' agenda. Antonina sought community control over basic environmental issues on an estate not given to much self-help in the past. Phil Cope condenses his considerable experience in Community Arts into a demonstration of how poetry can become a vehicle for change and solidarity (chapter 14).

For convenience, we have packaged some of the chapters together, and have given them brief collective introductions. Others defied inclusion in this way and so they stay, like mavericks, on their own. For those of you who like reading about community development, we hope that the bibliography will prove inspirational!

Meanwhile, we should like to thank all those who have helped us in this production, especially those who have put their work on the line for others to criticize. This is the most important step in community development – the refinement of our ideas and methods through sharing and learning from each other.

Steve Clarke, Antonina Mendola Byatt,
Martin Hoban, Derith Powell
Swansea
January 2002

yn frodorol. O Affrica y daw un o'r rheini: 'codi ymwybyddiaeth', sy'n astudiaeth ddiddorol mewn mudo syniadau. Ffeministiaeth, ysbrydoliaeth o'r gogledd yn ddiau, a ledodd gyntaf y syniadau am undod y 'personol a'r gwleidyddol'. Ond yn Simbabwe y daethpwyd ag athrawiaethau Paulo Freire (un o Frasil) – a osododd 'godi ymwybyddiaeth' i mewn i fethodoleg addysgol ffurfiol – at ei gilydd mewn llawlyfr ar gyfer ymyriad yn y gymuned. Erbyn hyn mae'r syniadau'n dychwelyd i ddylanwadu ar weithwyr datblygu cymunedol yn ne Cymru. Maent yn ffurfio'r model damcaniaethol i Derith Powell (pennod 4); hefyd, pennod Jenny Turner ar Fenter y Cymoedd (pennod 5); a disgrifiad Lyz Jones o waith yng nghwm Cynon (pennod 6) a sut y daeth ei syniadau hi ar ddatblygu cymunedol at ei gilydd.

Trafodir iechyd a'r amgylchedd ym mhenodau Maria Finnemore (pennod 12) ac Antonina Mendola Byatt (pennod 11). Cyfarwyddyd Maria yw adeiladu cymuned o gwmpas materion iechyd o fewn i'r Prosiect Cymunedau Iachus wedi'i leoli mewn practis meddyg-teulu lleol. Ceisiai Antonina reolaeth gan y gymuned dros faterion amgylcheddol sylfaenol ar stad nad oedd wedi arfer fawr o hunangymorth yn y gorffennol. Mae Phil Cope yn crynhoi ei brofiad sylweddol mewn Celfyddydau Cymunedol gan ddangos sut mae barddoniaeth yn medru dod yn gyfrwng newid a chydsafiad (pennod 14).

Er hwylustod rydym wedi pecynnu rhai o'r penodau â'i gilydd a rhoi iddynt ragymadroddion cyfunol byrion. Nid oedd hyn yn bosibl â'r lleill, ac felly maent yn aros ar eu pennau eu hun, fel rebeliaid. I'r rhai ohonoch sy'n hoffi darllen am ddatblygu cymunedol, gobeithiwn y bydd y llyfryddiaeth yn ysbrydoliaeth!

Yn y cyfamser, dymunwn ddiolch i bawb sydd wedi'n cynorthwyo gyda'r cynhyrchiad, yn enwedig y rhai sydd wedi gosod eu gwaith yn agored i'w feirniadu gan eraill. Dyma'r cam pwysicaf mewn datblygu cymunedol – cywreinio ein syniadau a'n dulliau trwy rannu a dysgu oddi wrth ein gilydd.

Steve Clarke, Antonina Mendola Byatt,
Martin Hoban, Derith Powell
Abertawe
Ionawr 2002

1 Community development work in south Wales – an introductory overview

STEVE CLARKE, ANTONINA MENDOLA BYATT, MARTIN HOBAN
and DERITH POWELL

Crynodeb

Mae'r bennod hon yn cysylltu ymarfer heddiw â chyd-destun hanesyddol datblygu cymunedol yn ne Cymru. Mae tair prif ffynhonnell i'r traddodiadau: hanes diwydiannol de Cymru ac anheddiad trefol; atgyfodiad yr iaith Gymraeg ers y 1970au cynnar gan ddod yn ffocws ar gyfer datblygu cymunedol; a thueddiadau'r llywodraeth tuag at fentrau lleol.

Mewn llawer o ardaloedd, ni lwyddodd trefnu'r gweithwyr gan yr undebau llafur a'u hymwneud â gweithgareddau adloniadol i oroesi dirywio'r diwydiannau cloddiol. Gadawodd hyn wagle enfawr yn sefydliadau cymdeithasol y trefi glofaol. Yn ne Cymru drefoledig, fodd bynnag, trefnai'r dinasyddion eu hunain yn erbyn grym a chynlluniau tra-awdurdodol yr awdurdodau lleol i ail-lunio eu cymunedau'n gorfforol. Gweithredai ymgyrchwyr a gweithwyr proffesiynol i gynhyrfu'r cymunedau, ac yna gwthiodd y rheini eu ffordd i mewn i'r broses gynllunio neu orfodi'r llywodraeth i gymryd sylw o'u barn. Bu dau fath o arbrofion gan y llywodraeth mewn prosiectau datblygu cymuned – ariannu uniongyrchol neu anuniongyrchol. Bu'r ymateb yn gymysg ond, hyd yma, ni chafwyd polisi penodol gan y llywodraeth ar gyfer datblygu cymdeithasol cymunedau yng Nghymru. Mae newidiadau diweddar mewn polisïau'r llywodraeth yn awgrymu posibilrwydd o batrwm cynhwysfawr o weithredu mewn adeiladu galluoedd lleol, cytundebau partneriaeth a chael y bobl leol i ymwneud ag atebion i faterion cymdeithasol dybryd.

Daeth yr iaith Gymraeg yn ffocws i strategaethau datblygu ar gyfer trefi bach ac ardaloedd gwledig. Gwelwyd cynnydd yn hyn o beth, ac mae'n codi cwestiynau diddorol iawn ynghylch technegau cynhyrfu cymunedau a ffactorau cymhelliad ar gyfer cymunedau'n gyffredinol, yn ogystal ag wrth hybu materion diwylliannol. Mae cymhariaethau a chysylltiadau â chymunedau Celtaidd eraill yn rhoi modelau cadarnhaol a diddorol i ni'u hystyried.

Introduction

There are unique challenges ahead in Wales over the next few years in dealing with the impact of social change, in particular the effects of new approaches to governance. This challenge is coming not only from the international and political forces that play all the time on our economy and culture, but also from the way in which social policies are being framed today. They represent a completely fresh approach to who is to be involved, how responsibilities and duties are to be allocated, and how accountability for outcomes is to be assessed. The public are to be connected to government, and there will be roles for stakeholders in completely different ways (National Assembly for Wales, 2000c and 2000d). This will have an immediate impact on the behaviour of professionals, and on the context in which they work.

These changes will affect everybody. In particular they impact upon those professionals in direct contact with the public or upon those who are planning changes in the way services are offered and the way in which decisions are made. If the constituency of involvement is to be widened, then these new methods of working will involve a far wider group of officials and non-officials adopting community development techniques and processes. This places an added duty on those who must ultimately take responsibility for changes in health, social welfare, economic restructuring and planning. They must henceforth ensure that they are conversant with the methods and underlying values and presumptions that go into implementing a participative, sustainable public-involvement structure. At no time in the development of professional expertise in the conduct of government, has there been a greater need to come to grips with the process of community development. This will affect the practice of health, economic support, planning and welfare services across all sectors – voluntary, independent and/or statutory.

We will show that, despite the good intentions, and the expenditure of a great deal of public and private resources, there is still no common agreement about exactly what community development is, how it is done and exactly what it is supposed to achieve. We hope to deal with all these issues and, at the same time, provide a detailed history of the way in which community development has made its impact on south Wales (and beyond). We will also show how we think it will develop in the future and, if the advice and predictions that are offered here are heeded, then we believe that in the future community development practitioners can get it right.

General background in the context of Wales

It is difficult to identify a date, or even a specific period of time when community development first emerged in Wales, and in south Wales in particular. As we shall see, there are many local instances of activity at the level of the community that could fit our definition, give or take one small factor or another. It is important to register that in Wales there is a rich cultural heritage of community involvement with most civic, social and economic activities. Cultural and political organizations have, together and separately, taken up the cause of community-building, and the agencies of government have moved resources and policy directives in and out of the sector as fashions and priorities changed. In some respects, Wales has followed the trends set by government and the larger voluntary organizations in the wider British context. In other areas, Wales has gone down a distinctive road of its own. We hope that we can shed some light on the history, and those features, which make the Wales experience unique. From these beginnings, present and future practitioners can appreciate something of what has gone before, and consider their own analysis of where we are going today.

Small-scale, community-building exercises emerged formally with the establishment of the independent chapel movement in the seventeenth century. Grassroots support, organized leadership, usually of the self-taught variety, sustained these spiritual and welfare institutions in the face of organized, institutional opposition. The rise of the formal usage of the Welsh language, and the spread of Methodism and the other Nonconformist churches were to make an indelible imprint on the distinctiveness of life across Wales (Morgan, D. L., 1988; Wearmouth, R. F., 1945). The dramatic impact of industrialization provoked a powerful social response to exploitation in the newly urbanizing population of the south. Political solidarity gained expression through the Chartist rising, and the eighteenth and nineteenth centuries were marked by communal riots over food, taxes and working conditions (Davies, J., 1939). In a small country, with a population of less than two million until the end of the nineteenth century, language and chapel sustained the rural communities during a period of significant social and economic change. In the urban and industrializing centres of Glamorgan and Monmouthshire, the population rose from 20 per cent of the whole in 1801 to 57 per cent by the census of 1901 (Davies, J., 1939; May, 1994). In the towns, workers' organizations, to a large extent, replaced the solidarity of the rural community. Whereas religion continued to flourish in these expanding commercial and industrial centres, the influx of large numbers of Irish and English immigrants heralded the formation of new spiritual and social loyalties. Communities had to be built from scratch from aggregates of people drawn in from many origins. Geographical settlement would now signify the boundaries of defensible space, social conflict and economic competition, as much as the old, traditional village had marked out the patterns of family networks and spiritual harmony. In addition to the economic differences from the countryside, immigration and industrialization produced significant divisions between rural and urban cultures. Two 'nations' began to emerge, which would have a decisive impact on the manner in which community development objectives would be pursued.

Self-help in the Valleys communities grew around the rise of the Miners' Welfare Society, and the trade union movement. Because of the repressive nature of labour law, many of the workers' 'combination' moves had to start out under the guise of Friendly Societies. Only in this way could their true identity escape the scrutiny of the magistrates (Brabrook, 1898). The Friendly Societies provided a working model of the power of communities to pull themselves out of dire circumstances.

Through self-help, and the great advantage taken by some 'enlightened' mine-owners of helpful legislation (the Miners Welfare Act 1921 and the Mining Industry Act 1926), the miners' welfare organizations gathered great strength and social impact as the twentieth century progressed (Ocean Area Recreation Union, 1931). A network of thriving social organizations, managed by workers, supported by the mines, and run for the welfare of those who worked deep underground, produced institutions which even today in some instances, provide a focus for the whole community. They compensated for the grimmest effects of the most brutal economic depressions and times of industrial unrest and social conflict. They have left an indelible mark on the culture of their communities – and not merely in sentiment and in the folklore.

Firstly, their determination to provide direct services, on a self-help basis, to those in most need of them, flew in the face of those who might say that self-help works for the profit of the bosses. The provision of pithead baths, healthy exercise for the young, community-building social contact, holidays and youth clubs may well add up to the 'social reproduction of capital', but without the social solidarity which emerged, the collapse of social life would have been inevitable.

Secondly, quite apart from the symbol of social and economic solidarity that these organizations represent, they demonstrate something fundamental to those who would introduce the notion of community development for the regeneration of the de-industrialized communities of the south Wales valleys. The miners' welfare clubs demonstrated without a doubt that the ordinary people could organize their thinking and resources towards socially responsible objectives. The people's organizations were, and could be, the spearhead for social planning exercises in full cooperation with agencies whose power and authority might at first glance seem to be totally alien to the workers. Before, during and after the Great Depression, the General Strike (and the miner's strike which outlasted it), through the Second World War, and into the days of nationalization, one institution symbolized the strength of the Valleys communities – the miners' welfare institute. Until the eclipse of the mines themselves, these miners' welfare organizations were unremitting in their desire to provide for the current and future needs of their members. The problem today is that their organizations are now in the same ruinous state as the post-mining communities that still crowd the shadows of the old institute buildings. In their heyday, they proved their potential for the mobilization of their members, but today the people lack the focus, the vision and the force to take the first steps. To date, those in authority have failed to divine the correct formula for sparking life once again into the process. It is the firm belief of the authors that community development, strategically planned and resourced, can deliver this impetus for change where people's organizations cannot rise spontaneously out of their own communities. As we shall see, this is not an unproblematic process, but within the south Wales area there is ample experience to draw from, and many examples to analyse for appropriate models.

The intellectual and policy climate: a view from the top

We wish to describe the general context of Welsh community development and to deal with the relevant issues in some detail. For this, we must start with a discussion of trends in community development for the UK as a whole from the 1970s onwards. We will then make the connections with the specific Welsh experience as issues emerge. We shall also introduce examples of govern-mental and other initiatives from Ireland and Scotland, whose experience may prove supportive to our task of illustrating the strengths and weaknesses of the approach in Wales.

A shorthand analysis of the changes that have gone on within community development over this period might read thus: 1970s – resistance and competition; whereas, for the 1990s we might read – cooperation and co-option. We will explain these trends and changes in some detail since, in Wales, as for the rest of the UK, the picture is very much the same.

The intellectual basis for community development has not gone through just one revolution during the period that we are studying but at least two. Professionals entering the field in Britain in the early 1970s had a limited range of choice over their theoretical framework and their practical approach to intervention. The 'colonial' model had been actively promoted by the University of London's Institute of Education (Colonial Office, 1943 and 1958; United Nations, 1955; UN Secretary-General, 1961; Batten 1957, 1965, 1967), and by the then new *Community Development Journal* (launched in 1966). They stressed heavily the role of professionals as consensus-builders, who enable 'desirable' social change to take place: those changes that had been planned and resourced from outside the locality or the local community. Local social institutions were to be built or adapted to suit official priorities. It was assumed that community development and social education approaches would be readily received by populations grappling with the pains of modernization. Whereas this model had been devised to assist British colonies cope with leadership development and the processes of democratization, no real thought had been given in official circles to the application of these methods at home.

During this period, official thinking in Britain was actually going in a number of directions at once, but this was not fully appreciated at the time. Firstly, there was the question of consultation, participation and the role of the state as a mobilizer of human resources for service provision. The Seebohm Commission was deliberating on the future shape and function of social services within local government. Its Report was published in 1968 (Seebohm, 1968), and it devoted a chapter to the function of and need for community development within this sector. Community development was recognized as being a necessary ingredient of public services, which would enable local communities to provide the bulk of social care in support of the mainstream, safety-net provision by the state (Seebohm, 1968, chapter 14, pp. 147–57). Beyond social services, official thinking extended into the realm of planning (Skeffington, 1969); New Towns (Cullingworth, 1967); primary education (Department of Education and Science, 1967) and local governance. The Housing Act 1969 called for 'environmental improvement', which required the active participation of residents, and the full cooperation of officials. All these government reports pointed to greater community engagement in local administrative processes. The teachings of Sherry Arnstein on participation (Arnstein, 1969), and the insight provided by contemporary American experiences, provided a timely yardstick for measuring local progress in real terms (Marris and Rein, 1967).

As the institutions of the establishment groped their way towards more openness in government, they also claimed the moral high ground for themselves. But a wide divergence became inevitable between their understanding of the issues, and that of the deprived citizens whose situation provided the rationale for the official programmes. The establishment sought the safe logic of consensus in society or, at least, 'managed' conflict and change. Unfortunately, this objective was probably never attainable at the end of that particular decade.

Secondly, and in parallel with, but apart from the various government commissions, was an unofficial body, the Calouste Gulbenkian Foundation study group. This was established to produce a blueprint for the indigenous training of community workers. Whereas the Seebohm Report emphasized 'participation in running the services' and a 'welfare through community' approach (p.149), the Gulbenkian Foundation tackled the question from a broader perspective. Their final report considered possible extensions of the 'participation' scenario. They conceptualized that, in addition to consensus-based neighbourhood work and social planning, situations of conflict would arise where citizens did not wish to share in common cause with those in authority. They saw the 'client' of community development to be the 'citizen', and that the objectives of the democratic society should be targeted (Calouste Gulbenkian, 1968, p. 79). The working group drew heavily on the content of the National Council for Social Service paper *Community Work* (Leaper, 1968), which itself addressed the relationship between 'community' and 'community care'. The 'alert and community-conscious citizenry' (Leaper, 1971, p. 69) must ultimately be responsible for the general level of welfare in society, it claimed. This was a line very much in keeping with the spirit of Beveridge, who envisaged full employment, rather than the state transfer-dependants of mass, continuing unemployment. A second Gulbenkian Report drew also, on the American community organization school, which allowed for constructive conflict within the general parameters of representative democracy (Calouste Gulbenkian, 1973).

Meanwhile, at a higher level of government cooperation, a more directly interventionist strategy was being created. This crystallized as the Urban Programme (launched in May 1968), and the Community Development Project (CDP – begun 1970), which fell under the Children's Department of the Home Office (Loney, 1983, p. 47). The CDP initiative attracted broad interest across government ministries at the highest levels. There were those in government who saw an urgent need to prevent an outbreak in Britain of the tensions and violence which were a feature of American cities at the time. Race issues and urban deprivation were the headline causes of this unrest. The aftermath of Enoch Powell's 'Rivers of blood' speech in 1968, inner-city tensions, especially frictions between displaced 'British' and 'immigrant' minorities seemed to mirror the American situation (Marris and Rein, 1967; Naples, 1998a and b). These were symptoms of a considerable distance between the governors and the governed. There were fears that flashpoints of urban violence might ignite as the year progressed. The irony of this situation was that in the

United States, by the end of the 1960s, official interest in community participation and the extension of the welfare arm of government into the community, was on the wane.

The CDP in England and Wales reflected a partnership between local and central government, with central government putting up most of the money (Higgins et al., 1983). Twelve local projects were planned as action experiments to assist the disadvantaged to come to grips with their problems. Communities in areas of urban deprivation, and particularly where there were tensions between minorities and the larger community, were to be helped to build fresh responses to their predicament through self-help and social-planning processes.

However, it was not long before the CDP workers, often in collaboration with their citizen partners, produced reports on local conditions and assisted in staging local political actions. These events confronted and confounded the local authorities, as well as their central government paymasters. They also shaped a model of professional militancy hitherto unknown in British public service. Within months of some of the projects being established, there were signs of considerable tension. The projects began to produce reports critical of the whole philosophy of corporate government: its patch-and-repair schemes for under-capitalized housing improvements, the lack of a structural analysis of poverty and urban deprivation, etc. (Benington, 1970; Community Development Project Working Group, 1974; Loney, 1983). It must be emphasized strongly that no comparisons could be drawn between the British response to this centralist intervention and the (inspirational) 'War on Poverty' in the United States. In the latter case, there had been dramatic instances of urban unrest, and the whole scheme ballooned into a wasteful and corrupting influence on local politics by the end (Blaustein and Faux, 1972; Marris and Rein, 1967). In the UK, 'unrest' manifested itself only as local protests, formal representations against bad conditions, and some thought-provoking reports by the CDP workers (Loney, 1983; Higgins et al., 1983). The sensitivities of British politicians and administrators proved much more pronounced than their American counterparts.

Of the CDP projects, it was said that local *frictions* caused breaches of contract, and accusations of misrepresentation of intent abounded (Butcher et al., 1979; Butterworth et al., 1981; Loney, 1983; Specht, 1976). But the truth of the matter appears to be that there were certain solutions to local problems that proved to be unacceptable to the policy-makers at all levels. Where these involved the active intervention of the citizen-as-planner, the frictions appeared to multiply (Butcher et al., 1979, Butterworth et al., 1981, Loney, 1983; Specht, 1975). By the time the initial five-year contracts for each of these projects had ended, they were all closed down. Thus ended a brief government flirtation with direct sponsorship of community development. In future, Urban Programme funds would be distributed differently. This showed how vulnerable publicly-funded schemes were if they did not fit local political philosophies.

The situation in Wales was slightly different from the mainstream experience of the CDP. The Upper Afan CDP was one of the first generation of projects. It was established in 1970, and immediately adopted a 'social planning' approach. The team spent the early months in isolation from the community, gathering factual information about their area of 'action research' and, during this time, the project adopted a rationale of full identification with the established civic structures for the attainment of social change. In so doing, they aroused some suspicion in the resident population (anecdotal evidence supplied contemporaneously by community activists in the area), and when the team did seek contact with the population it was on a strictly controlled basis (Penn and Alden, 1977, pp. 39 *et seq.*). No attempt was made to establish any local representative groupings of residents, and it was the elected representatives and their officials, at the three levels of local governance, who were adopted as the only appropriate channels for communication.

This approach conflicted sharply with the philosophy of other contemporary schemes. The projects of the Young Volunteer Force Foundation (YVFF – now Community Development Foundation) in Pillgwenlly, Newport and Cwmbrân, set up community-based structures to monitor and intervene in local governance matters, as well as to build the capacity of the local communities. The emphasis was on impacting directly on the process of local democracy. This translated as sensitizing the populations to the need for direct pressure on, and direct input into, social planning processes, and to ensure that the 'consultation' required of the local authority under the Town and Country Planning Act, for example, were adhered to in full.

In Cardiff, the Hook Road campaign (*Community Action*, No. 1, February, 1972, and No. 6, January 1973) developed a direct-action confrontational style which placed it at the radical extreme. Community activists mobilized residents' groups in the path of the planned road. Funds were raised, legal pressure was put on the planners and there was widespread public protest. By contrast, the Upper Afan CDP project represented the voice of control, accommodation and moderation. Community development workers at no time organized the community in protest against any of the major structural problems that confronted them. In Cardiff, simultaneous campaigns against large-scale urban renewal were sparked off in Canton, the city centre and in Adamsdown and Splott. These aroused widespread interest, and groups of professionals and students of the professions gave freely of their time and expertise to assist. Technical reports were provided, appeal documentation was compiled, and communities were assisted to mobilize around their respective causes. Identity-building photographic exhibitions were held, the new technique of video evidence was explored, and community newspapers began to flourish. Many 'community activists' developed a range of community development skills in this process, and some went on to become paid workers in the field. In the case of the Hook Road campaign (above), activists mobilized many Tory voters to vote Labour in crucial by-elections, and were successful in saving the bulk of their area (*Community Action*, No. 6, January 1973, pp. 3–4). Alas, most of the other protests were brushed aside by the authorities.

In the Afan Valley, local activists were simply ignored. It was interesting that despite the 'radical' and often doctrinal approach of many of the urban activists and professional workers of this time, no outright condemnation of the CDP was voiced. Some kind of conspiracy of silence between professionals appeared to be in place. For their part, the CDP largely ignored all other community-building activities outside their own area. In the case of the YVFF, permission was once denied to CDP staff to 'travel outside their own area' to see the work of others (work diary of the Pillgwenlly project)!

Thus, in south Wales by the end of the 1970s, there was already a tapestry of community development activity. It spanned a broad range of outlooks, expertise and aspirations. It tapped into the widespread discontent at heavy-handed, inflexible and time-wearied Labour Party administrations, and it sought (through all its differing techniques) to bring fresh insights and solutions to the pressing problems of the time. It tapped a fertile vein of creative and energized resources from citizens in defence of their own homes, through community arts, to dissident professionals. It dramatically confronted official attitudes towards social issues. Penn and Alden accuse the CDP nationally of not addressing the 'social pathology' view of community development, and of seeking, therefore, unrealistic solutions to social problems (Penn and Alden, 1977, p. 20). Nevertheless, at the local level in Wales, the evidence of political and administrative rigidity in the face of citizens' resistance to imposed solutions highlights a more basic flaw in the democratic process. At this point, it may prove instructive to consider whether other 'national' approaches differ from our own, and to consider how Wales might have benefited if alternative routes had been followed.

A Celtic fringe of community development?

The distinctiveness of the Welsh experience is clarified by considering parallel developments in Ireland (both in Northern Ireland and the Republic) and in Scotland. As in Ireland and Scotland, the solution to local problems in Wales drew out variants from models that had been devised centrally, and from which more generalized solutions might have been identified. It is true that Wales has not experienced the intercommunal violence of both Ireland and Scotland, nor has it witnessed the class oppression and enforced rural depopulation that was the hallmark of the nineteenth century in Ireland and Scotland. Nevertheless, Wales has seen many of the difficulties experienced by these other Celtic countries: concentrated industrial and/or urban prosperity followed by decline, the marked lack of competitiveness of its fringe agricultural areas, and the distinct division of the community into rural/agricultural and urban/proletarian elements. The fact is that there are many parallels of circumstance, and many similar lessons from which learning might have taken place. These all point to the conclusion that future cooperation between the 'Celtic fringe' nations in approaches to community development could prove beneficial to all concerned. The detail behind this assertion is outlined below.

The economy as the basis for community development

In Scotland, in the late 1970s, a governmental initiative took the lead in a departure away from the experiment in community-based, social welfare/education projects, which had been piloted in England and Wales as the CDP. The Scots targeted economic development at the local level as a mechanism for shoring up the community. As in England, where various commercial leaders were becoming greatly disturbed by the enduring and rising unemployment in the traditional industrialized areas, Scottish experiments in local economic regeneration were supported initially by the Highlands and Islands Development Board and then by regional authorities and other agencies. These rapidly became embedded in government policy, and many survive largely unchanged to this day (Calouste Gulbenkian, 1982; HIDB, 1982; McArthur, 1984; Hayton, 1984; Castro, 1986; Department of the Environment, 1990; Brotherhood and Thurley, 1998; see also *New Sector* magazine (1992–current). Whereas in England the problem of economic decline was perceived to be essentially an urban problem, in Scotland the issue was seen to stretch across industrial and rural areas alike. It is worth mentioning two pioneers in England, if only because of the extension of their ideas into both Scotland and Wales.

Firstly, in St Helens, the Pilkington Glass company decided that resources from industry could be responsibly placed at the disposal of the community (Calouste Gulbenkian, 1981; Miller, J., 1982). To this end they established a Local Enterprise Trust to promote and pump-prime small enterprises. From this lead, another (national) institution was developed which was to develop sustainable expertise in this sector – Business in the Community.

In Wales, it was the British Steel Corporation, itself building up to massive restructuring approaches to workforce and employment practice, which launched an initiative of practical and material support for locally based/owned business. Through their subsidiary, BSC (Industries) Ltd., they provided nursery space for small, new businesses. They made funds available for soft loans, and they gave and supported subsidies for 'housekeeping' costs on business-building sites, especially in north Wales.

In Scotland, the local arm of the state provided the vehicle for this in both urban and rural settings. In Strathclyde, the regional council used the Urban Programme to fund a project devoted to community economy-building for six years, 1978–84 (LEAP, 1984). A thriving network of community-based cooperatives and community enterprise centres came into being, supported by the Local Enterprise Advisory Project promotion scheme, under the direction of John Pearce, sometime director of the CDP Cumbria Project. The Lothian Region sponsored a Community Projects Foundation scheme in Leith (which gave rise to a significant publication of the late-1970s, *In and Against the State* (London Edinburgh Weekend Return Group, 1979; see also Ball et al., 1980)). It also gave financial and administrative support to such diverse schemes as the Wester Hailes Committee and Craigmillar Festival Committee (major local institutions for capacity-building and socio-economic development (Crummy, 1992), and a knitting cooperative in the shadow of Edinburgh castle (Miller, J., 1982; Vincent and Davison, 1984). On Clydebank, links between the national 'resource centre' initiative, funded by the EEC, and the local economic development initiatives were made possible (Lees and Mayo, 1984; Miller, J., 1982; LEAP, 1984) in the Govan economic initiative (see South Wales Anti-Poverty Advice Centre's experience in south Wales, p. 21 below).

Meanwhile, in the far-flung areas of the highlands and islands, the depopulation of remote areas had long been a critical factor threatening the survival of many rural communities. The Highlands and Islands Development Board was established by Act of Parliament in 1965. This development board had the brief of protecting the Highlands' economy from further decline and collapse. Its experience pointed to the importance of support for local economic development trusts, in order to sponsor community business and local economic enterprise, crofters' industry, cooperatives and the like (Miller, J., 1982). Today, Scotland boasts an independent community development agency, its own learned journal, and the ongoing commitment to linking social and economic development through the agencies of government at all levels.

From Scotland, Wales has many lessons to learn. The Scots have a preparedness to define community as an economic agent, and to include the training of professionals who would operate at community level in business formation and social ownership (McMichael et al., 1988). This idea, that social and economic responsibility can go together, has been nurtured in Scotland, despite some harsh analysis (McArthur, 1984). It has spread throughout the country that ordinary people, in their own environments, can play a direct role in their own material survival. This is as much the doctrine in de-industrialized Govan as it is in the Outer Hebrides. This provides a salutary lesson for Wales: that the philosophy of community development of 'can do' needs to be infused into the Welsh approach, especially from the top down.

In Wales there was no parallel policy to the Scottish model of championing alternative economic and social capacity-building, and limited learning from the legacy of earlier attempts at consolidating community development within its policy structure. It might be countered that Scottish conditions were unique, and that the disparity there between urban/de-industrializing areas and rural communities was far too different from the Welsh experience for imitation to be fruitful. But those in British Steel did think that there were lessons to be learned from, and in, both Scotland and Wales for its own initiative into local economic community development. At this time, too, came the foundation of the South Wales Common Ownership Development Agency in 1973 (a small, project-oriented organization), and the later emergence of the search for 'socialist' economic solutions through the Wales TUC Cooperative Development Unit. All these developments in Wales lacked coherence, and little official governmental support.

In Ireland, community development followed distinctively separate paths in Northern Ireland and in the Republic. In the North, communal protectionism became an art form as far as the Unionist community was concerned (see the essays in Frazer (ed.), 1981), with shadows of the same in the sectarian areas of urban Scotland (Bryant and Bryant, 1982, p. 19). Attempts to bridge the dividing line in the 1960s and 1970s with inter-faith, inter-communal projects, particularly centred on children's play and social activities, were quickly marginalized and discarded. Thereafter, community regeneration and other social programmes were mounted on discrete sectarian bases (Hughes and Carmichael, 1998; Lovett et al., 1995). More recently, the Health Boards have attempted to bring some coherence to their social planning by building accountable programmes into their local policies. They have recently commissioned a handbook on community development project evaluation from the Scottish Community Development Centre (Barr et al., 1996a and 1996b). The influence of the twenty-six District Partnership schemes, funded by the European Union through its Urban Peace and Reconciliation Programme, may make some progress, but much work has to be done to bridge the sectarian divide.

The Republic of Ireland presents a completely different picture, with a history of development and change, where the rural experience informed practice in the urban areas, and where the connection between the economic base of society and the focus of the community development policies were never very far apart.

This process all began, as did the bulk of the Welsh rural activity in this sector, with the formation of distinctly Irish, ethnic, community-based social and economic cooperatives. In Ireland these were known collectively as *Muintir na Tire* – People of the Countryside (Riley, 1967). This was a Church-backed movement, rooted in the traditional systems of the rural community, drawing extensively on its established leadership and communication functions, particularly those of the parish and the educated elite (Stokes, 1955; Bolger, 1977). *Muintir na Tire* established a stable and widely varied record of economic achievements over many years. Eventually, because of the combined forces of social and macro-economic change across Ireland as a whole, it was found to be unable to adapt appropriately. These forces brought the eclipse of *Muintir na Tire* by state-driven community enterprises and new social formations that elbowed it into the sidelines (O'Donohue, 1990).

As in Scotland, the Irish community movement was adapted to take advantage of the inflow of European Union funds from Ireland's accession, and the 'national, representative and coordination' functions of *Muintir na Tire* gave way to more market-oriented economic formations (Combat Poverty Agency, 1990; O'Cearbhaill and O'Cinneide, 1986; Kennedy, 1980). European funds raised the official government profile in community development overall. It gave rise to the launch of a serious experiment devoted to obtaining the maximum advantage from community development methods and values in order to tackle issues of national concern. The best use of community development methods was to be tested directly in the field. The prime target of this strategy was poverty, and a programme of thirteen projects was piloted between 1974 and 1980. This covered a range of rural, urban, social action and technical support initiatives. In addition, there was a central resource unit, and a considerable number of specialized activities were 'contracted out' to independent organizations.

The findings of this pilot scheme were mixed, but considerable insight was gained, both into the implementation of different models of community development, but also into the politics of mounting such a programme in the first place (Kennedy, 1980). Unlike the British CDP the central resource unit played a key role. It provided specialist advice across a wide range of policy areas, as well as legal, financial and other service functions to the projects, and to the Dublin area in which it was situated.

This pilot government initiative crystallized the thinking of activists and educators alike across Ireland. It also spurred the government to make a major contribution to the extension of community development as a necessary vehicle for addressing poverty. From 1986 onwards, with the new Combat Poverty Agency Act, the state began to exert a more purposeful influence over community development strategy and direction. It began directly to affect organizations and movements which had run sporadically and inter-mittently during the 1970s, for instance the women's movement and the tenants' movement (Hayes, 1990; Kelleher and Whelan, 1992). It also instituted a framework for the monitoring and objective-setting for the agency, which became a benchmark for other developments in the country as a whole (http://www.cpa.ie/agency2.html – accessed 3 February 2000). In 1989, a conference was held in Kilkenny, sponsored by the Combat Poverty Agency, the new government vehicle for this initiative. Representatives from training programmes, the state and a range of activists and project workers from Ireland and Britain shared their experiences and needs for the future (Combat Poverty Agency, 1990). In general terms, issues such as the influence of the widening gap between rich and poor, the role of the Church and the significance of the partition of Ireland were on the agenda of most delegates. In practical terms, the issues raised focused chiefly on the main victims of poverty – women, travellers and children in all locations (see Frazer (ed.), 1996). In 1997, the Irish government published its *National Anti-Poverty Strategy* which outlined a comprehensive approach to tackling poverty across a broad front, including education, employment, income maintenance, urban decay and the plight of the rural poor. Community development is central to this programme, and this is a major function of the Combat Poverty Agency (Taoiseach, 2000).

There are a number of factors that make the Irish experience significant for Wales. Firstly, it is the national ability to achieve integrated learning from a diverse range of community development experiences, either rural or urban, secular or parochial. Furthermore, the Irish found the capacity to translate a nationalist and traditional movement into a positive platform for more universal application. Then there is the ability to borrow from others (the British experience was studied during the launch of the pilot programme to combat poverty), and the acceptance of social phenomena which might disturb the status quo, such as the women's movement (Tobin, 1990).

One institution that has flourished in Ireland, but not in Wales, is the credit union movement. In terms of the urban/rural mix, the dependence on inward investment, and the general tendency for a social divide to open up between the 'haves' and the 'have nots' in the two countries, it might have been supposed that there would be closer parallels between them. The history of credit rotation and primitive credit unions goes well back in the general British context (Berthoud and Hinton, 1989; Drakeford, 1996; Todd, 1996), but it was not until the post-Second World War era that the formalization of credit unions took root. As formal institutions, credit unions were introduced into Ireland well before they came to Wales – the 1950s as opposed to the 1980s (Irish League of Credit Unions, 2000; Rhondda Cynon Taff County Borough Council, 2001). This is surprising, as the opportunity for relatively poor communities to reap the benefits of cheap credit, and to bypass the irregularities of 'loan sharks' and debt exploitation must have been obvious on both sides of the Irish Sea.

Of the two, it was in Ireland that the movement took root after 1958, and it spread rapidly to become a major instrument of social capital in the nation. It has now become an established and 'respectable' institution of collective stability, and has not embarked on a path to make itself a major force for social change and community development. In underdeveloped economic situations, the 'rotating credit' and credit union approach is established as an accessible and powerful mechanism of empowerment (Ardener and Burman, 1995; Harper, 1998; Hurley, 1990; Todd, 1996). The success of the movement in Ireland demonstrates what a potent force this could be, if only it were differently directed. In Wales, these fruits are still being sought, whereas in Ireland, the movement appears to have lost its momentum for social change. It is the Church in Wales that is now promoting credit unions in collaboration with the Wales Co-operative Centre, and training programmes in the south Wales valleys are being launched. In some respects, it is the legal framework that allows the Irish model to flourish, but which restricts any Welsh initiative (Berthoud and Hinton, 1989). Nevertheless, if the people have not put any real pressure on their elected members for changes in the law, then this is a statement of significant political weight.

All these factors are found in Wales, but as a nation-wide development and unifying mechanism, the 'nationalist' movement still has some way to go. The women's movement in Wales has been sanitized into a housing association for the accommodation of victims of domestic violence. The national resources of religious bodies have been largely ignored. These include: the significant contribution made by the (Anglican) Church in Wales through its *Faith in Wales* studies (Church in Wales, 1988a, b and c); the work of the Diocesan Boards of Social Responsibility in Swansea and Brecon, Monmouthshire, St David's and Cardiff, which are implementing the *Faith in Wales* recommendations; the engagement by Welsh theologians of the connections between faith and the community (Selby, 1985; Ballard, 1985 and 1990); and the capacity-building potential of the Nonconformist churches at the level of the people in all communities. Isolated chapel projects (for instance the youth facility in West Cross, Swansea) stumble on from one funding crisis to another with disinterest from all the official agencies. Tokenistic support is given to 'ethnic minority' groups, sometimes through their religious organizations, and in the particular case of the Somali community. In these situations, some resources have been placed at the disposal of ethnic women's organizations, but these have rarely gone beyond the needs of basic welfare, literacy and alternative and substitution provisions in keeping with the 'mixed economy of welfare'. The *Faith in Wales* momentum within the Church in Wales structure found other theological messages were more pressing in its rural areas (Church in Wales, Board of Mission, 1992). Generally, then, there is no positive encouragement, little financial support and no real insight into the nature and purpose of a community sector development that can operate within a locality without all the trappings of voluntary sector overheads and structures. This is borne out by the total absence of the community sector in the recently published 'community development' Compact document between the National Assembly for Wales and the 'Voluntary Sector' (National Assembly, 2000).

Having looked at the developments in the 'Celtic fringe', we return now to discussing the more general background to the Anglo-Welsh context.

Looking up from the street

From the beginning of organized community development/
community action/community work in England and Wales, the
feeling at street level, especially in the large and deprived urban
settings, was far more militant than in the contemporaneous events
that we have described in Scotland and Ireland. There was a
strident Marxist flavour to most of the organized community
responses to the negativity of the bureaucracy and the paternalism
of elected councils. These feelings were well represented in
Community Action (a magazine record of radical action and
technical support) and they later fed into a series of community
work (hardly 'community development') texts (Wooley, 1970;
Leonard, 1975; Corrigan, 1975; Corrigan and Leonard, 1978;
Bolger et al., 1981). They called for alliances with organized
labour, and conflict programmes organized along the lines of militancy and traditional trade unionism. Middle-class organizations
and professional community development workers actively added a
theoretical and analytical perspective to this process.

Following the 'rediscovery' of poverty by Abel-Smith and
Townsend in the mid-1960s (Abel-Smith and Townsend, 1965),
there was an upsurge of interest in homelessness, and social
alienation. As champions of the deprived, Shelter and the Child
Action Poverty Group had launched their attack on government
neglect of the poor and the homeless. Squatters' organizations and
community law centres vied with each other for the leadership of
people's movements. *Community Action* was launched to spread
the views of radical planners and social workers, together with the
citizens who shared their experiences of direct action in the
communities. Authoritarian government was the target: 'Action
groups can oppose ill-conceived policies, propose alternative solutions and obtain a greater role in formulation and implementing
policies, which affect the lives of their members' (*Community
Action*, 1, 1972, p. 2). In the same issue, *Community Action*
reported the saga of the Hook Road Public Inquiry in Cardiff (see
p. 11 above). Already active for six months, this inquiry was to
galvanize community workers in south Wales, and send very clear
signals to the local authorities about the intentions and capabilities
of locality-based community development personnel, especially if
they were supported by technical expertise. Local residents could,

and did, become an unforeseen element in urban renewal, and many groups took inspiration from this event. Weaknesses of local government were exposed, and professionals with technical and community-building skills forged powerful alliances. Alas, the theorists failed to identify either that consensus might provide a more beneficial outcome for all, or that the people in these actions were not the organized proletariat, but ordinary citizens going about their citizenship in an orderly way.

Indeed, this wave of seemingly militant, high-principled, almost revolutionary approach to citizenship was not to last. By the end of the 1980s its impact was all but spent. There was the Europe-funded South Wales Anti-Poverty Action Centre (SWAPAC), which was part of a national policy fudge. This British experiment, to explore a locally based approach to tackling poverty, followed the Boyle Report on community work by the Calouste Gulbenkian Foundation in 1973, and the launch of the European Economic Community Anti-Poverty Strategy in 1975. Six deprived areas were approved for European funding support, and six resource centres were established. These were managed by different non-govern-mental organizations as prototypes of local targeting. Alas, their impact was not evaluated properly (Lees and Mayo, 1984, p. 68).

SWAPAC was launched as a broadly based agency, which would target poverty as a structural problem, as well as offering direct support to self-help economic initiatives. The need grew from the chronic structural unemployment in the Valleys, due to the rundown and closure of much of the primary industry upon which the area was highly dependent for employment and prosperity. Could this new agency produce a fresh approach to the engage-ment of the poor and the unemployed in the local economies? Could this approach provide an alternative to the standard modern response – a fixation on 'inward investment', or on the historical dependence upon charity-supported self-help (Naylor, 1986)? Unfortunately, and before long, this ambitious scheme had to give way, not least due to shifts in government financial-aid targeting. SWAPAC became more and more concentrated on fighting job losses, trade union strategies, and linking the poor and the unemployed through their social organizations with the wider structural issues in the south Wales community. This led to the provision of advocacy, relief and targeted interventions, notably through welfare rights services, and the housing campaigns of the

South Wales Association of Tenants (Lees and Mayo, 1984, pp. 76–8). It meant that the broad objectives, and the attempt to influence directly the policy and economic activity of the district (Merthyr Tydfil), gave way to support for ideological questions. This drew the project somewhat into the same double-bind that had bedevilled the CDP projects – whether to integrate their activities into the ongoing structures of the system, or whether to demand more class-distinct, purist and anti-capitalist activities? (see Lees and Mayo, 1984, p. 145).

These dilemmas are well analysed by Fleetwood and Lambert (1982), where the contradictions between the aspirations of doctrinaire socialists and the immediate perceptions and needs of the poor are highlighted. One of the biggest problems, apparently stumbled into by successive waves of community development workers, is: when does a professional begin to be an activist leader of the community? This arises particularly when they are seconded to work in crisis and extreme situations that require incisive intervention and leadership. The descriptions of the Upper Afan CDP show how these pressures were successfully resisted to the extreme. Nevertheless, SWAPAC, the YVFF Pill project (see chapter 15 below), and the activist-dominated Hook Road and Canton/Riverside campaigns (see p. 11 above) highlight this dilemma. Perhaps, where the ideological issues are made explicit and built into the structure of the programme, sensitive questions might be easier to handle. As with the CDP, the government had its own agenda for managing difficult social conditions. This was not reflected in the real priorities of the workers on the ground, and so a clash was inevitable. SWAPAC's fortunes were bound up in this syndrome of discordant values. Its failure to fulfil official expectations sealed its fate, and it was allowed to wither away at the end of its funding contract. This left a legacy of bitterness and frustration, and another 'here today, gone tomorrow' development event.

The promotion of the Welsh language and culture appears to have been given a better run in community development terms. This has undoubtedly been given impetus by the passing of the Welsh Language Act in 1993, but in community development terms, things were very active before that. As has been shown (p. 4), in the mining communities the presence of a community-based and capacity-building mechanism proved extremely beneficial to social cohesion and survival in times of social change and economic depression. In the case of the Welsh-language and nationalist movements, the realization came that the continuity of the culture would not survive the steady erosion that was taking place. Unless they could be built up from within, and on a more community-sustaining and economic basis, rural communities would cease to provide a platform for the survival of the culture. This revival gained concrete impetus with the launch in 1979 of Antur Teifi, a valley-based economic and social initiative, which sought to bind together communities under the joint banner of Welsh culture/language, and economic self-help. In different forms, this activity has been replicated, and networks, such as Menter Iaith Myrddin in Carmarthenshire, have been developed to offer mutual support and contact for this socio-political endeavour. The whole movement to promote the Welsh language has embraced community development with gusto, and their training and publicity materials bristle with phrases like 'combating alienation', 'regeneration of the poorer areas', 'alleviating democratic deficit' and so on. They have adopted an aggressive policy to influence community life at every level, and have adopted social planning as well as locality development methods. Their mission is plainly stated and appears to be officially approved. Local *mentrau* can be found taking the lead in European Development Fund initiatives, and this approach to a 'national' development strategy might be instructive even for those without a specific 'cause' to expound.

In classical community development terms, this movement provides a positive example of integrated social and economic initiatives and integrated sustainable activities which augurs well for the future. The fact that they have prospered over the years gives credence to the argument that with gentle and focused governmental support, even a beleaguered community can take giant strides to pull itself up by its own bootstraps. Obviously the administration of Wales does not see the fostering of the Welsh language, and the promotion of its political culture, in the same light as it saw the SWAPAC venture. Similarly, numerous other local community development initiatives, which once drew their life-blood from the Urban Programme, perished with little trace. To date, it is the rural economies and communities that have benefited most from this movement. It has built on traditional lines of contact, and has offered positive examples of achievement to many that might otherwise have thought themselves to be powerless in the face of vast, external economic forces, especially in the countryside. Could such a movement produce equal success in an urban setting? The National Assembly for Wales may well get around to addressing this issue before long.

Of equal significance in social terms, is the impact that a movement like this will have within a culturally diverse community. In the Welsh context, 'nationalist' and 'linguistic' agendas are usually perceived as being in parallel and in concert with each other. The immediacy of a drive for linguistic collectivist solidarity will impact heavily on those who find themselves outside these boundaries. This is one of the inevitable consequences of community development anyway. Minorities (or majorities) who are not targeted find that they are getting unequal treatment, and are experiencing different life-choices as a result. The issue of the targeting of public funds towards a Welsh-language movement is one which professionals in community development will have to consider seriously. This could become the ideological divide of the future. From a 'welfare' perspective, and from the desire to produce 'socially inclusive' policies, community development workers in the Welsh context have to consider the effect that linguistic exclusivity may have on other 'priority' areas, namely the other ethnic and cultural minorities within Wales.

The contemporary scene

Since the early 1970s, the profile of community development has fluctuated, and yet the intellectual framework seems not to have changed profoundly. Current works on the subject reflect a great respect for the earlier advocates. The themes of non-directive approach, consensus, conflict model and so on, may have been replaced by participation, consultation and partnership, but the process required of professional community development workers appears to be similar. They are still required to intervene at community level. They enter into planning strategies with other professionals and introduce their special technical insight into the processes of social planning. They strive to create social situations that are amenable to the introduction of managed change or social stability. They deal in the development and allocation of power within the wider community, and with government (Clarke, 1996; Barr, 1996; Popple, 1995; Rothman, 1995; Thomas, D. N., 1995b; Henderson and Salmon, 1995).

What has changed significantly is the level of accountability that now surrounds these processes. The government is itself in partnership across international boundaries with the offices of the European Union. Government and EU funds are in partnership through contracts with the private and voluntary sectors, and there is a new urgency about value for money and time-fixed projects. Monitoring and evaluation, and even the concept of a contract for work done, was a rarity in the early days. Today it is the norm, rather than the exception. This is what was meant at the beginning of this chapter by the phrase 'cooperation and co-option'. There now does appear to be some convergence between the practice in Wales and that of the Celtic nations we have described. It will be interesting to discover whether or not some of the theoretical preconceptions have to be changed to accommodate this shift. Community development in Wales once demonstrated a wide range of degrees of freedom and autonomy between projects. We have to discover whether or not this range of flexibility still exists.

In 1987, an England and Wales initiative by the rural community councils began an ambitious scheme of Rural Appraisals. ACRE, an English rural charity, began a systematic programme to co-ordinate citizens in rural settings to audit their environment for facilities, area usage, population structure, household structure, infrastructure etc. This initiative spread to Wales through the establishment of Jigso, an environmentally aware agency (begun as Local Jigsaw Campaign in 1988; Day et al., 1998). Jigso has now established its own bilingual computer-software package to assist in this task and they, like ACRE, have instituted a self-help community development training scheme for community activists. They are now focused on sustainable development for Welsh rural communities, and are closely linked to the Wales Council for Voluntary Action policy development relationship with the National Assembly for Wales.

The National Assembly for Wales Compact with the voluntary sector outlines a wide-ranging reciprocal relationship. It includes definitions and mutual responsibilities, and is very much concerned with the ability of the voluntary sector to fulfil, with government support, many of the community-level support systems of the Welfare State. The emphasis is on transparent accountability, with expectations of monitored services producing dutiful citizens under the benign patronage of the national government. It does not mention the community sector or the need to invest in the grassroots and the informal community. It might reasonably be claimed that, if there is to be more depth to the 'voluntary sector' than the high-profile institutions and charitable activities, then direct investment in the social fabric may be necessary. Additionally, whereas there is a great need for proper accountability for the expenditure of public funds, and the need to infuse informal activities with proper evaluative processes, the sights of conformity have been set exceedingly high in this document (Welsh Office, 1998a).

This Compact has now been followed by a number of subsidiary consultation papers. They describe a six-year partnership pro-gramme which makes full use of the European funds available for community regeneration. From our perspective, it is the Compact Paper on Community Development, which is of the most interest. The theme is 'lasting regeneration' (National Assembly, 2000, p. 8), with the 'partnership' growing out of national priorities and strategies already categorized in the original bid for these funds. Strategically, funds are to be deployed in strengthening the employ-ment prospects for structurally excluded sectors of the community, and for the economic regeneration of marginalized and run-down localities. These are laudable aims, and no one will criticize them for what they are. Nevertheless, for a major allocation of resources in a social setting that has been deprived of an economic livelihood or has been faced with continuing decline for decades, more is required than just building for the future.

Were the community truly to be allowed to 'decide' on its own priorities to build mechanisms to sustain it into the future, it might decide to restore some of the losses to the social fabric, and seek a little joy for itself along the way. Across the world, the 'pie in the sky' message about prosperity being just around the corner is a well-worn myth. This mirrors some of the propaganda messages of the 1960s, prior to the cancellation of the CDP.

Today, we have had Strategic Development Schemes for local partnership; the Social Exclusion Unit's programmes for neigh-bourhood renewal and initiatives for economically excluded young people; European Structural Fund moneys; the *Better Health, Better Wales* Green Paper consultations on participation in health promotion and delivery schemes (Welsh Office, 1998a); community nurses being required to acquire competence in community development (UKCC, 1998); etc., etc. Here we find government actively seeking, at every level, mechanisms for uniting and unifying the resources of local and central government with the citizen-consumer. All should be set fair for local neighbourhood schemes for community-building and the taking of community responsibility for the welfare of the young people in their midst. But in Swansea in the late 1990s, for example, a planned community development project caused the most horrendous political row (see chapter 15). This forced a massive delay in implementation and distorted institutional relationships for several years. Why did this pattern mimic so closely the experience of the 1970s in Newport (see chapter 15)? Hopefully, something has changed.

Certainly, with the launch of the Objective One initiative under the assistance offered by the European Structural Fund (National Assembly for Wales, 2000c), a huge step forward has been taken. This will focus the institutions of government on the difficult processes involved in linking the people on the ground, in the communities, to national economic and social renewal strategies. Depending on your interpretation of what community development is all about (see chapter 2), then all of the six priorities of the Wales Objective One will need to be based upon and contain community development approaches. This is clearly illustrated in the National Assembly parallel document that related Objective One to health matters: Objective One's priorities 3 and 4 (community economic development, and developing people) are connected with health, lifestyles, the economy and the influence of the community (National Assembly for Wales, 2000d, pp. 9–15). We are optimistic that the intentions, written across so many policy and consultation documents, signify a genuine attempt to come to grips with the problem. The critical question is: has the government's rediscovery of community development offered the opportunity for a new 'take-off' period for professional activity, or will community development become encapsulated within the strictures of bureaucracy and accountability structures?

The need to take stock

One way in which to deal with this problem, is to seek a wider perspective, and to compare our local activities with the worldwide phenomenon of development and community involvement. We now have a feel for the many attempts to introduce developmental approaches to social planning and social change in Wales over the last century. It is very much a mixed bag of spasmodic government interest, local opportunism, and a confusion of political causes. There have been so many institutions, agencies and even individual citizens involved, but at no time until the present, has there been a concerted attempt to instil a wide range of public policies with one philosophy. The achievement of a coherent strategy for this purpose is still in the making. Before anything makes its mark in practical terms, we can step back a bit and see what lessons there are to be learned. We can benefit considerably from the historical events that we have described above. We can now begin to determine whether or not there were any underlying principles at work in these achievements. In addition, we can seek out any patterns in the work, and seek to tie them in with theoretical models that community development practitioners have sought to perfect in other settings. We may then find that we can better decide what values should underpin community development, and also discover whether or not there are circumstances that are special to Wales, and how they may shape our thinking. We begin with an exploration of community development: the essential definitions of its terms, and the most important influences in its progress.

2 Definitions of community development and the role of the practitioner

STEVE CLARKE, DERITH POWELL, ANTONINA MENDOLA BYATT
and MARTIN HOBAN

Crynodeb

Trafodir yma hanes datblygu'r term 'datblygu cymunedol' a'r cyd-destunau amrywiol y defnyddir ef ynddynt. Rydym wedi penderfynu bod tair elfen allweddol: y gymuned a'i hamgyffrediad o rym; y gweithwyr proffesiynol; a chyd-destun gwleidyddol y fenter.

Bu'n rhaid i ni wneud rhai penderfyniadau ynghylch diffiniadau, a chytunwyd bod rhaid i ni fod yn eglur yn yr hyn rydym yn ei ddweud, hyd yn oed os bydd eraill yn anghytuno â ni – efallai'n ddwfn. Felly, rydym am amddiffyn y syniadau hyn: (1) mai cysyniad mympwyol yw cymuned, ac fe'i diffinnir gan y rheini â'r grym i'w wneud – hyd yn oed os nad ydynt yn hanu o'r ardal neu'r boblogaeth eu hunain; a (2) mai gweithgaredd un proffesiynol cyflogedig wedi'i hyfforddi ac yn atebol yw datblygu cymunedol, a hanfod gweithgareddau datblygu cymunedol yw'r tensiynau sy'n codi rhwng rhinweddau'r bobl hyn, yn ogystal â rhyngddyn nhw a chyflogwyr, ymgyrchwyr yn y cymunedau a'r dinasyddion yn gyffredinol. O ystyried yr amgylchiadau economaidd-gymdeithasol a gwleidyddol, diffinir a chyfyngir datblygu cym-unedol gan faint mae'r amgylchiadau hyn yn gosod gwir gyfyngiadau ar ryddid y gweithiwr. Mae datblygu cymunedol yn rhoi 'gymuned' i mewn i ddatblygu. Datblygu yw'r crynhoad o adnoddau materol a dynol ar fater cym-deithasol/economaidd, ac fe ymgyfeirir at wir newid. Mewn enw, datblygu cymunedol yw'r dimensiwn moesol o 'ddatblygu', ond mae cymaint yn dibynnu ar rinweddau sydd y tu allan i reolaeth y gweithwyr a'r 'gymuned'.

Introduction

The origins of community development stem from a wide variety of sources, both here in Britain and around the world: the desire to develop self-government in colonial peoples; the need to create representative structures in rapidly changing economic conditions; the forging of self-help organizations; class-solidarity movements; the need to resist imposed systems of control; attempts to salvage membership for belief systems; and a myriad of individual examples. The lessons of these diverse processes are still being absorbed by professional practitioners, community organizers, activists, educators and public administrators alike, and this chapter will attempt to provide some focus. We hope to make a reasoned contribution to this process, and also to assist those in Wales who may also be seeking clarity on the critical questions of why community development is done, by whom and how.

This chapter involves a detailed discussion on the key issues and, to set the scene, we have selected a short list from the mass of formal statements on our subject. These statements have been used over the years by some of the most powerful agencies to justify the creation of national, international, and local policies. They show, even if the specific words used may have changed over the years, just how consistent the thinking has been, particularly the central place given to the community as a necessary agent for real change to occur.

Sample definitions

Colonial Office (1943)

We wish to show in fuller detail the inter-relatedness of the various factors in community life and the consequent necessity for co-ordination of the efforts of the various agencies concerned with the improvement of that life . . . [which] . . . depended above all for its success on the interest taken by the people themselves in the work of the agencies . . . [Africans] must be the main agents in improving . . . life . . . participation involves the training of all . . . who are to take a share in that work . . . If we are to secure the improvement of the life of the community . . . that improvement depends upon the training of the community as a whole . . . more systematic and energetic than any which were contemplated before . . . designed to enable them both to maintain their own cohesion under the stress of powerful influences and to reap for themselves the advantages which the changing conditions of life may offer. (pp. 5–6)

Murray G. Ross (1955)

Community organization . . . is . . . a process by which a community identifies its needs or objectives, orders (or ranks) these needs or objectives, develops the confidence and will to work at these needs or objectives, finds the resources (internal or external) to deal with these needs or objectives, takes action in respect of them, and in so doing extends and develops co-operative attitudes and practices in the community. (p. 39)

United Nations (1955)

. . . a process designed to create conditions for economic and social progress for the whole community with its active participation and the fullest possible reliance upon the community's initiative. (p. 6)

US International Co-operation Administration (1956)

Community development is a process of social action in which the people of a community organize themselves for planning and action; define their common and individual needs and problems; make group and individual plans to meet their needs and solve their problems; execute these plans with a maximum reliance upon community resources; and supplement these resources when necessary with services and materials from governmental and non-governmental agencies outside the community. (du Sautoy, 1962, p. 122)

Younghusband Report (1959)

Community development is primarily aimed at helping people within a local community to identify social needs, to consider the most effective ways of meeting those and to set about doing so, in so far as their available resources permit. (p. 183, cl. 638)

Ministry of Housing and Local Government (1967)

Community development: The processes by which the efforts of people themselves are united with those of the authorities to improve the social and cultural lives of their communities.

. . . the worker is an enabler and a catalyst, setting up groups and associations and the administration of community centres He encourages co-operation between the statutory and voluntary bodies. 'Community work' includes social planning and advice, public relations, and providing research and information. (in Leaper, 1971, p. 178)

Calouste Gulbenkian Foundation (1968)

C.D. is mainly associated with the problems of rural people in underdeveloped areas. Its purposes are to help people to improve their economic and material conditions and to rouse them from the apathy and fatalism of the centuries. (p. 155)

Liverpool CDP (1977)

Thus community development involved three separate activities – first to improve the performance and co-ordination of services at the local level, second to strengthen the organization of community groups, and finally to develop techniques and institutions that would bind the community groups effectively together, providing a coherent structure to which the local authority could relate. (Topping and Smith, 1997, p. 27)

Standing Conference for Community Development (1992)

Community development is about the active involvement of people sharing in the issues which affect their lives. It is a process based on the sharing of power, skill, knowledge, and experience . . . [it] . . . seeks to enable individuals and communities to grow and change according to their own needs and priorities and at their own pace, provided this does not oppress other groups or communities or damage the environment. (SCCD News, vol. 12, p. 1)

Rubin and Rubin (1992)

Community organizing is a search for power and an effort to combat perceived helplessness through learning that what appears personal is often political. Organizing is a way of collectively solving problems like unemployment, deteriorated housing, or sexism, and racism. The message of organizing is that a better world is achievable if people work together as a community . . . community development occurs when people form their own organizations to provide a long-term capacity for problem-solving. (p. 1)

Departments of Health and Social Security and Northern Ireland (1999)

Community development is about strengthening and bringing about change in communities. It consists of a set of methods which can broaden vision and capacity for social change and approaches, including consultation, advocacy and relationships with local groups. It is a way of working, informed by certain principles which seek to encourage communities . . . to tackle for themselves the problems which

they face and identify to be important, And which aim to empower
them to change things be [*sic*] developing their own skills, knowledge
and experience, and also by working in partnerships with other groups
and with statutory agencies. (*Baseline Study of Community Development approaches to Health and Social Wellbeing*, Coopers and
Lybrand, in Department of Health and Social Services, 1999, p. i)

Making sense of the definitions

We have seen from the varied definitions of community development in the literature, that a number of preconceptions are
involved. Many of these definitions clearly reflect the values,
expectations and boundaries that suit particular practitioners and
theorists. They reflect an individual predisposition towards the
community and its development. Many others (not cited here)
attempt to provide us with an overview and analyse the salient
themes and ideological approaches to the subject. They describe
the polar extremes of community development: from social control
and manipulation on the political right, to revolution and social
unrest on the left (see Popple, 1995; Mayo, 1975; Thomas, D. N.,
1983; Calouste Gulbenkian Foundation, 1973; Brager and Specht,
1969; Rothman, 1995). Very often, when they come to make their
own summary, they wind up in a form easily recognizable as one of
the classic definitions from the early days.

   We have attempted to derive our own definition of community
development from within this array. We have sought to distil out of
the proliferation of values and models of intervention a scheme
that suits our own needs in the south Wales context. We wish to be
inclusive in our scope, but also we wish to attempt to identify
approaches to social intervention, which are helpful to our overall
cause. We are determined to make as explicit as we can the value-
base we have assumed, and our rationale for making the distinctions that we have made. We will attempt to provide a framework
against which other forms of community intervention can be
discussed (but not judged). It will then provide us with something
constant and concrete. It is against this that we will make some
analytical appraisal of the case examples which provide the
substance of this work. We believe that the cause we are pursuing
is much needed in the south Wales context, since so much has been

achieved in the field and yet it has been virtually ignored in the serious literature.

What is our 'cause' exactly? Our cause is to inspire practitioners, past, present and potential, to deploy their talents across a wider spectrum of opportunities. Our motivation also is to assist them carefully to examine the values and objectives that they are pursuing. We hope that the presentation of a framework will support them in this endeavour. We recognize clearly that there has been a refinement of thinking within community development practice. We are anxious to discover just what has been gained from this process, and whether or not anything has been lost.

We wish to promote a dialogue about the nature of community development. We wish to consider its values, and the ethical limitations in which workers find themselves. We wish to examine the differences that location, funding mechanism and individual and personal characteristics bring with them to the scene of their activity. We are aware that there are moves in official circles to 'reinvent the wheel' insofar as community development is concerned. 'Partnerships', 'community health development', 'participation', and even 'community development' itself are becoming the essential cue-words in official reports and planning documents. We hope that we can assist all who are in the habit of using these phrases to gain some insight into their meaning, so that all discussion on the matter can be better informed.

We have isolated some of the key words from the definitions and the themes in the case materials. It is an ambitious list of aspirations for the professional. The key words are: community; grassroots; development; professional; participation; organization; power; social change; planning; politics; oppression; rights; diversity; class; social welfare; consensus; conflict; process; outcome; leadership; imposed; organic; housing; poverty; structural. We can group some of these together, and discuss them in a composite way. In doing this, we will achieve an analytical discussion of what are often contentious subjects. Many of them are seen as 'necessary' descriptions of practice, and are recited as a litany. As such, they are in danger of becoming clichés. Nevertheless, there is no easy way through the controversies that they tend to create.

Additionally, one of the most important aspects of community development, and one that makes it so suspect in the eyes of many other professions, is that it always involves risk. Risk is the certainty that 'things' are bound to work out 'wrong' to some extent, or that the getting it 'right' is going to be an uncertain experience. Even defining 'right' is often an impossible task. Plans go awry even before they are implemented: objectives are too vague, or too tightly delineated, the 'players' refuse to play, have agendas of their own or have not understood what is happening.

No law defines the rights and duties of the community development worker, and every intervention has to be negotiated. The very right to take part has to be agreed by the participants, and any authority and recognition of the value of a practitioner's usefulness has to be hard-wrung from the situation. So much depends on creating, and then capitalizing on, the goodwill that is generated. Nevertheless, it is not so much a wonder that anything works at all, but that it actually *does* work most of the time, despite the odds. Perhaps it is for this reason that the practitioner accepts these difficult conditions as part of the job. It galvanizes personal and professional energy for the challenge, and requires one to become philosophical about its outcome, whatever it may be. The art of community development is forever to be 'unfinished'. Today's objective, successfully attained, becomes the means for tomorrow's new objective, and so on until the contract runs out.

As the objectives change, so do the participants – both the workers, and citizen activists. They all find that the passage of time affects them. It also affects social practices, the community's sense of self-awareness, its values and the conditions of the physical environment. As a professional activity, community development work tries to produce some stability over time, by anticipating the pressures from within the change processes, and creating the mechanisms to manage them. It strives to allow reflective and coherent thought to take place on the pressing issues of the present, whatever their history may have been and whatever threatens to be their future. There are few heroics here, just an attempt to bring some rationality and deliberation to the processes of constant social change. Community development work enables people and the people's processes to exercise some control over events, through creating and managing the appropriate structures (organizations). It is through these that they can work towards meeting their needs with some sort of stability, and with some predictability.

Stability, however, is a false god, and it breeds for itself the need and the means for disruption and change. Forces that tend towards stability create interests that are vested in the status quo. They depend upon established status, ways of doing business, and mediums of exchange which are comforting and conservative. Change will destabilize these qualities, but change will and must come if the dynamics of society are to be absorbed and communities are to remain resilient. There has been a tendency to build into the ethos of community development the idea that conflict is an unhealthy trait to be avoided, and that consensus is the ultimate goal (Brager and Specht, 1973).

Community development is concerned with the analysis of power and its distribution between interest groups (Clarke, 2000). Engagement in community development entails an explicit statement about power relationships, identifying the parties involved and managing the process of pitting them against each other. This statement about the quality and nature of any particular experience of community development resolves itself after the action plan is defined, and the tally is made of the objectives won. Which pattern of objectives has been accomplished, and how does this reflect the balance of interests that are involved in the process? Who then has established a dominant influence on the way things are done? Whose scheme of things will shape the future? Which leadership faction will control the way in which the proceedings are reported, and whose 'logic' will preside over describing the way forward?

Too often, these questions are left unasked, let alone unanswered. The outcome of this is a frustrated sense of involuntary collusion for those who do not find their needs being met. The weaker parties defer to the more powerful, and the balance of power remains unchanged. Is this a reflection of the failure of community development? Is it the role and the imperative of the professional community development workers to ensure that they are not found to be lacking in this fluid and exciting arena? Can the particular skill and knowledge of the professional enable this difficult process to be managed and contained? How some practice falls short of reaching towards these questions is described below.

We will be dealing with some of the most contentious aspects of this activity, such as the definition of community; anti-oppressive practice pitted against 'free-market' expressions of power;

professional 'control' over process, communication and information; and the creation of dependency. A vital element begins with drawing the frame of reference for the professional, including the boundaries of time and context, and decisions which identify the contending parties in the frame. If the professional is employed by one of the major power elements in this process, then there are limits set to the freedom that the professional may perceive as being permitted. On the other hand, it may just require that different tactics be employed to reach certain necessary objectives for the other players.

Thus, there is no clear run towards the 'process goals' of development. The great advantage is that the professional is aware of the possibilities, and can help prepare all parties to recognize their needs as things unfold. One of the most interesting aspects of this is defining the boundaries, or limitations of participation. Interest groups may feel that they have a clear picture of who is involved, whose interests have to be accommodated, what barriers there might be to gaining some necessary agreements, and what resources have to be mobilized to achieve their objectives. It is the quality of, and the level at which participation takes place that reflects the capability of interest groups to express their power (Arnstein, 1969; Burns, 1991). Who gives consideration to other interests that may have a legitimate case for being involved? The fact is that some parties may either not be aware or even capable of participating in the process. Some parties may actually possess some form of a veto on proceedings, and will use it when their interests are threatened. All factors such as these have to be considered and brought into the equation. The identification of such issues is the special talent of the professional community development worker.

Community

Much of this process falls within the scope of something called 'community'. Each party will have their own idea of what the term means, and how it might be applied to a particular situation. Most people will recognize communities of geographical location, whether or not any 'community' exists there in spirit or not. Many communities are defined passively, by outsiders, who seek to clarify things for their own purposes. In this way, people's status is ascribed without their consent, and many may even remain unaware that they have been included in this way. In modern, urbanized societies, there is less evidence of aggregates of people actively and spontaneously defining themselves as communities. It may be 'us' or it may be 'them'. Who is 'us' and when might 'them' become 'us' as well? It can be seen that the defining process is capable of drawing lines according to various criteria.

One example of how the shift can take place, is reflected in the rise of the social movement. Here, people who subscribe to a cause operating at the local level through small formations, constitute a national, or even an international, force for change. They represent a body of people who all identify together with their particular beliefs or objectives. Greenpeace and Amnesty International are two of these. They are both organizations at the local and national levels but also constitute an international collective will. Developmental activities with constellations such as these certainly contain aspects of 'community', but it will readily be seen that the boundaries may have to be drawn pretty arbitrarily once activity becomes formalized in any way.

Even community of interest in apparently identifiable groups is difficult to define, especially from the inside. People have their own subjective perception of group belonging, and most belong to more than one group, anyway. Even if group attachment is acknowledged, an individual may have distinct preferences as to which grouping is of primary or secondary importance. Policy-makers, on the other hand, may seek to justify and demarcate categories for reasons of economy or convenience. In this way, they may create a pattern for the distribution of society's resources that does not conform to the needs and expectations of the most appropriate beneficiaries.

The whole concept of 'community', as used by community development professionals and planners to define the boundaries of their intervention methods, has come under serious scrutiny. Critics of the traditional approaches (geography and interest group) point to the considerable diversity within all these arbitrary divisions. Of more searching importance is the insistence that the power relations in society be taken into account when attempts are made to demarcate targets for the distribution of social resources, and plans are made for the reshaping of the social and economic order. Factors like gender, race/ethnicity, disability and economic class all have their effect, and distort the presumptions that plans can be implemented and objectives gained through objective criteria and rational strategies (Anderson, 1999; Antrobus, 1991; Chambers, 1998). It is when the specifics are analysed within the more sensitive 'participation' and 'integrating-women' models that the contradictions between rational analysis and actual social change achievements became clear (Brohman, 1996; Chambers, 1998; Friedmann, 1992; Oakley, 1991). 'Community' can contain many conflicts and tensions, which are very much a part of its dynamic process. Community development must come to terms with this dimension, and not define for itself the idea that 'development' must mean integration or consensus.

It is evident that here there is a vital task for the professional: to engage the participants in an active discussion about the nature of community and how it is to be defined for the purposes that confront their interests, at this time, and in this situation. It is the role of the professional to strive for the best degree of 'fit' between the composition of the group making the decisions about the objectives of development and the legitimate interests of groups which will be affected by those objectives. This also includes the processes of attaining them. As the objectives of development will change as circumstances change, so the necessary composition of the decision-making group will have to change. It is incumbent on the professional to ensure that the decision-making group remains open to involving new interests as this process develops, and that the interests of the decision-making group do not become so entrenched that they become desensitized and exclusive. It is further incumbent on professionals to target oppressive pressures within the community process, and develop methods of dealing with them.

Another professional task is to try, carefully, to build a *community* out of all the participants in an action/planning initiative. But will this produce a limiting sense of exclusiveness, which excludes others from taking part? How does the professional explore these real or apparent boundaries, ensuring that the original community is secure in its identity, and can accomplish the tasks that it sets for itself? The capacity to become inclusive, rather than excluding, is a great test for a community. It is the community's component elements that must recognize that their commonality of interests is what makes them a 'community' and that there are bound to be points of irreconcilable difference which must coexist with the contractual agreements to go forward on issues of mutual concern (Clarke, 2000).

In this chapter, we try to discover what comprises the constituency of the community development worker. Many of the definitions which appear in the literature fudge this question. When many of them state that the definition of community is a matter of circumstances, then are they avoiding vital questions about the nature and direction of professional community development work? Many of the definitions confuse the distinction between 'locality development' (Rothman, 1995) and the feeling of being involved with and answerable to the 'grassroots' elements in community, with the consequences of engaging in 'problem solving' (Rothman's description of this is social planning), and the engagement of institutional forces in the wider community. Does the community development worker have a greater loyalty to the 'grassroots' elements in and activity than to the other agencies involved? Does not 'solving the problem' depend on engaging all the participants on equal terms, and must an element of positive discrimination be employed to provide some mechanism for levelling the playing field?

Powerful forces are ranged against the citizen, and the citizen's organizations. These can be professional cultures, traditional institutions, accepted power centres in society, and vested interests of all kinds (Cockburn, 1977; Midgley, 1981 and 1986; Clarke, 2000). Many of these may be hidden in the participant agencies of change themselves, including the community. They constantly strive to undermine change, to limit the scope for action, or to do away with resistances to their own way of doing things. Sometimes, things get very messy (see Clarke's case study in chapter 9).

Considering these forces, is the role of the community development worker to continue to organize and prepare all sides for the engagement? The professional must be personally aware and prepared for what those pressures might be. Can a route be plotted towards achieving the community's objectives? There is no place for naivety or collusion in this process, but cynicism is a constant and seductive threat to personal integrity. Much of what is written distils the experience of practice into a well-controlled, positive analysis of history, with many warts concealed. There are a few candid exceptions, but they are few and far between (Landry et al., 1985). In the United States, is has long been accepted that the 'community' has to be constructed by the professional organizer, who creates a broad-based coalition of groups, using common interest as the motivational factor. Groups may have to be built up from scratch where none exist, and the ensuing organization is a political mechanism, which has to be actively maintained through determined professional motivation and support (see chapters 4, 5, 11 and 16; also, Alinsky, 1972; Delgado, 1986; Boyte, 1984; Fisher, 1994; Holman, 1998; Rogers, M. B., 1990).

We have grouped below some well-known types of community development practice. They reflect some of the major influences on professionals, including some of their own motivations and value positions. We hope that after considering these differing perspectives, we will be able to analyse our own position. We will then have a context within which we can discuss the case studies that follow.

The charismatic leader or idea

The histories of many modern democracies are studded with the bright stars of political and social events. These may have emerged from local and/or national liberation struggles, or their role may have created landmarks in social history. These 'stars' became legends in their own time, as their actions entailed political confrontation of great intensity. Sometimes this may even have led to the bloody overthrow of an unpalatable regime. In the background to these events stood the communities which gave succour to their political figureheads and inspirational revolutionaries. Sometimes the shining star of the movement for change was also the spiritual leader of the community, as well as being the marshal of the forces for change. The Gandhian movement called for passive resistance and essential purity of action and thought (*Satyagraha*). In contemporary India, Panduranga Shastri is forging a spiritual movement based upon a belief system and a community-building process (*Swadhyaya*), with millions of adherents (Roy, 1993). Dalino Dolci employed powerful charisma in his struggle to unite the Sicilian peasants against the stranglehold that the Mafia held over their lives. The stoicism of Nelson Mandela was the inspiration to millions as the dreadful contradictions of apartheid worked themselves out. The formid-able resolve and organizational ability of Cesar Chavez held the workers together throughout the California grape boycott. These figures have passed into legend, and now command a special place in the community development worker's mythology (Gandhi, 1951; Dolci, 1959; Rogers, M. B., 1990).

All these 'leaders' were sustained by their communities in different ways. In return, they all contributed to the capacity-building of their communities, and focused their members on the necessities of the movement or struggle for their cause. They were all political leaders but, more than that, they embodied the organic spirit of their peoples as well. They led from the front, but they also sought to create sustainable structures behind them to ensure that the movement could survive their own passing. They com-bined a 'life philosophy' with a political objective. This kind of activity presents special problems for community development. Are these leaders to be considered community development workers?

What organizational model do they apply? Are they each inventing their own approach, or do they tailor something more basic to suit their own requirements? How do local circumstances determine which model or method should be the most appropriate? Each movement will be bound by the general needs of all organizations: resource accumulation; management systems and delegation; internal consumable resources such as information, training and technology; planning and decision-making machinery, and so on. Do the special characteristics of charismatic or powerful leadership demand the establishment of tightly focused centralized structures, and the (probable) prominence of one individual?

Sometimes, charisma is combined with a deep-seated under-standing of the community development purpose, and this may cause some dilemmas. Here the capacity to lead, and the perceived virtue of leadership, becomes confused with the need for self-determination, self-help and the need to grow through the personal and organizational experience of the risk that change brings. Some community development workers become legends in their own time and, in the United States, Saul Alinsky was one such. His capacity to win, and his prominent role in organizing the struggles of citizens against authority and vested interests, saw him pilloried by those who feared that he was destroying the very fabric of society (Hasler, 1990; Alinsky, 1969; chapter 15 below). Another was Rabindranath Tagore, the Indian poet and international figure in the arts. His hands-on commitment and leadership by example gave impetus to the Indian *panchayat* movement of model-village development in the poorest rural areas (Dasgupta, 1961). To what extent does the mystique of this kind of leader distract the people from the purposes of conscious self-improvement?

Leadership from within

Another theme, which runs through many of our definitions, is the imperative that the 'community' itself must define the way forward, equating *felt* need with *true* needs. But how is this 'community' to be identified? The disciples of Paulo Freire and Robert Chambers will testify that it is the 'wretched of the earth' who must first be raised into a state of consciousness and active, independent action – conscientization (Fanon, 1967 and 1970; Freire, 1970; Chambers, 1983).

> Men will be truly critical if they live the plenitude of praxis, that is, if their action encompasses a critical reflection which increasingly organizes their thinking and thus leads them to move from a purely naïve knowledge of reality to a higher level.
>
> (Freire, 1972, p. 100)

Awareness, integration of ideas into reality, and reflection are the key to conscientization. (Freire always has a way with words!) Once this is in motion, then the process of social change can begin. This is a pedagogical model of the highest correctness, but it usually describes people who must survive the outrages of deprivation under the harshest of circumstances. These people are in no condition to rise up and achieve conscientization without considerable support and encouragement (Freire, 1970; Clarke, 2000). It is the very essence of community development to enable this process to happen, but in many instances the change and growth process is hijacked by ambitious indigenous leaders. Once in a position of power and influence, they take over the show for themselves. These people are not necessarily evil, but their opportunistic assumption of leadership must retard the raising of consciousness across the whole 'community', however it is defined.

The essential difficulty with the indigenous leadership model lies in the degree to which the quality of participation is degraded. Examples of this are found in ideological movements that are linked to specific communities. The leaders who emerge are home-grown, but they command the authority of powerful voices and moral virtues.

We feel that this is of special relevance to understanding the experiences of communities in Wales when the combined forces of language, national identity and economic decline require immediate and focused responses. Delay may be perceived as weakness of position or lack of resolve. Tailored organizational structures are needed through which to sustain a community effort. This must take on a clearly identifiable political and cultural character to reflect the nature of the community. These qualities may come mixed up with fundamental religious beliefs or cultural symbols, and may render complete rationality powerless. The quality and characteristics of leadership on this situation are crucial. Minorities must intrinsically trust their leadership, put up with its eccentricities, and revel in and celebrate its triumphs. When communities are caught up in these processes, it is easy to see how debate might be stifled in the name of 'progress' and how dissent might be understood as a challenge to the leadership structure. Focused, determined and well-organized leadership, with firm control over the interpretation of cultural symbols, can retain control and determine the strategy for shaping the direction of any development processes.

As even the most uncompromising of experts will testify, it is the situation and power of the professional workers that hold the key to the quality of the development exercise (Chambers, 1983, pp. 215–17). People may vote with their feet, undermining the impact of resources and planning. At the same time, there are often sufficient people who will benefit directly from some specific changes to enable specific leadership decisions to be rationalized. It was Dalino Dolci, speaking at a fund-raising function in London in 1970, who was challenged from the floor about who decided the priorities for social action. He replied: 'Who can stand aside in a time of crisis? He who sees the way forward must act decisively!' (notes taken at meeting by one of this chapter's authors – Clarke – who also asked the original question!). He was appealing for the right to lead from the front, as the 'community' was fragmented, oppressed and unsure of the path forward.

Direction from without

The great majority of community development initiatives in Wales have originated in the planning offices of local authorities or large national voluntary organizations. The social planning process begins to deal with the issue of how to involve the 'community' once the basic decisions about desirable change have already been taken. One of the most tragic examples of this was the efforts of Swansea City Council in the late 1990s to enlist the goodwill and energies of the Townhill community in deploying up to £10 million of European and other public funds in a strategic development scheme. Imposing structures on the community resulted in years of delay, hopeless speculation over the possible objectives of such an exercise and severe divisions within the community.

Since the introduction of the Urban Programme in the early 1970s, local and central government have failed to come to grips with the problem of empowerment of communities. Successive joint funding arrangements, the lack of comprehensive community development policy frameworks and the absence of any genuine will to consult with people on the ground ensured that members of the community were often the very last to know that they were to be 'developed'. The essential reason for this lies in the short-termism of policy around the 'community' sector. Long-term planning and action programmes appear to be outside the comprehension of those who administer and structure public financial matters. From the arbitrary curtailment of the CDP in the 1970s, to the recently closed Save the Children Cynon Valley Children's project (Thomas, A., 1999), the history of community development in Wales has been one of 'project culture'. Locally targeted action research, shifting focus to meet fashion whims in the administration, underspend schemes and the like have fostered a climate of marginality within the profession. There is a total lack of career structure, a culture of low pay and short-term employment, fragmented pension prospects and a belief that they will be the first to be dispensed with. European funding in Wales appears to be allocated according to the same ideas, whereas, in Ireland, the Combat Poverty Agency has demonstrated how consistent application of development resources can produce a lasting effect on the underlying problems faced by socially excluded groups.

We can see how certain ideologically acceptable agencies can be enlisted on an almost monopolistic basis for implementing some aspects of national policies. Groundforce and Communities that Care (1997) are two that come to mind. In these initiatives, local participation begins once the decision to engage the agency has been taken. There appears to be no investment anywhere in south Wales by local or central authorities to develop the planning capabilities of communities per se, prior to the need for them to engage in predetermined social change exercises. This contrasts with the central government's initiatives to tackle the considerable risks of engaging the divided communities of Northern Ireland. Since 1993, the Voluntary Activity Unit of the (Northern Ireland) Department of Health and Social Services began to explore a strategic approach to the difficulties facing their divided society. The EU began to fund a Peace Programme in 1995, and this gave a boost to the philosophy that communities had a significant contribution to make to developing workable policies at the level of the community (Department of Health and Social Services, 1999). It remains to be seen whether or not the Active Community Unit outlook that 'self-help can make good the so-called democratic deficit of representative government' will be taken up (Home Office, 1999, p. 1).

The hired leader

The situation in which leaders find greatness or fame for themselves has translated itself into a commercial product for others who have been quick to learn the skills of community mobilization without possessing the flair or drive of their idolized mentors. One of the clearest examples is that of those who came in the steps of Saul Alinsky in the United States. Alinsky set up the Industrial Areas Foundation (IAF) to exploit the financial potential of 'community organizing', and to spread the message of his particular form of democratic action for change (Stayton, 1986).

The Alinsky formula for successful community organization was as follows: the employment of a professional organizer by a financially independent community organization, together with a team of social researchers; the assessment of 'felt need' within the community – across every aspect of social, economic and political life; the audit of all social and quasi-social organizations within

the community, plus an assessment of the disposition of commercial and other outside agencies operating within the community; the identification of indigenous leaders, and giving them total
support (this group would probably have invited the IAF in
originally); the formation of a broad-based organization com-
posed of existing and new organizations which now unite on the
most prominent of 'felt-need' issues as identified; the establishment of a strategic plan for the attainment of the objectives
identified by the needs; implementation of a programme of
'actions' which target attainable goals. All of these are evaluated in
minute detail; adopting the philosophy that there is no 'ideology'
save for the right to democratic participation and the fulfilment of
the American dream of equal opportunity (Pitt and Keane, 1984).

The essential element centres on the employment of the highly
trained and tightly focused community organizer, who becomes the
chief orchestrator of the community effort. This role is designed to
be purchased 'off the shelf' on a contracted basis. The complete
package comes in return for a substantial fee (theoretically raised
from the resources of the hiring community), and the organizer
virtually guarantees success in the social change objectives
presented by the community. Apocryphal stories have been told of
how Alinsky once overcame the corporate might of Eastman
Kodak, using the most underhand tactics of moral blackmail, but
there are many corroborated stories of his successes, and the
Industrial Areas Foundation is still a thriving training and action
agency (Boyte, 1984; Pitt and Keane, 1984).

From this beginning, other movements and approaches to
community organization have been established. The second
essential 'Alinsky ingredient' for success is the mobilization for real
power around issues of commonly held interest. Where specific
community size or resource potential are insufficient for the task to
become successful, then a broad-based organization becomes the
vehicle for establishing community-will over interests and issues
upon which they can all agree. This approach has been adapted
by organizations which have survived for decades, and are 'federa-
tions of membership-based community organizations'. The
most famous of these is ACORN (Association of Community Organizations for Reform Now) which now commands the
subscribing support of hundreds of local affiliates spread across
the United States.

These ideas have been slow to catch on in Britain, where, perhaps, the prospect of a national Welfare State has diverted marginalized communities from seeking their full opportunities as citizens. However, there has been one serious attempt to subvert this 'welfare state' lethargy, and this stemmed from a seemingly unlikely source: the Church of England. Working through its associate charity, the Children's Society, specially selected professionals were sent to the IAF for training. At least one of this band of community organizers came from Wales, and worked for the Children's Society in Wales continuously until retirement. Fortunately, or unfortunately, we were spared any consequential demonstration of the 'conflict model' of community organization, which IAF espouses. Also, despite plentiful literature on the subject, and the availability of at least one local course at university level, there is no evidence that this kind of experience has developed any roots (Clarke, 2000; Alinsky, 1972; Bobo et al., 1996; Henderson and Salmon, 1995; Rothman, 1995). A Welsh brand of community development appears to be remaining constant to the conventional consensus model.

In England, there were some immediate results from this initiative, which came as the Church of England was to publish its swingeing critique of the failure of the Welfare State effectively to combat poverty. The Church published its *Faith in the City* in 1985 (Archbishop of Canterbury, 1985), which attacked the lack of social awareness of the Church with regard to poverty and the plight of marginalized communities in close proximity to Church buildings and established parishes. The Church called for social action and active advocacy for and with the poor. In response to *Faith in the City*, the Church set up its 'Urban Fund' to finance action in the worst areas (Jameson, 1998). In Bristol, citizen action resulted in the formation of a city-wide community organization network, where local communities cooperate for their collective needs in dealings with the local authority (Henderson and Salmon, 1995). In Gloucester, in the mid-1990s, organized direct action ousted the housing manager, and forced the reinstatement of the city's Law Centre. Both these campaigns were led by Children's Society IAF-trained community organizers.

In this model, the members of the community are considered to be the shareholders in a business which expects success, profit-maximization, and full accountability. The 'shareholders' are also the means of production, as they have to do the work by staging their own 'actions' and put up their own resources. They then have to agree to learn, actively, from their successes and failures. They contract themselves to follow the leadership and strategic thinking of their hired organizer. 'You gets what you pays for!'

Professional tyranny?

Control of the processes of change comes to a head in and around the decision-making arena. There is always going to be a tension between the perceptions, interests, needs and culture of those sponsoring a developmental exercise, and those vested with the responsibility of carrying it out. In some sense, there is an inverse correlation between the ability of a core management structure to manage community development directly, and the degree of complexity that goes into the make-up of that body. On the one hand, if the professional is met by divided priorities, or intensely politicized factions within management, then either fieldwork becomes paralysed through indecision, or the worker can take charge of the decision-making processes for day-to-day events. Conversely, if the employee perceives that an employer operates from a cohesive structure, and has a firm grip on the managerial system, then there is a strong likelihood that the word of command will be obeyed.

We have seen from some of the models described above, how seductive the leadership profile within a developmental process might be. These roles may attract leadership personalities who seek the consolidation of power in their own hands, and who revel in the spotlight which prominence in the social change structures can bring. Perversely, often the reverse situation is found in the majority of professional practice situations. We have described the relative weakness of even the skilled community development professionals in a process that is specifically dependent upon their capabilities, loyalties and integrity. Even more specifically, the professional is under personal pressure – and under scrutiny from a highly articulate and critical peer group – to justify field practice in terms of an identifiable ethical approach, which strives to achieve the shibboleth-like objectives of 'maximum feasible participation'. Under these circumstances, community development projects highly contradictory images of its power, structural position and direction of preferred practice objectives. This can add up to a classic example of workplace exploitation, where the apparent 'expert' is actually deprived of any real freedom of action, unless an unacceptable degree of control is taken arbitrarily. We have seen, also, that the community is rarely in any position to make demands of external funders and social planners because of their lack of collective consciousness and their inexperience of working within the system. In most situations, the community usually lacks a seat, or an articulate presence, at the decision-making table.

We must decide whether or not the role of the professional deserves to be fully recognized, and what the pitfalls and/or advantages are of putting the professional in the key management position in this process. A discussion on this topic raises the issue of whether the community development process itself is to be judged by results; what those results are supposed to be; and how those results are to be assessed. It is apparent that, where there is already in place an agency-directed strategy for the direction of change, then 'productivity' is going to be assessed against how output corresponds to the expected outcomes of these centralized policies.

As a 'professional', the worker might justifiably assume that, given the complex mix of resources which have to be coordinated to achieve the objectives of most development programmes, the strategic priority should be under professional jurisdiction. It is the person on the spot who must decide what tactical process should be engaged, adapted or abandoned at any time during the running of the scheme. 'Why hire a dog and bark yourself?' Surely, those putting up the resources for a complicated system of investment and change realize that they cannot hope to control the process from a distance. It is to the professional on the ground that they must turn for results, as well as direction, progress interpretation, information, guidance, ethical balance or on-the-spot decision-making. It could be argued that it is the professional, through being on the ground, and in touch with all the competing interests involved, who is in the only position to decide what is 'best' for the programme. It is surely a wimpish and defeatist doctrine to assume that the professional must be 'wrong', given all these advantages, as well as professional training and practical experience, being selected for demonstrating integrity, and being contracted to deliver a certain array of 'results'. Clarke (2000) argues that this is the only tenable position. Professionalism must demonstrate that it can exercise all the qualities that are expected of it. Given that the process of development also involves political manoeuvring, the delivery of quid pro quos and the balancing of the powerful (and the not so powerful) interests of the participants, no one else can be trusted.

This position has been attacked as being neo-colonialistic, imperialistic (Midgley, 1981), corrupt and elitist, and it has not been presumed to be the correct way to work since the classic writers of the 1950s and 1960s. Nevertheless, we must recognize that the pressures of reality produce situations for workers in which they have to exercise speed in decision-making. They have to rely on their experience, and they come to exercise considerable authority and responsibility in the running of programmes. They usually have to make do with very scarce resources, which does not make their task any easier. Without these themes being made explicit there would be a tendency for a vacuum to develop, and everybody would begin to blame everybody else, without taking responsibility themselves.

Defining community development

The literature is full of examples that demonstrate the corrupting influence of centralized programmes on the more purist expectations of community development pundits. In countries where there is a marked distinction between the (external/foreign) donor and the (internal) development agency and, again, between those agencies and the ultimate beneficiaries, a well-worked analysis exists in the literature. The debate is pointed, and professionals agonize over the contradictions (Kelly and Sewell, 1988; Popple, 1995; Thomas, D. N., 1995 and 1996; Clarke, 2000). This debate is not well developed in Britain with regard to the same relationships in contemporary community development, and has yet to surface at all in south Wales. The most recent development is the 'Compact' between the National Assembly for Wales and the voluntary sector (Secretary of State for Wales, 1998). In this document, the rights and obligations of both sectors are spelled out. In support of this Compact, five documents were produced to provide substance and meaning to the process of cooperation. One of these was entitled *Community Development*, and it provides a framework within which the state recognizes the nature and purpose of an active community role in the process of social, economic and political change (National Assembly/Wales Council for Voluntary Action, 2000).

This document goes further than most in trying to provide positive encouragement for the active community and the responsive state. What it does not do, and we may well wonder at the political sensitivity of the issue, is provide a working framework for the professional community development worker to play an active role in the process.

> Capacity building is, apparently, a process community groups go through to increase their effectiveness'. Support for 'catalysts' or 'animateurs' within the community whether they be insiders or outsiders, community workers or other professionals, or a person/persons from within a group of local people is important in helping community based organizations to become strong and self-sustaining. (pp. 3 and 5)

This is as close as the document gets to suggesting that there is a job of work to be done in getting the 'community' to play an equal and dynamic role in creating sustainable local economies and social structures.

In Britain, there is an incredible coyness about recognizing that the only way in which communities are going to be able to 'compete' in the way a document like this describes, is to have professional support built into the process. This includes communities playing an active role in the mixed economy of welfare, in the local economy, or in the struggle to overcome social impoverishment. This means the establishment of permanent resource personnel, trained and strategically placed such that they can enable the processes so hopefully expected of communities by the Compact. We justify this position in the following analysis.

Community development for south Wales

We have taken a hard look at the definitions of community development and recognize the serious contradictions that they contain. The first stems from the confusion between whether or not community development is a 'process' or whether it is some form of change-interventionist activity, practised by professionals (or others). Is it possible for it to be both: a passive community engaged by the professional, plus the ensuing change process that follows that engagement? Of immediate relevance to these questions is whether or not the 'community' can be said to be capable of developing itself (the explicit message of the Compact, pp. 51–2 above: National Assembly/Wales Council for Voluntary Action, 2000).

Next, we have to discuss whether we should look for an ideal type of community development or settle for something that is less than perfect? In this volume, we are responsible for bringing to the attention of a wide audience the painstaking efforts of practitioners from all walks of life, in all sorts of social and economic circum-stances, and within a wide range of social/economic/political situations. To what extent are we justified in throwing back in their faces the 'fact' that their dedication does not come up to scratch compared with the idealized view of armchair editors? We are not for one minute suggesting that we accept anything less than a realistic view of the world in which community development must either thrive or else wither away. We believe that these descriptions of community development in south Wales deserve a framework that reflects the real world, rather than a fabricated and abstracted position. Consequently, we are also convinced that community development should not be taken for granted. It should be judged for what it does, for what it claims to be able to do, and the real effects that it has on the lives of the people who are engaged through it.

It is time that the context of community development in Wales was explained, and analysed intensively. There are lessons to be learned in all sectors from the diversity which is found here. For these reasons we have decided to make a firm statement about community development. We do this by defining the essential components, and then combining their essential components into a definition of our own. This will provide the lens through which the case material in this volume may be evaluated.

Development

This has been described as a 'totality': 'It is an integrated cultural process, comprehending values such as the natural environment, social relations, education, production, consumption and well-being' (Lopes, 1994, p. 37). In south Wales, where the effects of de-industrialization are still deeply entrenched in the social fabric, it must be a bitter irony to reflect on the range of economic recovery models that have been tried out to revive the declining economic fortunes of the population. The collapse of the mining industry made the vulnerability of this 'one-product economy' starkly apparent. The economic theories of 'take-off', postulated in the post-Second World War desire to stimulate the economies of post-colonial nations, has been dramatically tested in Wales, a member of the 'developed world'. It is as pointed here as it is in the faltering economies of Central Africa (Rostow, 1964; Schuurman, 1993). It became readily apparent that, even where there was unforced labour, free markets and entrepreneurial spirit, local capital formation might not take place. When this failed to materialize, social progress suffered incalculable setbacks.

Following the decline in the mining industry, governments have tinkered around with economic intervention, but nothing of substance has come up to restore the economic fortunes of the area. There is still the belief that neo-liberal economic models of the free market will allow the marginalized areas of the British economy to avoid the 'Brazilian effect' of poverty and affluence existing and persisting side by side for generations (Rahnema, 1993; Wolfe, 1996). It is no wonder that the policy-makers have concentrated on development-led community regeneration. These policies have been building up over the years, but their impact has been a mixed blessing to the settled communities where their fortunes have been bound up in the shifting fashions of the European Union, and the limited vision of most politicians towards inward investment. We are suggesting that the whole concept of 'development' be expanded, and that the force of the community, even the poorest communities, be brought to support the national regeneration effort.

Development theorists are now intrigued by the attempts to move beyond pure economic theory to produce models for social and economic revival. Alas, these are not yet apparent in the south Wales area. If we were to take a leaf out of the international aid agencies' notebook, we might consider the employment of socio-economists and anthropologists rather than just bankers and regional assistance programmes (Booth, 1994). If there are serious doubts about the prospects of economic revival using 'traditional' economic development methods, then at least social development approaches might be allowed to try alternative routes (Midgley, 1995; Toye, 1993).

Powerful arguments have been raised about the 'relevance' of development in the purely economic sense. If development does not result in the empowerment of the people but leaves them still vulnerable to the power of external decision-makers, then the benefits become illusory when the economic plug is pulled (Edwards, 1989 and 1993; Booth, 1994). This is the more serious backdrop to our study of community development approaches in south Wales. We begin with an exploration of 'development' in order to discover what our ultimate objectives might be. If, on the other hand, we are not successful in achieving the economic reformation necessary to restore the fortunes of south Wales, then other proactive approaches to enabling the social fabric to survive must be allowed to engage with the remaining social issues that will affect the people.

Development can be elaborated as a historical change process, where deliberate efforts are taken to achieve positive or progressive outcomes (Thomas, A., 2000, p. 42). Development could also be viewed from a neutral standpoint, as merely the passage of change. When value is attributed to its direction and to the notional 'worth' of any outcomes, then value systems have their part to play in the selection of targets for change, and in the subsequent interpretation of change processes as they occur. For this approach, it is necessary to impose a framework of ethics, which can itself be the subject of critical scrutiny. We are happy to apply the framework developed by Goulet, where ethics become the 'means of means' (Goulet, 1995, p.12). These 'means' allow for a resolution of the tension between the following factors: the action requirements of solving the problem facing the community; the legal, policy and cultural framework within which the work has to be done; and the idealized values of the professional or of the society where the action is taking place (see chapter 3). Ethics allow choices and decisions to be made, and action to follow. They are the framework for compromise which allows morality to be tempered by the other rational demands of survival. They demand reflection and consciousness, and not mere rationalization. But they exist to permit the possible rather than only to demand the impossible (Corbridge, 1993; Goulet, 1995).

In this volume, many of the contributor studies may be anything but impartial. They reflect the crucial vulnerability of the south Wales economy and its communities as they struggle to survive. Our own attempts to analyse the essentials of these studies will also expose the contradictions suggested by Goulet's framework for seeking ethical practice. But we do believe that there is a good-practice objective. Because we are considering the implications for targeted social intervention, it is necessary to make this statement as explicit as possible: community workers seek development, and development for us means the positive or progressive change brought about through planned material intervention and investment. If development in the economic sense comes without the parallel attainment of the population to achieve sustainable social and economic well-being on their own account, then we do not consider this to be 'development' within the definition we seek.

Community

We have seen how difficult it is to define and engage a 'community', due to the diversity of the population, the shifting allegiances of the participants and the complicated policy objectives of state and other interventionist agencies within the context of a locality or area. Insofar as the aspirations of 'communities of interest' can be accomplished within the framework generated by the idea of 'locality', then we acknowledge that a formation geared to specific group-membership qualifications may have some validity. Our position on this is that it is the concept of citizenship that we see as the most generalized and justifiable focus for the objectives of development. Dividing the 'community' into sub-sections, with the notion that 'exclusion' or segregation is fully legitimate, diverts attention from and, thus, investment in, the full potential of the community to benefit from change. The whole ecological community will be affected by any changes that take place in a specific part of it, in any event. To exclude the whole from an initial analysis and programme design is wasteful and, ultimately, divisive and disruptive.

We recognize that funders, planners and architects of social change have to target segments of society and discrete areas of the environment. When the process of community development is applied in these circumstances, this distortion must be acknowledged, and possible shortcomings in the outcomes identified.

Where there are divisions within 'communities' due to the forces of outmoded traditions, imposed power structures and cultural factors such as gender relations, then the professional must attempt to obtain acknowledgement of these forces. They must strive for an acceptance of realism by stressing that objectives will not be attained if exclusion and oppression of vital parts of the community are maintained.

From this it can be seen that divisions in 'community' may be lasting, and even permanent. The realization of commonality must come through engagement in problem-solving and interaction, even if taboos and custom make this difficult. It must be seen that it is the human, social, political and economic institutions of society that make up community, 'warts and all'.

We have looked at the examples presented by Ireland and Scotland (chapter 1), and we can see clearly that in Wales the advantage of building on the experience of the Community Development Programme was lost. The growth of community development in the other nations has been pronounced by comparison, and they sought out the lessons from the CDP, and prospered by them. But Wales is a special community. It is gradually moving towards bilingualism, which has immediate significance for community-oriented professionals, and the countryside/town divide is being marked by the drive towards rural Welsh-language development schemes, and community-rooted projects. Those interested in realizing the potential that 'community' presents have seen that the Welsh language is a potent lever when it comes to affirming identity and collective effort.

Community development

Community development is about putting the 'community' into the development process. This is no easy task and the risk elements are high. High-quality control is demanded for the management of the forces of change, and also for the management of the forces of resistance to change. The same qualities are required for the identification of issues, and the speedy resolution of value conflict. We consider that these are best achieved through the employment of specially qualified, trained and contracted professional workers. The achievement of 'progressive' change outcomes, and the necessity to engage society at all levels of organization simultaneously in the achievement of these objects, requires great application and skill. For many of the 'participants', the ordinary citizens who are not protected by institutional employment conditions, the consequences of the failure of development are serious indeed. For them, the investment of scarce resources, and the requirement to devote both time and effort could amount to a major sacrifice if it proves to be misguided and a project fails. This is so for everyone, but it is especially true for those in marginalized social conditions, who are the target for much community development activity.

Progressive development requires that the change processes be well informed and planned to the fullest possible extent. Preparation for change must extend downwards and upwards through all levels of the community that will be affected. Every effort must be taken to ensure that those who are to be engaged, consulted, or considered relevant to the objectives of the development are included in the preparation process. Unless resources are released for this purpose, then there are going to be deficits that will bear negatively on future outcomes.

With community members unused to the processes of planning, and still further unused to anticipating the outcomes of planned change, specialist skills are required to ensure their participation. Their capacity will need to be advanced progressively as the nature of the problems they are forced to solve become more and more complex (Hambleton and Hoggart, 1988; Eade, 1997). As the technical requirements of change increasingly require highly specialized applications, so there is an obvious need for a highly trained, professional generalist to provide a particular form of leadership. This person needs to be in command of the basics of all these specialisms and to be able to procure expert assistance for all participants. This generalist's skills have to be known and respected by all other participants as a necessary input into all planning and action activities. This is the real meaning of the term empowerment – people being ready and capable to play a full part in planning and creating change for their own environment and socio-economic systems. But even empowered people are not full-time development personnel. They need support, expert advice and trained people to assist them, facilitating the process of acquiring new skills, assimilating new information and executing new strategies.

Not only do they need these inputs as specific challenges arise but they need them as the impact of ongoing change unfolds. A community development input is required on a sustainable basis if sustainability is to be a feature of enlightened and meaningful public policies. This is the special ingredient provided by the community development worker – as the servant to the process of change. To some large extent, the professional worker becomes the custodian of the values of the democratic process as it is enacted. What, then, are these values? How are they to be applied? We go directly into this discussion and then, armed with a package made up from our history, the theories of bringing about change and the philosophies that we choose to guide us through the process, we can explore the case materials. This will provide us with a clearer view of how to interpret their effects, successes and problems. These case studies will also give us a clearer insight into how to measure the impact of the community development worker, and to discover whether or not the claims that are being made here are justified.

3 Values and current issues in community development

STEVE CLARKE, MARTIN HOBAN, DERITH POWELL and
ANTONINA MENDOLA BYATT

Crynodeb

Rhoddir strwythur i'r drafodaeth o werthoedd a moeseg datblygu cymunedol gan y pynciau grym, cyfranogi a phroblemau'n ymwneud â chodi ymwybyddiaeth. Mae materion dosbarth a dylanwad cymdeithas prynwyr yn cymylu'r diffiniadau o amcanion a modelau ar gyfer ymyriad. Mae gwahaniaethau sylweddol rhwng ffyrdd traddodiadol, Prydeinig o wynebu awdurdod o'u cymharu â'r rheini yn yr Unol Daleithiau. Trafodir y rhain yn ogystal â'r gwerthoedd a gysylltir â gwleidyddiaeth ddosbarth draddodiadol yng Nghymru. Y cwestiwn hanfodol yw a yw'r adnoddau a phrosesau sy'n gysylltiedig â mentrau cynlluniedig a strategol yn troi gweithwyr datblygu cymunedol yn *élite* neu beidio. Mae rhan sylweddol o'r bennod hon hefyd yn trafod sut mae delio â'r dimensiwn hwn.

Mae camau diweddar gan y llywodraeth i sicrhau adnoddau'r gymuned wrth ddarparu gwasanaethau'r 'Wladwriaeth Les' wedi arwain at yr angen i archwilio polisïau'r llywodraeth 'Lafur Newydd', ac i ystyried swyddogaeth datblygu cymunedol yn y sefyllfa hon. Edrychir o'r newydd ar rai o faterion y gorffennol – megis cynlluniau 'gwneud gwaith' ac ildiad awdurdod lleol i Ddeddf Ariannu Tai 1972 – ac ystyrir hefyd rôl sefydliadau fel Cymorth i Fenywod. Nid yw'r angen am gloriannu a hunanfeirniadaeth yn llai erbyn hyn nag y bu yn y 1970au.

The case studies that form the substance of this volume are part of a continuing history of community development in Wales. They demonstrate that their contribution, through investment in social capital and professional support, can have a marked influence on the lives of many people and their communities. They influence the way in which people appreciate their environment, and they have changed and will continue to change people's material, spiritual and political expectations and aspirations. These case studies describe the settings, the elements of the action and the populations involved in their work. They reflect a blend of the workers' own understanding of what has happened, and the priorities which time, resources and the employers imposed on the work.

In community development, outcomes are often measured in terms of their paper objectives, and these are most often described only in terms of material or tangible social change, for instance groups formed, moneys raised, activities run, membership harnessed and so on. At the start of a project, after the planning stage and once a project is up and running, there is often a discernible shift of interest within it: from the abstract towards the purely practical and pragmatic. The ideal of attaining praxis through testing theory in practice usually gives way to managing routine events, and solving the crises as they arrive. Consequently, investigations into any real progress on the underlying rationale of any project can be neglected. Instead, shallow reports might be prepared on how the bare bones of policy are being met, and these can be put forward to funders. Additionally, materials might be gathered together in preparing publicity material. There may well be a great deal of soul searching in the proverbial expresso bar, but not much of this translates into effective planned modification of the work being done.

In light of this inexorable pressure within the work situation, it follows from our discussion of the ethics of development in the previous chapter, that we consider in some detail the whole question of values in community development. Are there any underlying values that professionals should strive towards in their work? What factors dictate what those values should be, and how are they realized in practice? Do these values apply similarly to the communities that undergo the changes of development as well as to their professional change agents? These values may have a higher or lower profile within the work. Either they might be stated distinctly throughout a project or process, or they might only be identified historically, after the workers have left. It is especially important that values are not ignored, and we will try to make them explicit in this section. Through this, we hope that readers will be better able to judge the histories described in the case studies, and also obtain a better perspective on their own work.

Through this discussion, we need to discover who are the real beneficiaries of community development interventions. Just what is reality when it comes to setting expectations? How significant are the sentiments behind the rhetoric? Is there scope for idealism and/or ideology, and how tightly are the boundaries drawn about the workers? We will examine these questions through the prisms of some of the most frequently used slogans in the trade.

Another factor emerges from the literature, the histories and the case studies. This is 'factor X', the qualities and the motivation of the people doing the work (Francis et al., 1984; Baldock, 1977; Gallagher, 1977; Bobo et al., 1996; Kelly and Sewell, 1988; Chambers, 1997; Eade and Williams, 1995). Are professional community workers driven by their own agenda? Do they accomplish what they do through a combination of personal beliefs, energy, foresight and/or determination? What drives them towards the achievement of some personal fulfilment? Will this 'factor' ever become public knowledge? Some are driven by a sense of injustice, or, perhaps, by some form of guilt. Others may be inspired by the sheer challenge of picking up the threads of an entire community, and mobilizing it against or towards some new barrier or hurdle.

Practitioner ethics and values

The ethics of development are usually discussed more from the bottom upwards than from the top downwards. Nevertheless, the process of development all begins with macro-economic policies set in the halls of the World Bank, or in the chambers of the national or local government. By the time policies or resources find their way to the streets of the neighbourhood, many decisions have been taken, and the directions they are to take are more or less fixed. The literature on practice and the public pronouncements of the workers are seemingly united around some strict principles based on natural justice, anti-oppression, ownership, participation and change through empowerment. Most of the texts take these principles for granted or spend a great deal of space refining points and setting out plans for their attainment. Case-study material does not usually concern itself with such lofty matters, but tells us of objectives that have been gained. The actual response from the citizen on the ground is largely absent, as are the heart-felt feelings of the professional practitioners who put the process into motion (Burghardt, 1982; Brager and Holloway, 1978).

Is it a practical proposition to discuss ethics, morals or values alongside the work while it is happening? In the face of poverty, misery, oppression and social exclusion, is this discussion just a luxury for those who can go home at night to the comfort and security of the suburbs? Goulet sees the ethics of development being the compromise between the need of politics to achieve the achievable within the means available, and the fundamental values of society and the professional class (Goulet, 1995). This allows a range of latitude between expectations and outcome, between principle and action. Banks draws this division more starkly by highlighting the distinct divide between personal/professional values and those of the market place (Banks, 1995). The tension here springs from the gap between externally assessed prescriptions for a particular local need, and the actual outcomes that become possible when the work begins. Midgley's plea still stands today: for local accountability (indigenization); training practitioners for the attainment of the objectives of need, rather than the objectives of prescription; and, thirdly, actually to target the needs of the oppressed and excluded, rather than focusing on externally devised priorities. This stands up well in the 'developed world' as it did when written for 'developing economies' (Midgley, 1981).

The difficulty today starts with defining a community. There are grounds for ignoring 'community' when addressing the questions that arise in a mass, urban society. Goulet suggests concentrating on a 'community of need', that is, one that has been identified externally because of its special characteristics (Goulet, 1995). 'Community' is a sentimental term in a materialist and consumerist age, smacking of the rhetoric of street politics more than the need to engineer change of a practical nature. This approach is faced up to by Oxfam (Eade and Williams, 1995, chapter 1; also Perlman and Gurin, 1972; Midgley, 1986). Most writers confine themselves to an overview of sociological writing on the subject, and then get on with the rest of their message (Mikkelsen, 1995; Thomas, D. N., 1983), whereas others see participation as being essentially an individual activity. The involvement of the greatest number then becomes the essence of development (Oakley et al., 1991; Etzioni, 1993). The point is that just because there are no absolutes when it comes to defining a 'community', the concept is a real one for those responsible for mobilizing people on the ground. Whether or not community actually exists, something is (or has to be) created to serve as the medium for exercising the collective will in the processes of change. Once this medium is identified, it has to taken very seriously indeed.

If community has to be defined by the practitioner, then considerable power rests with that practitioner. This leaves wide open the question of the personal agenda of that worker. In an age of consumerism, an age where the idea of 'instant gratification' holds sway, people are distracted from addressing basic issues in their search for greater satisfactions (Ritzer, 2000; Chambers, 1997; Adams, B., 1993). People will more readily be directed towards activities and aspects of life that appear to reinforce the trends of fashion. Workers, already tied to the needs of their employers, may seek openly, or not so openly, to pursue ends that meet a wide range of possible needs. The question of worker values is addressed clearly by Perlman and Gurin (1972), in which they caution against allowing radical, personal agendas to subvert the needs of the people that may not be met through the directed pressure of the professional. We welcome all cautionary advice because we never know when we may need it ourselves. However, we need to decide for ourselves whether or not personal values play an important necessary part in the role of a community worker.

We can illustrate this by examining the most simple of concepts: neighbourhood work. When a practitioner enters a locality with the intention of changing the dynamics of the community through the creation of new local organizations and groups, there are some crucial distinctions that have to be made. Does the worker have a public or a private agenda behind the initiative? Does the deployment of the resources which the worker represents both in person and as a representative of an outside agency have any bearing on the direction to which the worker will direct any initiatives taken by the community? Does the professional have any 'professional' objectives for the outcomes of the work, and/or are there personal objectives which will claim precedence in the priorities that have to be set? In addition to these crucial questions, is the practitioner aware of these issues/questions, and how competent is the worker to deal with the demands of setting and delivering an agenda on any of these themes?

Participation and empowerment

Participation was the slogan of activists in the late 1960s, and Arnstein's enduring *Ladder of Citizen Participation* provides a classification of the hurdles and barriers that limit a citizen's influence on public life (Arnstein, 1969). This 'ladder' is constantly being reviewed and adapted to suit many sectors of welfare and community activity (for instance Hart, 1992). From a community development perspective, the best of these is that of Burns, who extended the analysis deeper into the political meaning of participation. He shows how 'participation' is offered and effected by those who hold power, particularly in areas where the consequences of 'power-sharing' make little immediate impact on the overall power-holding position. Power is seldom given away voluntarily. Participation is often confused with consultation, and other therapeutic activities, especially by hopeful participants. It becomes more difficult for those without power to make any impression: the greater are the vested interests, the more impact real change may have, and the more complex the action needed (Burns, 1991).

In Britain, participation originally gained currency through the Skeffington Report, in the context of town planning (Skeffington, 1969). Here, the concept was woven into a fabric of 'top-down' procedures that ensured that the participants' contribution only came at a point after the main decisions of principle had been made. Nevertheless, a whole generation of community workers saw this report as a breakthrough in a process which might one day democratize planning and problem-solving in the public arena. For the first time, communities at the bottom of the economic ladder found that there was expertise available to progress their claims for more involvement in environmental issues. Most importantly, it introduced the concept of planning into the repertoire of paid workers who, hitherto, might have wondered why spontaneity and ideological purity were not enough in the business of social change.

The analysis of public participation in planning depends heavily on an accepted northern cultural view of the nature of society and the way in which decisions are made. More radical models have emerged from developing economies, where the structure of society appears more fluid, and the institutions of state and commerce have not established a stranglehold. Participatory Action Research (PAR), through which members of the 'consuming' community set the agenda, and evaluate progress themselves, is one way in which the humane objectives of development can be salvaged (Rahman, 1993, pp. 74–91). PAR draws heavily on the Freirean notion that change has to be organic (endogenous: Rahman, 1993, pp. 217–18), and that the subject of the experience must carry the change forward.

The question, however, remains: whether or not 'popular' participation, conscientization, and collective effort for and by the oppressed working on their own agenda, has to wait until all the participants somehow change into 'purified', aware citizens before any real progress is achieved? Freire must surely expect too much. Rahnema paints a more realistic and, overall, a more pessimistic view. He recognizes the spiritual value of participation and the 'staggering contagion of intelligence and creativity' which it creates. Nevertheless, he fears more the 'often invisible and structural processes of addictive manipulation' of an 'economized' life and culture in a globalized environment that lures the oppressed away from their true liberation (Rahnema, 1993, p.123). The joys of instant gratification will overwhelm rational thought and planning – 'McDonaldization' (Ritzer, 2000). Do community workers wilfully blind themselves to the seemingly tiny impact that they make on global forces such as these? Would the final realization of their marginality deal the deathblow of disillusion to what they do for a living? We will leave this in abeyance for now.

The term 'empowerment' has now come to replace 'participation' in the vocabularies of those professionals who have the responsibility for involving ordinary people in solving pressing social, welfare and micro-economic problems. It is found particularly in locality-based initiatives. This term, coupled with another, 'sustainability', is now well established in the thinking of 'partnership schemes' and urban regeneration programmes. On the one hand, the concept of empowerment can be interpreted as misleading or paternalistic. On the other, the one element of political life which the poor and oppressed lack is power. Perhaps intervention into their lives by professionals can only ever be justified if it is to rectify that imbalance.

Empowerment can also imply that the preferences which people have taken all their lives do not reflect their 'true' potential. There is a 'better' solution waiting – just add empowerment, and it will be attained! It is not often marketed as such to those whose participation is solicited. People are focused on 'perceived needs', and then shown, step by easy step, how to attain them. In this way, professional agendas are then engaged to plot how people can be supported. Most often, empowerment is a concept reserved for processes of evaluation and described by professionals in reports to their employers, or to the funders of social programmes. Indicators are devised to measure the degree to which people have been induced to change, to 'take charge' of their own lives, and develop activities in line with the programme's plans for change. This is usually done in terms of identifiable outcomes, objectives to be reached or targets to be met

Direct calls to take up power are seen as being revolutionary, and not part of the 'development' process. Histories of discrimination, exploitation and manipulation are to be played down. Instead of seeking to explain the past, and deploy resources to recover losses or reverse exploitation, the people are usually defused into 'constructive' activities. Fears of the potential impact and significance of conflict, either engineered by professional intervention, or arising out of fresh insight into social predicaments, is likely to be greatly distorted in the perceptions of established interests. We will discuss the implications of this on communities, institutions of government, and employer agencies when we consider analytical models below.

Friedmann describes the 'rational' power of the self-serving, independent citizen in a market economy, and contrasts it with an idealized situation in an 'alternative economy'. In the latter, individuals are sensitized to the common good, and their own best interests are understood as being dependent on the whole (Friedmann, 1992). In this alternative view, people are empowered if they are aware that all dimensions of life are integrated: their own activities and the environment in which they move. This embraces their social situation (domestic and social stability), their political experience (enfranchisement without structural oppressions), and their psychological perceptions (personal sense of wholeness and capability) (Friedmann, 1992, pp. 30–4). In 'alternative development', the objective of the process, and, thus, the goal of the practitioner, is to achieve this state of conscious interdependence for all individuals in the community. Friedmann's view is commonplace, in that it does not describe the confrontation with non-alternative systems from which the 'power' has to be wrung. Instead he describes models through which Non-Governmental Organizations (NGOs) can be and are successful in winning the confidence of oppressed peoples and starting them on the road to democratic control through small local actions. He agrees that the poor are unlikely to spark off their own organizational development, and seeks leadership in progressive projects from the NGOs (Perlman and Gurin, 1972; see also Clarke, 1996, on professional control of the process). Somehow, the agents of the state and of these NGOs are to act benignly, and 'allow' the progress to be achieved. Susan Holcombe describes how tightly centralized control can be combined with openness at the base of the organization and transparency in its procedures, but this is a rare example indeed, and one which we will have to import if we are to learn how it works (Holcombe, 1995).

This combination of openness and centralized control contrasts markedly with the view of Stevenson and Parsloe. They have decided that the objective of 'empowerment' is purposefully to limit the aspirations of the oppressed population. Rather it should steer them towards objectives that are divined to be within their capabilities (Stevenson and Parsloe, 1993, pp. 6–7). This has been described as 'the myopia of good intentions' (Jack, 1995, p. 22). Citizen capabilities and insights into the underlying problems are sacrificed uncritically, and a gloss is put on the necessity to deliver services. Against this, we can quote even the most gentle of revolutionaries, Paulo Freire, when he writes, 'There can be no "conscientization" without denunciation of unjust structures . . .' (Freire, 1970, p. 76). It is obvious that, with interpretations so widely apart on the same topic, there is considerable confusion and lack of common cause amongst those working for the 'empowerment' of the people.

'Empowerment' is limited by the relative power of those who offer it. It is, therefore, only a partial offer to those on the receiving end (Friedmann, 1992; Jack, 1995; Nelson and Wright, 1995; Rowlands, 1997). But it is a solution offered by mainstream social workers as a mechanism to justify their actions within the mixed 'economy' of welfare and community care (Adams, R., 1996; Banks, 1995; Stevenson and Parsloe, 1994; Braye and Preston-Shoot, 1995). In practice, as social workers in Britain do not offer 'development' but 'empowerment over self', it offers little to the 'participants'. The power equation is seldom addressed in full. In the 'classics' of British social work literature, 'community work' is sometimes listed (usually last) alongside other 'methods of intervention', but more often not at all (Coulshed and Orme, 1998; Davies, 1985).

The limits of the neighbourhood perspective

While the horizons of community development have widened greatly over the past fifty years, it is nevertheless evident that the methods used by practitioners to stimulate grassroots activity have remained mostly unchanged. Further, it is 'grassroots' activity that appears to dominate perceptions of what practice is all about. Stimulating 'community groups' is seen as the essence of 'community work'. Community development in this mould will certainly have its effect, and will influence those exposed to it in particular ways. Nevertheless, this is a very limiting view, which actually describes only a small part of the picture. 'Locality-based development', as it is called, or neighbourhood work, sets the horizons for workers very firmly within a framework that can be gravely unambitious if followed slavishly. It will restrict the limits that they set for themselves in terms of change objectives and in terms of the skills and insights that they recognize will be required by them for the job (Goetschius, 1969; Henderson and Thomas, 1987).

Over the years, at the grassroots level, the sameness of the professional approach is reflected in the similarity of content between the 'how to' guides to intervention (Batten, 1962; Biddle and Biddle, 1965; Goetschius, 1969; Henderson and Thomas, 1987; Association of Community Workers, 1981; Pinder, 1995; Skinner, 1997). They all stress the need to introduce 'non-directive' methods to generate group solidarity (Batten, 1967). They then direct the worker to establish groups and create an organizational cohesiveness with them. Sustainability has to be established, and then the worker has to withdraw from the relationship. All are rather vague on how they actually achieve the necessary changes in their citizen-clients, and all are thin on establishing any theoretical basis for their work. The question for us is: are these 'guides' being coy about something, or are certain truths revealed only in practice? The outstanding feature of the work behind these vagaries is that something definitely seems to 'work' in practice. We hope to discuss some of the underlying issues behind these phenomena in this chapter. We hope that by unpacking some of these 'traditional' approaches, we will discover some of the strengths, weaknesses and potentials in community development practice in south Wales.

It might be claimed that Jack Rothman had said it all when he classified the work of community development workers into three distinctive settings or roles: locality development, social planning and social action for change (Rothman, 1995). These terms translate into: (1) the creation of local, neighbourhood groups for local service activity; (2) working with organizations for problem-solving of larger social issues across wider horizons and between cooperating agencies; and (3) the building of organizations for confrontation tactics. Rothman presents us with some difficulties. Firstly, as an American, albeit one of their most eminent theorists on the subject, he remains virtually unread in Britain. Secondly, the impact of the local social context on community development methods and expectations is considerable and it is therefore difficult to graft on foreign guidelines without considerable modification. Lastly, the underlying values of society at community level are completely different. The endless competition between factions and settled minorities are well documented in the USA, and their situations allow unlimited opportunities for community organizers and the creation of self-help institutions (Bailey, 1974; Boyte, 1984; Naples, 1998a; Rubin and Rubin, 1992). The traditions of British community development workers within a Welfare State culture have grown from a different cultural set. Ideal outcomes such as the primacy of needs over wants, the redistribution of wealth and the attainment of social justice through changing the institutions of society command a powerful place in the perceptions and folklore of the workers (Goulet, 1995; Bolger et al., 1981; Mayo, 1979 and 1994).

The most obvious difference between American writers and practitioners and their British counterparts is the basic pattern of objectives that they are seeking. In America, there is no clear statement about social justice along an ideological continuum between capitalism and socialism (there are exceptions, for instance, Burghardt, 1982; Bobo et al., 1996; Fagan, 1979; Miller, 1987;

Naples, 1998a, etc., but they do not get much of an airing in the established publishing houses). Instead, there is a notion that interest groups in society are competing against the established order (and, by implication, against each other, somewhat) for their slice of the 'American Dream', and a meaningful voice around the table of democracy. In Britain, the crisis of socialism is the crucial element which has swamped the public rhetoric for decades. This has diverted community development workers from focusing on those elements of professionalism which might make them more effective and more persuasive in the corridors of power. Whether or not community workers should ever enter the corridors of power is still very much a live issue in Britain, and the advent of the 'contract culture' has induced a tense atmosphere. As we shall see, it is a dilemma which stretches all the way back to the days of the Manpower Services Commission and make-work programmes (see below pp. 81–2).

Another difference between British community development 'programmes' and those in the United States, is that in the USA, national and local government has had decades of experience of dealing with local organizers, local community corporations, ethnic organizations, women's organizations and focused pressure groups on a large scale (Bailey, 1974; Marris and Rein, 1967; Blaustein and Faux, 1972; Swedner, 1982). Yet another difference is that the tradition of self-interest rather than ideology proving to be the main motivation has been woven into the essence of community organization in class, ethnic and ordinary citizen action-planning since the beginnings of their democratic system. Professional organizers, such as Saul Alinsky, Mike Miller and Ed Chambers, are nationally respected figures, whereas there are no comparable figures in the annals of British community development.

In Wales, we are faced with a very different situation from those elsewhere in Britain or in the United States of America. Wales is a small country, with a small population, spread across many small communities. Although these communities, rural and urban, reflect the problems of cities and countryside in larger political constellations, social issues in all settings appear more immediate, more relevant to the others within the nation. They are recognized as being part of one's own situation and perspective on society as a whole. It is obvious that the economy and political destiny of Wales is tightly bound in with the global forces which shape the whole of Europe but, nevertheless, there is a feeling of 'neighbourhood' about the whole country. The advent of the National Assembly for Wales has helped to give more focus to this feeling, whatever the individual voters' original views may have been at the time of the referendum. The launch of Community Development Cymru in March 2000 is a testimony to this.

This notion of 'togetherness' may be a delusion, but there is definitely a resurgence of feeling about the nature and purpose of community development to which this volume wishes to contribute. However, this book has to be more than just a rallying cry for political opportunists. We have to get right inside the subject matter, and present the readers with a meaningful analysis of the subject, its underlying values and the issues which confront it today. We hope that, by doing this, we may make a contribution to the future of community development in a resurgent Wales. We must not be seduced into thinking that, because we now have the ability to seek our destiny from within ourselves, we are going to find it in our own back yard. Community development workers who are preoccupied with the purely 'local' issues will lose perspective. Wales has issues of macro-policy which need to be addressed, both at the local/national level and at an international one: for instance the Welsh language and bilingualism; structural unemployment; development tourism; and other matters which also have great resonance in development debates around the world (Chambers, 1992; Goulet, 1995).

Planning and elitism – posing the question about role and purpose

There is much more to community development than (mere) work in the community and, once the pattern of work shifts outwards, into the social planning and problem-solving plane, a dramatic shift in expectations arises. Social planning and problem-solving demand thorough-going changes in methodology and in the behaviour of practitioners. It represents a completely different ideological approach to social capital and to the capacities of communities to conceptualize, create, plan and manage their own affairs. It requires a transformation in outlook for the people in the communities and groups, for the practitioners in the field, and for the agents and officers of public institutions and private enterprise that may have an interest in the proceedings. We will attempt to describe the forces that are at play in establishing this divide, and hope to uncover some of the obstacles for people at all levels in the community in intervening effectively in a variety of ways in social, economic and political issues. We will draw a little more on the history of the south Wales area to set the scene for this discussion.

Over the years, there has been a profound change in the language used to describe the nature and purpose of professional community development activity. These changes have accompanied a shifting focus for the work into new settings, and have kept a lively debate alive within the profession. In Wales, this 'debate' has come in flurries, as the fashion for community development has waxed and waned. In the 1970s, there was a lively interprofessional grouping which included planners, architects, social workers, environmental health workers, community activists and many more. Direct action by 'residents' was the main vehicle for progress, and professionals fed into the projects and initiatives as and when their skills were required. One persistent dilemma was the concern about how professional knowledge, even if simplified, might become generally understood across a wider population. On the one hand, speed was of the essence if plans generated elsewhere were to be challenged effectively. But for this to be possible, awareness had first to be raised, a reasonable understanding achieved across as wide a social base as possible, and informed decisions taken in line with the citizens' choice.

The problem was (and still is) that decisions in the statutory sphere were taken by professionals based on complicated problem analyses and the technical solutions required to implement them. 'Development' was the task of corporate officials, and the involvement of the community was introduced at a later stage. In fact, the integration of a 'community development' process into their scheme was not often on the official agenda at all, despite the Skeffington Report! Complicated questions would not fully be aired at community level but, somehow, informed advocates had to make up this deficit and represent community views and interests within the unyielding official protocols. These advocates might be drawn from the communities themselves; they might be hastily trained leaders of protest groups; very rarely, they might be ward councillors, who risked excommunication from a party caucus if they did so. Most often in the early days, they were drawn from the ranks of professional community workers, or from the bands of professionals from other disciplines who freely offered their services.

An exemplary case of this was given by the Shelter Community Action Team (SCAT), two of whose members were seconded to the Newport Polypill project in 1973 (see chapter 15). 'Alternative' planning and other technical advice was put at the disposal of community groups struggling to overturn a council redevelopment plan. Technical education with a wide base across the community was achieved through intensive street work, followed by group activity. Once preferences and priorities had been chosen by the community using this information, the SCAT input changed to one of advocate for the community. The community was then represented by them, and by members of the Polypill project, at public inquiries (usually opposed by the town clerk, or legal officer). And so, despite the apparent militancy (in the council's eyes, at least) of these community activities, and the citizens' relative sophistication in their subject material, professionals-as-advocates still had to wage most of their struggle within the system as it stood. They had to conform to the protocols of public inquiries, and also to maintain a certain amount of professional contact with the 'opposition' in order to obtain information. Because of this, constant caution had to be exercised if professionals were not to be co-opted into the planning machinery. This gave rise to a lively exchange of views about objectives and methods and, on occasion, accusations arose from residents about the loyalties of the workers.

In south Wales in the 1970s, because of the successes of campaigns and local actions, such as the Hook Road scheme (see p. 11 above) and the Polypill project (chapter 15), the struggle between governmental planners and residents' and activist groups at times became very bitter. Few signals were received that the system would ever bend to the will of the grassroots organizations. This hardened opinions in communities, and gradually the line of thinking within the 'alternative' professional caucus began to crystallize into a firm Marxist analysis. For some, this was a 'shut-out' process, as the associative grouping of professionals contained a wide spectrum of opinion within a general 'structuralist' framework. From then on, the firmness of a coherent 'line' seemed to kill off the discussion about ways and means.

Meanwhile, in 1971, outside the hardening Marxist pale, the CDP project in the Afan Valley put its own approach on display, in a rare public appearance. Despite this being hidden away in the Great Western pub in Blaengwynfi, community workers from all across south Wales made the pilgrimage. There were workers from the quasi-government sector (CDP), different tiers of local government (Glamorgan County Council; Glyncorrwg Urban District Council), national and local voluntary sector (Young Volunteer Force Foundation; Cardiff Council for Voluntary Service, Cwmbrân Community Resource Centre, Cardiff Student Community Action), civil servants (Welsh Office), other individuals from the 'professional support groups', the private sector (independent companies established to implement the 1969 Housing Act 'General Improvement Areas'), and a few residents. The CDP model was a highly technical and sophisticated social planning approach, with lots of flow diagrams, trend projections and bar charts. It provoked a lively encounter with the project workers. The latter were employed in many and diverse backgrounds: housing estates, adventure playgrounds, street-level projects, and neighbourhood resource centres. This was a particularly poignant event because of the CDP's steadfast denial of a well-established activist group in the Glyncorrwg area where they were based, and that group's demands for radical action on employment and transport. Despite the 'in-your-face' acrimony that this 'top-down' approach described, the CDP model left a host of questions unanswered on all sides (Lees and Mayo, 1994).

Social planning, being so closely tied in with town and country planning in this government-sponsored setting, created a quandary for workers about the most appropriate role for professionals to adopt. The CDP's decision to work from an 'objective' and community-audit standpoint flew in the face of adversarial politics espoused by many of the community-based project workers. The very idea that a 'consensus' model could achieve anything for the 'people', and that their target collaborators should be the elected members and their officers, was a highly contentious issue at the time (Penn and Alden, 1977, pp. 185–6). From outside the Upper Afan CDP, there was a broad consensus that it was a 'top-down' approach that reinforced traditional class interests and was elitist in the extreme.

The spate of 'slum clearance' schemes implemented by local authorities in the 1970s had created havoc with traditional, urban

community life. This process coincided with the structural adjustment of the UK economy (MacInnes, 1987; Cornia, 1987). This
began with spiralling inflation and unemployment in the early
1970s, and then became official when the Wilson/Callaghan
governments accepted the International Monetary Fund's imposi-
tion of monetary policies. In this, south Wales was to experience
rather worse effects than most other areas. Unemployment began
to rise markedly, and community workers were unable to handle
the dynamics of community decline and economic decline at the
same time. This was partly because their recently acquired Marxist
ideology did not come with a ready-made application model in
non-militant demoralized communities. A 'bottom-up' approach
was anti-elitist; it tied in well with the structuralist analysis and
was, potentially, revolutionary. But the community workers were
having difficulties in mobilizing the masses, and as the economic
situation got worse, so the whole task appeared to be an exercise in
futility. This left the professionals endowed with considerable skills
and insight into the way in which the system was working against
the common citizen, but what the communities lacked were
coherent bodies of militant, informed and focused grassroots
organizations with which to confront the decision-makers. The
professionals were then forced either to adopt an 'advocate' role or
to step aside from the process altogether. Many opted to stay
involved, but this underlined how elite their position was within the
system of development. To those to whom this was never an issue,
such as the Afan CDP, and the Cwmbrân Community Resource
Centre, they just carried on with their own work and did not
concern themselves with schemes elsewhere.

In or against an elite?

The simplicity of the enduring and conventional 'grassroots'
approach is contrasted with the more radical, and hard-line
requirements of the traditional Marxist school of the 1970s and
1980s (Corrigan, 1975; Corrigan and Leonard, 1978; Bolger et al.,
1981; Leonard, 1975; Smith, J., 1978 and 1981; Mayo, 1979;
Wooley, 1970). Under a Marxist strategy, the grassroots movements
of the people must be combined in a grand alliance with the
organized labour movement. Together, they would struggle to

overcome the oppression of capitalist domination. How this need for solidarity was to be transmitted to the 'rank-and-file' membership of the trade unions was never explained. 'Alliances' had to be formed, presumably with the union leadership. The political muscle of the unions would be harnessed for the benefit of the 'struggle' in the 'centre for the reproduction of labour' – the home environment (Cockburn, 1977; Gortz, 1977). In Newport in 1971, one of the editors was evicted from the local Trades Council for suggesting that the unions should ally with the neighbourhood organizations (mainly 'housewives') to resist the destruction of their home community through planned council redevelopment. Fifteen years later, and well into the Thatcher era, the same organization was solicitous of a relationship with the same work at community level.

Implementing this solidarity model contained a number of difficulties. Firstly, the union leadership held the key to access to their members. The tight, centralized leadership model of the unions did not, and still does not, fit with the more fluid, participative structure of community organizations. Community workers may be prepared to focus on the purely 'political' objectives of power organizing, but community organizations are interested in more prosaic things such as house repairs. Meeting the unions face-to-face means 'elite-to-elite'. The role of elites, and the way in which strategic plans are forged under these conditions, requires a change in the relationship between the elite and those being led. In the 1970s, the collective voice of the trade unions was the much neglected Trades' Council. This lacked any real political leverage. At the level of the community, people were becoming tired of following 'representative' leadership, only to find things get worse and worse. Some even doubted the effectiveness of the current form of organized labour, and sought other tactics (Landry et al., 1985; Fleetwood and Lambert, 1982). Divisions between the 'worker' and the community were being recognized, and social movements organized along lines of class and social issues began to claim the skills of activists and professionals (*Community Action*, 1980, No. 50).

The top priority for community development workers is how to develop and ensure the maximum number of participants, while ensuring that they have the greatest amount of information and ability. Their function is to help these participants claim a place within the dynamics of power development, power-sharing and decision-making for a sustainable future. At this time, it clashed completely with the Marxist theorists' call for industrial solidarity, led by a proletarian vanguard. Jones, and Fleetwood and Lambert, have described how disillusionment with formal trade unions was growing, and how the defence of the Welfare State was degenerating into a defence of services and the service approach (Jones, 1983; Fleetwood and Lambert, 1982). The dilemma was crystallized in the decision by the Case Con collective, a radical group of social workers, to focus their confrontational efforts for change on the trade unions that represented social workers. They stepped out of the arena for general social change in the cause of setting their own house in order first (Case Con Manifesto, 1975; Jones, 1983). An era of 'single-issue politics' was dawning, and the 'new social movements' were stirring (Castells, 1977; Foweraker, 1995; Byrne, 1997). The left was calling for activism, in the hope, perhaps, that the ever-failing unions might follow. There was a role in this for community development workers, especially those with a highly developed streak of entrepreneurialism. For the majority, however, it was a question of raising the quality of representation within the existing democratic system that mattered most (Smith, T., 1980; Barr, 1991).

Commentators at this time may have been excused for seeing things as being more dramatic than they actually were. For example, Jones complains that the 'community social work' approach of the Barclay Report (Barclay, 1982) was an example of how the Thatcherite state was attempting to cut services still further (Jones, 1983, pp. 150–1). From a community development perspective, established social work (individualization, 'clinical'/ pseudo-scientific therapies, policy-bound service structure) was already indefensible. The Barclay Report was a lot closer to creating the conditions for an 'alliance' between professionals and the community, than would ever be possible through established practice. Had the community social work model been generally adopted, social workers would have been placed in a face-to-face relationship with poverty, exclusion and the reality of people's daily life experience (especially the more 'collectivist' Appendix A of Barclay, 1982, pp. 219–35). In South Glamorgan, social workers refused to implement a patch-based (Barclay-inspired) reorganization because, *inter alia*, workers felt that they would be at risk if asked to work so close to the people!

The second big fissure between the Marxist approach and the groundswell of radical community work activists was the unions' approach to women. Female members of the proletariat were acceptable on the terms of the male leadership, but the feminist view of patriarchy, the needs of women in the home as well as at the workplace, and the primacy that should be given to children and the domestic safety of women was something else (Cockburn, 1977; Dominelli, 1990; O'Malley, 1977; Wilson, 1980). In addition, the parallel issue of ethnicity and racism emerged as another glaring contradiction within the 'labour movement' (Centre for Contemporary Cultural Studies, 1982). As the Thatcherite hammer-blows began to fall on the union strongholds of manufacturing and the extractive industries, these divisions highlighted just how ill-prepared the old message of labourism was. The unions had no community base either. No one explained to the members of the emergent 'centres for the unemployed' why the trade unions were embarrassed by their presence, and that they could not be admitted to full membership. Marxist community development theorists were left high and dry, and no one had really asked for intellectuals to play their part in any revolution (Gramsci, 1971).

Make-work, community care and the drift into welfare

By the end of the 1970s the prolonged recession was having serious effect, and the emphasis had shifted within community work. Training-for-activists schemes were being set up in south Wales by the newly formed Federation of Community Work Training Groups. There was considerable concern about the impact of government training schemes on the employment of 'community workers', and about the plight of council tenants following the 1972 Housing Finance Act – the 'Fair Rent' Act (South Wales Tenants' Association, 1982; Lees and Mayo, 1984; Fleetwood and Lambert, 1982; *Community Action*, 1972–83, Nos. 1–63 inclusive). Council housing maintenance became a major issue, as the government began to shift moneys away from the local authority, and the provision of public housing began its decline, which continues to this day. The South Wales Association of Tenants galvanized direct action campaigns and, in this, they were assisted by a cadre of professionals drawn from the public services and the universities. This grouping had many years of grassroots organizing and representation behind them (*Community Action*, 1980, No. 48). Rents continued to rise regularly, and housing associations became the only major source of new accommodation for people in housing distress (*Community Action*, 1980 No. 50 and 1981, No. 53). From 1978, the 'winter of discontent' of 1978/9 seemed to drag on for a decade, and unemployment, poverty and the collapse of the Valleys economies became virtually complete. For community workers with a more corporate interest, there was the board of directors of the new Cardiff Broadcasting community radio to take up their energy (*Community Action*, 1979, No. 44, pp. 16–17)!

A major diversion for community workers in south Wales came with the promise of cash for new projects and for a real 'structural' issue, the long-term unemployed. Beginning in 1975, government 'make-work' programmes had targeted first youth, and then, increasingly, the army of long-term unemployed, through the creation of temporary work and training for them in the community. These schemes were known variously as Training Opportunities Scheme (TOPS; 1973), Community Industry (1972), Job Creation Programme (1975), Youth Opportunities Programme (1978), Special Temporary Employment Programme (STEPS; 1978), Centres for the Unemployed (1980), Community Programme (1982), Community Enterprise Programme (1985), Youth Training Scheme (1983), and they made increasing inroads into the function and nature of community development organizations. They began to devour a great deal of their time, distorted their perspective and threw their 'principles' into disarray. The whole idea of cooperating with a government that had failed the working population and allowed unemployment to remain above half a million was, at first, inconceivable. These schemes began in earnest with STEPS in 1978 under a Labour government, which made the scenario even more unlikely. Under the Conservative government of Margaret Thatcher, the number of these schemes increased, and the funding of many established community projects became either dependent on short-term funding for their own work, or predicated on the administration of such schemes. They were boycotted initially and, gradually, a gap began to widen between the professionals and the actual needs of the local people.

The people themselves, in the communities, began to organize for themselves. It began with youth unemployment, when parents began to take up offers of government cash for the Job Creation Programme. As these schemes spread into adult unemployment, the voluntary and community sectors were drawn into the process more and more. The benefits seemed two-fold: employment for the unemployed, and useful work in the community, such as community arts, environmental work, the refurbishment of community buildings, etc. Ideologically, it flew in the face of socialism, and it diverted 'community work' into safe areas, acceptable to the (government) Manpower Services Commission (MSC). By 1983, the strongly socialist Workers' Education Association had compromised considerably, and a Centre for the Unemployed was opened by them in Torfaen using MSC funding (WEA, undated). It seemed as though the capitulation by professional development workers to the forces of the 'liberal' and unregulated economy was total. A survey for the TUC's Centres for the Unemployed in 1984, found that the negative effects of constraining the centres from campaigning against unemployment were outweighed by the benefits of obtaining secure funding from the MSC (*Community Action*, 1986, No. 73, pp. 11–13). The temporary short-term nature of the schemes that regularly changed their focus, and thus the basis of funding, certainly ensured that public moneys were not often harnessed for any political agenda, however mild (Benn and Fairley, 1986).

Involvement in these schemes required a critical shift in thinking, particularly a break with street activism and a move into an alliance (possibly unholy) with the MSC. Professionals began to follow the money into social planning exercises that developed from the hitherto therapeutic activities with the unemployed into the management of services for targeted groups. The government's Urban Programme moneys, that had given sustenance to so many of the community projects of the early 1970s, became focused on short-term, increasingly structured activities based upon work experience and training. An example of this is the Polypill project in Newport. The project spurned the early schemes, but eventually one of the community organizations started by the project called in the MSC for consultations about youth unemployment in the area. Within weeks, a youth employment project was started, and the community group was its manager. The community worker supporting the organization became, de facto, the treasurer of the MSC scheme. By the end of the 1970s, there was a full-blown make-work scheme in operation with up to fifteen 'community workers', training managers, overseers, administrators and many more trainees. Eventually, the whole project came on board and managed its own scheme with community participation in its management.

The philosophy of the professionals had begun to drift away from the social change model of the earlier years. In their way, the MSC mini make-work schemes paved the way for the 'contract culture' of the mixed economy of welfare. More tellingly, it revealed that many of the professionals saw a role for themselves around the planning table, and in roles which allowed them to play a direct part in shaping directly the direction of community change. This movement drew a line under 'locality development', and consigned it to being the workface/workplace of community development, rather than the preparation ground for social change. The successors of this shift are to be found today in the Strategic Regeneration Schemes, Healthy Living Centres, and the Objective One proposals (National Assembly for Wales, 2000b). 'Partnership' with the community is based upon integrating the established (or invented) community leadership. This is the safe option for setting out to develop the vehicles for mobilizing community opinion and organization so that they can shape these government-led initiatives for themselves.

The slide into welfarism

Baldock had begged community development workers to consider welfare as a legitimate focus for their skills, both at the time when they had just been made ineligible for membership of the British Association of Social Workers, and later on when the heat had been taken out of the rift (Baldock, 1974 and 1983; Cox and Derricourt, 1975; Popplestone, 1971). The Seebohm Report had made explicit the need for community development within the new social services (Seebohm, 1968), and in 1982, the Barclay Report demonstrated how traditional social welfare expectations would best be met through developmental approaches (Barclay, 1982; Smale et al., 1988). Some local authorities in Wales had taken up the message and, by 1989, Swansea had appointed ten community workers. Their difficulty was that, in the almost incessant restructuring of social services since 1974, the role of specialist community workers had been sidelined into a micro-project role (for instance, managing a temporary play-scheme, arranging for the distribution of Christmas gifts for poor children, and so on). When the time eventually arrived for a thorough-going justification of the need for this input (during the reorganization of 1990), the community workers failed to make their case. All were summarily redeployed or allowed to retire. Swansea's example contrasts starkly with that of the London Borough of Barnet where, with the input of a consultant from Wales, the team of Barclay-inspired community development workers were able to justify their continuation as part of a revitalized Housing and Social Services Department. By contrast, a great opportunity was lost in Swansea to consolidate the professional status of community development within a statutory welfare agency. No other Welsh local authority had embraced this approach so enthusiastically, but the decision to terminate the resource was taken arbitrarily on a 'value-for-money' basis in competition with a day-centre.

Again, following the 1988 Griffiths Report, and the 1989 White Paper *Caring for People*, the debate for and against community development as an agent for generating community welfare capacity was put into stark relief (Griffiths, 1988; Departments of Health et al., 1989). As the social services departments geared up for Care Management (Cooper, 1981), and the voluntary sector prepared for rich pickings within the 'mixed economy of welfare', no one considered that a 'community sector' might be a legitimate candidate for funding from the welfare budget to swell their own, marginalized local economies. Community development workers followed the road of becoming managers of 'initiatives' in area-based schemes of local design, while Charles Murray's predictions of an 'underclass' slowly emerged as a reality. Protracted unemployment, the failure of the state to bridge structural poverty and the widening welfare deficits produced a huge divide in society (Murray, 1990 and 1994). Community Care has now become an industry, and few have 'faith in the poor' any more to build vitality back into community life (Holman, 1998). The question that needs to be asked today is: has the triangular space between theory, values and practice opened up to the extent that they are now totally and permanently detached from each other? Is another set of values now needed to cope with the new millennium?

The power to play God, or managing director

So many problems, dilemmas and conflicts of interest have been faced by community workers in south Wales before today's crop of issues came along. This history is both seductive – the approach that 'we are destined to repeat it unless we learn from it' – and misleading. It is misleading because of the basic flaws in the structure of the profession, and the way in which it is applied. Work is usually set up on 'project' lines (the area/time specific approach); it is seldom fully evaluated (see below pp. 89–91); and the workers themselves are not selected, trained or bound by any common element of skill, ideology or career structure (Chanan, 1992: Thomas, D. N., 1995b and 1996). These facts will not, nevertheless, stop us from exploiting what we do know, and hoping that general lessons can be gleaned from the past as well as the present. This section reflects on the inordinate power that can be devolved onto, or be assumed by, the professional who is at the right place at the right time.

Considerable unrest and resistance greeted the implementation of the 1972 Housing Finance Act, which introduced market-related rents for council housing. Cwmbrân was one of the last local authorities to capitulate to the threat of personal financial surcharging of councillors if their councils refused to implement the Act (Clay Cross, in Derbyshire, was eventually left on its own, in defiance). It was the power of the local tenants' association that first held the official refusal together, but, when the decisive vote was finally taken to implement the 'Fair Rents', there was traumatic fallout in an unexpected quarter. The Cwmbrân Resource Centre team was found to be totally and irreconcilably divided, and it fragmented under the strain. It seemed that one faction of the team had been working for a 'sensible' solution to the impasse (and assisted in the delivery of a 'yes' vote on the Council), while the other was passionatly supported militant resistance and the 'no' vote. The 'Ayes' had it, and the team split up.

The political intrigue in the Council involved a large degree of social planning intervention at a high level. This process was certainly facilitated by the skills and forcefulness of particular personalities, whose final hand was not revealed until the process came to its climax. Nevertheless, when the result was in, the relative power of the respective players was revealed. The 'winners' remained in post and carried on the work and the 'losers' had to find fresh pastures. Minorities (the tenants' association) had to put up or shut up. The dissenting professional worker was summarily fired! This is a clear example of the strategic role that a well-placed professional can play when the stakes are high. Who has the 'right', what is the duty under these circumstances, and when do you know you have been correct to act as you did? Was this an isolated case, or is there more opportunity today to behave in this instrumental way and to exert powerful influence where it can have the most telling effect? Whose career is in the firing line, and does this factor influence the direction in which the pressure is placed?

Let us consider the role of the 'modern' community development worker-manager in an 'initiative' within a local authority's developmental programme, under the auspices of the new managerialist culture of 'best-value', evidence-based, targeted initiatives. There has been a massive upsurge of openings for community development initiatives since the election of New Labour in 1997. Many of these opportunities were around for some time before New Labour, but they remained subdued, awaiting a change in political climate. There have been the Strategic Development Scheme moneys (successor to the Urban Programme of the 1970s), Communities in Need programmes, Leader Projects (based on European Union Objective 5b of the Maastricht Treaty/European Social Fund). There are initiatives in partnership with local authorities such as Communities that Care (community development at the local level targeting child-related projects), Community Safety projects and many more. Community development workers have been employed and there has been a great deal of local-needs assessment and participatory research by local communities. Much of the work has been on short-term contracts, however. The latest bonanza comes from the 'Health' budget, in the form of Family Health Centres, the New Public Health (through local 'Health Alliances'), and Strategic Health Action Research Projects (Better Health Better Wales).

The broad description of one, the Communities First initiative (National Assembly, 2000a), stresses long-term commitment, targeting Wales's most deprived communities, a non-prescriptive programme and promotion of real partnership. This has the appearance of pleasing everybody, but the power-weighting in the delivery has an air of immediacy about it, which might, in reality, deny the community an opportunity to develop the capacity to participate in anything, except on a 'catch-up' basis. Under 'Basis for Partnership', the 'principle' is that 'coalitions of service providers working in close partnership will achieve more than when they work in isolation' (p. 6). It goes on to mention the role of local authorities, and the voluntary sector, but slides over reference to the 'community sector' with a passing reference to 'community based development groups' (p. 7). The grassroots element in the process will be hopelessly outgunned in the power relationships of this arrangement. This is a centrally planned programme, to be driven by professionals, who will coordinate over the best way to spend government resources. While there is an urgent need for local authorities to take advantage of these new funds (£81 million is promised), in addition to mainstream initiatives (National Assembly, 2000e) the question of how ordinary people are to be drawn into the planning and decision-making processes must be addressed urgently. To do this effectively, managers in local authorities will have to develop the skills for managing community-level projects, and for protecting them from political assault. The sensitivity of local politicians (and officials) to the voices of participation is no longer acceptable if 'bottom-up' partnerships are to have any meaning (see Clarke, chapter 15 below). Professionals in this new 'community development business' urgently need training opportunities, and the National Assembly must consider this if they are to take their own agenda of partnership seriously. Without a fully 'joined-up' approach to this issue, very mixed messages will emerge. At least this, with other policies, represents a long-term commitment to the process from a powerful, central source. Thus, Communities First must be given a firm welcome. It represents the only real attempt by government to consider a Wales-wide, 'bottom-up' approach to community development and to the general welfare of citizens since the demise of the Urban Programme.

The overriding feature of these initiatives is their link with a national development strategy, based upon a basic ideological construct – central control over economic regeneration. New Labour's target is the integration of as much public expenditure as possible into pushing the economic recovery of all marginalized areas and peoples. The safety net of welfarism is being cut back to residual proportions, and the onus for non-health services is to be placed upon the individual, preferably at the level of the nuclear family (Mayo, 1994). The critical element in these initiatives is the role and agenda of the community development worker/manager of these schemes. The upside of this is that community development workers are now expected to demonstrate some managerial competence, and there is now some recognition that financial control, accountability and adherence to prestated objectives are a part of their responsibility. This means that practitioners are expected to be able to understand far more about the economic circumstances and the drift of public policies insofar as they affect communities than they ever were before.

Difference and discrimination

Historically, there is a rich pool of writing on the subject of minority interests and the scope and direction that community development should take in order best to serve them (Cheetham et al., 1981; Curno et al., 1982; Dalla Costa and James, 1972; Fish, 1973; Freeman, 1975; Lapping, 1970; Ohri, Manning and Curno, 1982; Mayo, 1977; Wilson, A., 1978). The advance of feminism and its dialogue with traditional political and other value systems is at the disposal of community development workers of whatever gender or cultural background, and its influence on the published debate on the values of practitioners has been considerable. There has been an explosion of writing on race and other issues, such as disability and sexuality (Lucia-Hoagland and Penelope, 1988; Solanas, 1983; Swain et al., 1993).

At the micro-level, community development methods are the most efficient way of both allocating resources to marginalized groups and appearing to confront the political problem of being seen to be fair to minorities. At the same time, these very tactics can be the vehicle for mobilizing the powerless against exclusion and discrimination (Gilroy, 1987; Mackintosh and Wainwright, 1987; Segal, 1979). Given the pivotal power of the professional at the interface between a funder and the community, especially when particular priorities are backed by the system, then official approval for an initiative can become a double-edged sword for minorities. They may have no alternative source of support if their own priorities are at odds with those of officialdom.

In south Wales, the plight of the victims of domestic violence gave rise to the creation of a national organization, staffed by the first generation of community workers and bent on raising the profile of all women, as well as those in violent circumstances. This movement/organization began in Cardiff and then developed into a national representative and promotional body, Welsh Women's Aid. From the early 1970s, it and its offshoot local refuge organizations, got domestic violence out of the shadows of male collusion and into the mainstream of discussion and action. From the start, Welsh Women's Aid planned refuges, national education campaigns and local and central support for women who needed it, when they needed it. There were also ambitious plans for local rehabilitation schemes and community support for women in distress.

Today, the organization is the manager of a major housing initiative, and the agent of the state for managing the effects of continuing domestic violence. In effect, the main thrust of the organization is that of a housing association, providing a direct service. It is now institutionalized in a form that best serves the administration of the housing processes of the local state. Because of this, it cannot now pursue the objective of changing culture at the local level with the same vigour. It no longer has the profile of being an uncompromising advocate of changing women's position in society, and yet it is in an unchallengeable position to report on that situation. The reason for this is two-fold. Firstly, from the start, women's organizations in Wales, and in the UK as a whole, have been forced to operate at meagre subsistence levels. Their energies and motivation have been cynically exploited by the state at all levels as they were expected to provide high-quality support around the clock to all who needed it. Totally dependent on grant aid, Women's Aid has always had a frugal existence. This consigned women in need to the margins of welfare support, and those that provided it to the extremes of self-help and idealistic duty. The women funded their own service to a great extent. Secondly, the extreme reluctance of (male-dominated) local authorities to recognize the validity of domestic violence as a proper service need, had cumulative effects. It ensured that, year after year, this women's movement exhausted its resources in fighting the political battle for recognition, instead of being able to upgrade its services and development functions. That it managed to provide for the most needy of victims, and offer a valuable service at that, is to its credit. The consequence of this was that these organizations were not able to realize their more proactive and preventative developmental objectives (Southall Black Sisters, 1990). Their recent recognition in the housing service has not brought in increased resources for public education. Thus they do not provide the sharp focus for social change that they once promised. They do not have the time, nor do they have any surplus resources once the housing association work is done.

Can we see a similar pattern in respect of ethnic and other minorities? Does the provision of a Somali Advice Service have the same effect on a group of people who are now forced, through providing a service, to kiss the hand that feeds them and to refrain from campaigning for change in an oppressive culture? We can readily understand why those in authority seek to offer feasible and tangible solutions on practical issues to potentially militant victims of exploitation. Were they resourced to make their own demands, they might well threaten the fabric of the system as it now stands (Collins, 1990; Mama, 1989).

Evaluation

Most professionals who intervene in the lives of others will wish to discover how they have done, and yet there is something about the ethos of community development that makes practitioners draw back from making a thorough evaluation possible. We wonder whether this is because of the ambivalence of the value system of community development. We must consider just what it is that we are trying to measure, value, compare, learn from, extrapolate, analyse, provide a context for and, of course, judge. Firstly, there are few records of the myriad of community development projects which have 'flourished' in south Wales over the years. This may stem from the culture of short-termism which has always been a feature of 'projects'.

It is ordained in the culture of community work literature that 'workers must make themselves redundant' and then move on. This is a preposterous assumption, and one which stems from the colonial origins of the trade. Colonial 'masters' of government and administration had to 'go home' when independence was given, and the colonies were allowed to revel in their new-found freedoms – unsupported, and in a world which was preparing other ways to exploit them (Colonial Office, 1958; Batten, 1957; Biddle and Biddle, 1965; Henderson and Thomas, 1987; Lees and Mayo, 1984; see also Clarke, 2000, for the opposite view). The idea that an enterprise should deprive itself of its managing director at the point where it becomes profitable is absurd in a business context. A 'community sector' is obviously not to be considered seriously alongside the established interests of 'development': the statutory agencies and the voluntary sector. The anti-elitism of community development ideology and the short-termism of government and other funding mechanisms combine to make a virtue out of something which should not even be considered.

In the United States, the situation of the practitioner has not been circumscribed in the same way, but financial criteria (the ability of the community to pay) is a limiting factor (Pitt and Keane, 1984; Gittell and Vidal, 1998). In the developing economies of the world, grant aid, donor programmes, and limited state initiatives set the time boundaries (UN Bureau of Social Affairs, 1955; UN Secretary-General, 1961; Eade and Williams, 1995). Where some continuity is to be found is where NGOs are able to bring some stability through ensuring that, from outside sourcing, funding is maintained at a level and over a timescale that enables an ongoing developmental process to emerge (see Hulme and Edwards, 1997; Edwards and Hulme, 1995; Moser, 1993). Through these contrasting settings, it is possible to discover a pattern which can only be satisfactorily explained through the examination of values, and the contract between the development worker and the community.

The community changes, the problems shift, the dynamics of the wider community/society ebb and flow, and the community must remain resilient to these changes. The community does not understand community development. Its members understand needs, wants, leadership, organization (perhaps) and the failings of representative government. Professional practitioners understand the need to abstract and project from the present just how the future may develop, and how the community in question must adjust or fall behind. They draw upon their special qualities and from the mass of technical information which their training prepares them to absorb (Mondros and Wilson, 1994). The essential tool in this process is the ability to monitor and evaluate the process, preferably from the beginning of the exercise. There is a proliferation of approaches to evaluation, but most of these stem from work in the developing economies (Overseas Development Administration, 1995; Rubin, 1995; Patton, 1997). It is only recently that thinking in Britain has been updated from the two-page apology in Henderson and Thomas (1987) or Key, Hudson and Armstrong (1976). The Voluntary Activity Unit Belfast commissioned the first thorough-going analysis of what was required in 1996, and now a nation-wide survey of evaluation methods is underway with a view to bringing evaluation techniques up to date in the UK (Barr et al., 1996a and 1996b). This document outlines explicitly the values of community development and the evaluative framework which flows from it. It reviews structural, cultural and process dimensions, and produces a set of indicators which can be applied in reaching an understanding of progress and objectives attained.

Evaluation provides the worker, the funder and the wider community (potentially) with the means of measuring the effect-iveness of any particular work, and to find how that work rep-resents a trend in application of resources targeted on social change. Has community development, in a society polarized by old class-divisions and new consumption patterns, but with an ethos of mutual support through a benign Welfare State (and, therefore, state funding), produced a state of mind within the profession that is scared of declaring its hand in case its true motive is found out? Is it a post-colonial mentality, and (justifiable?) concern that resources might be wasted, that requires the present beneficiaries of our overseas aid to also receive progress monitors who are appointed by our government. They observe 'progress' and report back to us how 'they' are getting on.

Conclusion

We have shown how community development values have been influenced over the years by a number of contending forces: the practitioners themselves, other professional reference points and, most strikingly, government and other funding sources.

It seems that the internal tensions that have persisted over the decades are no closer to being resolved. Some constant issues remain central: how do practitioners reconcile any gap between their own personal motives and values, and those of an employer agency? Can they manage the power that accrues to them, and can they handle the frustrations of slow progress and small gains? How does a practitioner reconcile a similar disparity between personal values and those of the community, or segments of the community, in which the work has to be done? How do prevailing cultural influences dictate how a developmental initiative will take place? How 'autonomous' is the worker, and are there commonly agreed ethical standards that should be followed at all times?

4 Pwysigrwydd cyfranogi a rôl dysgu anffurfiol o fewn prosiect adfywio cymuned: Menter Drefol Townhill

DERITH POWELL

Summary

This chapter considers the importance of participation and the role of informal learning in the community of Townhill in Swansea which recently experienced a period of socio-economic transition as a result of an Urban Initiative Programme. The author describes in this chapter her role in providing and facilitating opportunities for members of the Area Committees to come together for informal learning sessions. She describes how training sessions were used to inform and empower the community through the exchange of information and the encouragement of dialogue and debate. The author concludes that meaningful consultation and participation in decision-making processes is fundamental to the process of change within communities. However, individuals firstly need to be equipped with the necessary tools to be able to engage fruitfully and take part in regeneration strategies. After all, it must never be forgotten that they are the experts within their own neighbourhoods.

Fy mwriad yn yr erthygl hon yw tynnu sylw at bwysigrwydd cyfranogi ar sail cymuned, a rôl dysgu anffurfiol o fewn y broses honno. Cymuned Townhill yn Abertawe yw'r cyd-destun ar gyfer hyn – cymuned sy'n profi cyfnod o newid economaidd-gymdeithasol o ganlyniad i weithredu Menter Drefol. Fy rôl i o fewn y fenter hon oedd darparu a hwyluso cyfleoedd dysgu anffurfiol ar gyfer aelodau pwyllgorau'r pedair ardal fel eu bod yn cael eu defnyddio mewn ffordd mor adeiladol â phosibl o fewn eu cymunedau, ac yn cael eu paratoi'n well ar gyfer delio â'r newidiadau sydd o'u blaenau. Mae'n rhaid pwysleisio, fodd bynnag, er mor bwysig yw'r agwedd hon o'r gwaith, mai adran fechan iawn o'r cynllun cyfan ydyw.

O'r persbectif hwn rwyf am geisio dangos sut y gall dysgu anffurfiol fod yn fodd i hwyluso cyfranogi. Mae hefyd yn ffordd o sicrhau bod ymgynghori'n golygu rhywbeth i drigolion lleol, wrth iddynt ymdrechu i weithio mewn ffordd bwrpasol o fewn cymunedau sy'n profi newid. Mae hwn yn ddisgrifiad o sefyllfa gyfredol go iawn lle mae trigolion Townhill yn dod i delerau ymarferol â'r hyn y cyfeiriwyd ato gan Kemmis a McTaggart fel a ganlyn:

> Cymunedau o bobl, wedi'u hymrwymo i ddarganfod mwy am y berthynas rhwng amgylchiadau, gweithredu a chanlyniadau eu sefyllfa bersonol, ac sy'n rhyddhau eu hunain o rwystrau sefydliadol a phersonol sy'n cyfyngu ar eu gallu i fyw yn ôl eu gwerthoedd cyfreithlon eu hunain. (Kemmis a McTaggart, 1988, t. 23)

Menter Drefol

Mae Townhill yn gymdogaeth â phoblogaeth o 13,450 sy'n cynnwys tair ward etholiadol. Wedi'i lleoli lai na milltir o ganol y ddinas, mae'n ardal sy'n amlwg yn dioddef o amddifadedd cymdeithasol, daearyddol ac amgylcheddol dybryd. Yn nhermau mynegeion amddifadedd, nodwyd yn 1994 etholaeth Townhill fel y trydydd uchaf yng Nghymru. Roedd bron 80 y cant o'r boblogaeth yn economaidd anweithredol a hanner y cartrefi gyda neb mewn gwaith; yn 20 y cant o gartrefi gyda phlant doedd neb mewn gwaith; roedd ffigurau diweithdra a rhieni sengl yr ardal yn uchel.

Yn ei hanfod, amcan y Fenter Drefol yw adfywio'r gymdogaeth, gan wella morâl cyffredinol y trigolion ac adfer eu balchder yn y gymuned. Yng nghais gwreiddiol Menter Drefol Townhill, nodwyd yn nadansoddiad y gymuned fod ymrwymiad aml-asiantaethol i newid er mwyn gwella a magu partneriaethau. Er bod llawer iawn o dlodi ac amddifadedd o lawer math, yr hyn oedd yn bwysicach na dim o'm safbwynt i oedd fod yna ysbryd cymunedol cryf yn parhau o fewn rhai grwpiau, a bod yna botensial i roi hwb i fentrau datblygu cymunedol yn seiliedig ar rwydweithiau lleol. Roedd y cais gwreiddiol felly yn cydnabod mor hanfodol bwysig oedd cyfranogiad y gymuned i ddatblygiad a chynaladwyedd y strategaeth. Yn wir, mae'r bwriad cyffredinol yn cynnwys y dymuniad i roi pŵer yn nwylo'r gymuned.

Lluniwyd y strategaeth yn sgil ymgynghori â chynrychiolwyr y gymuned a darparwyr gwasanaeth. Roedd y cais ei hun yn gynnyrch ymgynghori ag asiantaethau allweddol a grwpiau o'r gymuned. Roedd yn argymell defnyddio rhwydweithiau a grwpiau ymgynghori a oedd yn bodoli eisoes, megis y rhai oedd ar gael o fewn meysydd addysg gymunedol a thai, yn ogystal â datblygu rhaglen o gyfranogi cymunedol o fewn grwpiau nad oeddynt yn cyfranogi i lunio datblygiadau cymunedol ar y pryd. Rhagwelwyd y byddai nifer o fecanweithiau ymgynghori a chyfranogi amrywiol yn cael eu defnyddio, gan gynnwys holiaduron a chyfarfodydd cyhoeddus a oedd yn cynnwys cynrychiolaeth ar sail diddordeb yn ogystal ag ar sail ddemograffig a daearyddol. Rhagwelwyd y byddai'r broses hon yn parhau y tu hwnt i gyfnod y fenter drefol. Roedd y 'strategaeth ymgynghori' hon wedi'i seilio'n amlwg ar broses o roi pŵer yn nwylo'r gymuned tra, yn y tymor hir, roedd angen galluogi'r trigolion i helpu eu hunain a chyfranogi mewn ffordd ystyrlon i ddatblygu'r fenter a'i rhoi ar waith, yn ogystal â chynnal y gwaith yn y tymor hir.

Pan oeddwn i'n rhan o'r cynllun, roedd cynrychiolwyr y gymuned eisoes yn gweithredu ar sail y pedwar grŵp o bynciau a oedd wedi'u cyflwyno yn y ddogfen gais wreiddiol, sef:

1. Adfywio'r gymuned
2. Hyfforddiant galwedigaethol ac addysgol
3. Datblygu economaidd a chreu swyddi
4. Tai a'r amgylchedd

Roedd pedwar pwyllgor wedi eu sefydlu – y grwpiau partneriaeth lleol – ar sail y themâu hyn, a phob un yn gyfrifol am un ohonynt. Yn ogystal, roedd Townhill wedi ei rannu ym mhedair ardal ddaearyddol, a phob ardal â'i phwyllgor ei hun yn cynnwys cynrychiolwyr lleol. Felly, rhyngddyn nhw, roedd yr wyth pwyllgor hyn yn gyfrifol am oruchwylio datblygiadau yn ôl ardal a thema. Yn ogystal â gwneud penderfyniadau, roeddynt hefyd yn gyfrifol am gyfathrebu ac ymgynghori â'r gymuned a sicrhau bod y gymuned yn cyfranogi.

Erbyn i mi ddod yn rhan o'r peth felly, roedd Townhill wedi gwneud cais llwyddiannus am Fenter Drefol a fyddai'n dod ag adnoddau a chyllid newydd ac arwyddocaol i'r gymuned. Roedd gan y prosiect cyfan fwriadau ac amcanion clir ac ymrwymiad amlwg i roi pŵer yn nwylo'r gymuned yn y tymor hir, a hynny ar sail ymgynghori, cyfranogi a chymryd rhan. Sefydlwyd strwythurau lleol i adlewyrchu'r ymrwymiad hwnnw.

Ond, er gwaethaf hyn daeth yn amlwg yn fuan yn ystod oes y fenter mai ychydig oedd yn digwydd o safbwynt mewnbwn go iawn gan aelodau'r gymuned nad oeddynt yn gynrychiolwyr ar y pwyllgorau ardal. Daeth yn amlwg nad oedd y peirianwaith ar gyfer rhoi pŵer yn eu dwylo yn cyrraedd y tu hwnt i gyfyngiadau'r wyth grŵp. Nid oedd y broses yn darparu pont ystyrlon rhwng cymuned a phwyllgor ac, o'r herwydd, roedd sail ac ystyr cyfranogi yn gyfyngedig tu hwnt.

Er mwyn ceisio deall pam nad oedd y strwythurau a fwriadwyd i ysgogi'r gymuned i gyfranogi yn gweithio o fewn y gymuned, mae'n rhaid deall hanes a phrofiad cyffredinol y gymuned honno. Bydd cymunedau lle mae penderfyniadau canolog wedi rheoli eu bywydau, eu gwasanaethau a'u penderfyniadau yn ei chael yn anodd ar y dechrau dderbyn patrwm newydd o weithredu. Rydym yn gwybod mai'r rhai sydd â hanes o gyfrannu a chyfranogi yw'r rhai mwyaf tebygol o gyfranogi mewn menter newydd, pobl sydd eisoes yn meddu ar yr hyder a'r adnoddau i'w galluogi i fanteisio'n uniongyrchol ar y profiad. Roedd y trafodaethau cyhoeddus traddodiadol yn cael eu rheoli gan gynrychiolwyr y *status quo*. Bydd y rhai hynny sydd wedi profi effeithiau gwaethaf difreiniad neu gamwahaniaethu yn ei chael yn anodd iawn mentro cyfranogi. Yn ogystal, mae drwgdybiaeth naturiol o fewn y grwpiau ymylol oherwydd iddynt brofi, wrth gyfranogi yn y gorffennol, 'delay, incorporation, co-option, legitimisation and tokenism' (Croft a Beresford, 1992).

Ar ben hyn oll, roedd Townhill yn cael ei hadnabod fel cymuned lle roedd yr aelodau yn meddu ar lefel isel o gyfranogi mewn addysg a hyfforddiant galwedigaethol, ac ystyriai'r grŵp a gynigiodd y cynllun fod hyn yn cyfrannu at ddiwylliant o ddisgwyliadau isel o safbwynt cyraeddiadau dysgu a lefel isel o sgiliau perthnasol. Mewn ardal lle roedd canran uchel o'r rhai oedd yn gadael yr ysgol yn gwneud hynny heb dderbyn unrhyw fantais academaidd yn nhermau cymwysterau, ond yn hytrach gyda phrofiadau dysgu negyddol, daw mater gwybodaeth a'i pherthynas â'r gallu i ysgwyddo pŵer yn arbennig o berthnasol o ystyried amharodrwydd i gymryd rhan mewn prosesau cyfranogi.

O fewn y sefyllfa yma, felly, y deuthum yn ymwybodol y gallai'r strategaethau a'r ymarferion dysgu anffurfiol y bûm i'n ymwneud â nhw ers peth amser gyfrannu'n ymarferol a phragmatig i alluogi cymryd rhan a chyfranogi. Roedd y ffordd hon o fynd ati wedi ei seilio ar egwyddorion syml ond sylfaenol.

- Yn gyntaf, mae mynediad i wybodaeth, dysgu a hyfforddiant yn hanfodol i dwf personol, a thrwy hynny i gyfranogiad. Mae'r rhai sydd heb sgiliau sylfaenol yn debygol o ddioddef amryw anfanteision, er enghraifft o fewn y farchnad swyddi ac o fewn ymgynghoriadau cyhoeddus, ac yn sgil hynny, maent yn llesteirio cyfranogiad cymunedol. Mae cyfleoedd hyfforddiant a dysgu perthnasol ac ystyrlon y gellir cael mynediad iddynt felly yn hanfodol bwysig i'r unigolion yn y gymuned. Mewn cymunedau fel Townhill, dylid mesur y graddau y gall addysgu o'r fath gyrraedd y rheini sydd â'r profiadau addysg mwyaf negyddol. Wrth geisio cyrraedd y bobl hyn, teimlem ein bod yn cyrraedd y rhai a oedd yn teimlo fel eu bod wedi'u dieithrio fwyaf gan strwythurau'r gymuned ac, o'r herwydd, y rhai mwyaf ymylol o safbwynt cyfranogiad.

- Yn ail, sylweddolwyd bod perthnasedd, amseru a mynediad yn hollbwysig. Yn Townhill, roedd y pwyslais ar roi blaenoriaeth i anghenion unigolion yn ystod y cyfnod neilltuol hwnnw o'u bywydau pan allent fanteisio ar unrhyw ddarpariaeth berthnasol.

- Yn drydydd, dibynnai'r dull hwn o weithredu'n fawr ar ymrwymiad i gynyddu'r broses drwy feithrin ac annog partneriaethau ar sail y problemau cyffredin a oedd yn uno pobl. Gellid ystyried bod hyn yn gwrth-ddweud ymrwymiad i sgiliau perthnasol unigol, a thrwy gydol f'ymwneud â Townhill roedd tensiwn wrth gydbwyso'r materion hyn. Wrth gyflwyno rhaglenni dysgu cyfranogol, roedd yn ofynnol i'r polisi ystyried y tensiwn hwn.

- Yn bedwerydd, roedd y dull o weithredu yn annog y cyfranogiad mwyaf posibl gan y cyfranogwyr. Roedd yn gofyn am gyfranogiad unigolion ar y cychwyn fel eu bod yn gallu

penderfynu ar ystod o sgiliau a oedd eisoes ganddynt ac yna
nodi anghenion hyfforddi neu ddysgu arbennig. Gall unigolion
wedyn gyfrannu'n ystyrlon i gynllun, cynnwys a dull cyflwyno'r
profiad dysgu.

• Yn bumed, mae'r dysgu yn seiliedig ar broses o rannu, a
phroses o rannu lle mae profiadau unigolion yn cael eu
defnyddio i alluogi dysgu eraill o fewn y grŵp. Sgiliau, syniadau
a phrofiadau yw cynsail y dysgu sy'n digwydd.

Mae hyn yn fwy na dweud bod oedolion yn dysgu'n fwy effeithlon
pan fo'r gweithgareddau'n cyd-fynd â'u profiad hwy eu hunain – mae'n
datgan bod profiadau pobl yn werthfawr ynddynt eu hunain.
(Skinner, 1997)

Yn y ffordd hon, mae'n amlwg bod y syniad o berchenogaeth a
pherthnasedd yn flaenoriaeth. Mae'r datblygiad personol sy'n
digwydd o ganlyniad yn gallu bod yn arf allweddol wrth adeiladu
cymuned effeithiol, gan ei fod yn cydnabod profiad y gymuned ac yn
chwilio am ffyrdd o adeiladu ar ei sail. Mae addysg ymhlith
oedolion yn fwy effeithiol pan fo'u gwybodaeth a'u profiad yn cael
eu gwerthfawrogi, eu cadarnhau ac, yn y pen draw, eu datblygu.
Mae'r broses hon yn gwella galluoedd cyfranogi, sgiliau ac
ymrwymiad oedolion. Drwy adeiladu ar sail profiadau dysgu sy'n
gyffredin neu brofiadau dysgu y gellir eu rhannu, mae dysgu
cyfranogol anffurfiol yn galluogi'r cyfranogwyr i fod yn fwy proactif
wrth wynebu dewis neu wrth wneud penderfyniadau. Wrth wneud
hyn, mae'n hwyluso ystod gweithredu a dyfeisgarwch ehangach o
fewn y cymunedau yn ogystal â datblygu sgiliau newydd i unigolion.
    Gweithwraig leol y datblygiad cymunedol a oedd yn rhan o'r
cynllun a ofynnodd i mi gymryd rhan. Roedd hi'n bryderus ynglŷn
â materion yn ymwneud â chyfranogiad a chyfraniad gan y
gymuned ehangach, ac roedd hi'n deall potensial y manteision a
allai ddod o raglen ddysgu anffurfiol. Roedd yn gyfle i roi'r cynllun
a amlinellwyd uchod ar waith, mewn ardal yr oeddwn i'n
ymwybodol o'i hanghenion lluosog a'r gwaith a oedd eisoes yn
cael ei wneud gan y rheini a oedd yn chwarae rôl allweddol o fewn
y Fenter Drefol.
    Roeddwn i'n ymwybodol o rwystrau megis mynediad cyf-
yngedig, a phrofiadau personol negyddol o addysg, ac o'r diffyg

hyder cyffredinol – hyder a oedd yn angenrheidiol wrth ddechrau ar raglen o ddysgu anffurfiol. Roedd yn rhaid i'm ffordd i o fynd ati fod yn seiliedig ar anghenion ac ar gydweithio ac roedd yn rhaid sefydlu'r materion hyn yn fuan er mwyn sicrhau ein bod yn cwrdd â'r anghenion dysgu o fewn amgylchedd a oedd yn newid ac o fewn diwylliant cymunedol a oedd yn newid.

Cytunwyd ar amcanion y rhaglen ddysgu anffurfiol ynghyd â'r cynnwys a'r dull o'i chyflwyno drwy gydweithio. Nid oedd nifer o aelodau'r grŵp wedi cael unrhyw gyswllt ag addysg/dysgu ers blynyddoedd, ond roeddynt, serch hynny, wedi dysgu llawer iawn am lwyddiant a methiant drwy'u hoes, a hynny yn 'ysgol profiad'. Roedd yr unigolion o fewn y grŵp yn dod o wahanol gefndiroedd ac roedd i bob un ei gryfder, ei wendid, ei obeithion a'i ofnau ei hun. Roedd llawer yn ddihyder ynddynt eu hunain fel 'dysgwyr' neu 'gyfranogwyr' i ddysg. O ganlyniad, roeddynt yn tanbrisio eu galluoedd. Roedd eu hagwedd yn golygu eu bod yn amharod i rannu ar y dechrau rhag iddynt wneud camgymeriadau neu ymddangos yn dwp neu fethu mewn unrhyw ffordd.

Mae'r ymateb hwn yn gyffredin iawn ymhlith y rheini nad ydynt wedi cael profiadau da ym maes addysg. Gall y ffactorau hyn fod yn rhwystrau i oedolion sy'n ddysgwyr, yn enwedig os ydynt yn gaeth iawn i'w hagweddau ac yn arddel syniadau amdanynt eu hunain a all eu llesteirio. Mae'r rhain yn rhwystro dysgu oherwydd eu bod yn rhwystro unigolion rhag rhoi ystyriaeth ddifrifol i newid agwedd, a datblygu dull mwy cydweithredol o ddysgu. Gall y safbwyntiau maent yn eu harddel rwystro dysgu a'i gwneud yn anos iddynt ddod i delerau â syniadau ac ymddygiad newydd.

Ar y dechrau, roedd llawer o densiynau ymhlith cynrychiolwyr y pwyllgorau ardal – roeddynt yn amheus iawn o bob dim ac yn amharod iawn i gyd-dynnu. Flwyddyn yn ddiweddarach, nid oeddwn yn gwybod a oedd yr amheuaeth yma'n dal i fodoli. Rwy'n credu i'r cysylltiad rheolaidd yn ystod y rhaglen hyfforddiant daflu goleuni ar y sefyllfa i ryw raddau gan ddatrys peth o'r gwrthdaro.

Ond fe ddaeth yn amlwg i mi'n fuan iawn y gallai'r mwyafrif o'r aelodau, er gwaethaf y rhwystrau, roi'r addysg a gawsant ar waith yn ymarferol yng nghyd-destun y gymuned ehangach. Dyma rai o'u geiriau nhw:

> Doeddwn i ddim yn gwybod mai fel hyn fyddai hi. Dwi wedi mwynhau fy hun – er mawr syndod i mi!!!

Roeddwn i'n meddwl y byddwn i'n teimlo'n dwp – felly ar y dechrau roeddwn i'n ofni dweud dim.

Rwy'n edrych ymlaen at y pwyllgor nesaf, gan mod i'n gwybod nawr sut *ddylen* nhw gael eu rhedeg.

Dwi ddim mor ofnus i gyfathrebu nawr, gan 'mod i'n sylweddoli 'mod i'n gallu gwrando'n eitha da. Dyw rhai pobl sy'n rhan o'r Fenter hon ddim yn gwybod sut i wneud hynny.

Mae fy mhrofiad i o werth wedi'r cyfan.

Townhill yw fy nghartref i. Dwi wedi bod yma ers bron i 50 mlynedd. Pa hawl sydd gan y crachach o bant ddweud beth sydd orau i ni? Mae'n rhaid i ni wneud yn siŵr eu bod nhw'n ystyried ein teimladau ni. Dyna pam mae'r hyfforddiant yma mor bwysig.

Dyw geiriau mawr ddim yn codi ofn arna'i. Rwy'n gwybod beth maen nhw'n golygu nawr.

Nid diben ynddo'i hun yw dysgu anffurfiol, felly rhaid rhoi sylw i ddatblygiadau'r dyfodol ac i faterion a nodwyd yn ystod yr hyfforddiant. Roedd nifer o'r cyfranogwyr yn teimlo eu bod wedi'u hymylu a'u neilltuo gan fodolaeth y Fenter Drefol. Mae'r hyfforddiant wedi rhoi cyfle i hyrwyddo partneriaeth waith a chydweithio, gan gynnig dulliau o fynd i'r afael â'r gwrthdaro sydd o reidrwydd yn codi o fewn sefyllfaoedd fel y rhain.

Mae pobl yn fwy tebygol o fod eisiau parhau i ddysgu o ddarganfod fod dysgu'n ddefnyddiol ac yn werth chweil, eu bod yn elwa ohono a bod iddo fanteision di-rif. Roedd nifer yn synnu o sylweddoli, er enghraifft, fod dysgu yn digwydd yn yr isymwybod yn barhaus.

Rwyf o'r farn nad yw'n bosibl cefnogi pobl wedi'u ham-ddifadu'n economaidd er mwyn lleihau'r anghyfartaledd o fewn cymunedau heb yn gyntaf roi'r arfau angenrheidiol iddynt wneud hynny – arfau sy'n cynnwys cyfleoedd dysgu. Heb wybodaeth, addysg a sgiliau o'r fath, ni fydd gan unigolion yr arfau angen-rheidiol i gyfranogi'n ystyrlon o fewn eu cymunedau. Bydd perygl hefyd na fydd partneriaid a chynllunwyr yn cwrdd ag anghenion y cymunedau cystal.

Dyna pam mae hyfforddiant cyfranogol a dysgu anffurfiol yn
anhepgorol bwysig ac y dylent fod yn rhan annatod o
ddatblygiadau unrhyw fenter newydd.

Pain of the change process

Introduction to chapters 5 and 6

> Transformation rises from the energy within a person or community. The animator's role is to nurture this energy and this spiritual power.
>
> (Hope and Timmel, 1984, p.10)

Previous attempts to regenerate poor areas in south Wales have been marked by their failure to involve local people in the process of transformation. A cynical view might be that participation was never really on the agenda. Outcomes were predetermined by powerful interests and residents were merely regarded as the objects of their intervention. This mode of thinking assumes that outsiders know best and that local people must be led to the 'Promised Land'.

An alternative approach is to start with the concerns, energies and ideas of local people. One of the chief exponents of this approach was the Brazilian educator Paulo Freire. Freire (1972) argued for an educational (development) process that worked *with* people rather than *on* or *for* them, a process that leads to critical awareness and action for social change. Since the 1970s, the work of Freire has been adapted by workers, particularly in East Africa, South America and Ireland, and has led to the development of such programmes as Training for Transformation (Hope and Timmel, 1984). This programme emphasizes the principles of Freire – social analysis, working 'in community', the development of strong local organizations and networks, team approaches and long-term commitment.

The following two chapters from Jenny Turner and Lyz Jones argue strongly for a new form of practice based on trust, dialogue and participation. Essential to this practice is the need to link personal change with social changes at local, national and global levels. Such ideas create new opportunities and challenges at a time when the market economies of the western capitalist nations reign supreme. New approaches are urgently needed to address the increased polarization between the 'haves' and the 'have nots' both within and between nations.

5 Supporting active, educated and enterprising communities in the south Wales valleys

JENNY TURNER

Crynodeb

Mae'r bennod hon yn archwilio'r rôl bwysig y mae addysg a dysgu yn eu chwarae yn y broses o adnewyddu cymoedd de Cymru a symud tuag at dyfiant economaidd cynaladwy. Mae'n canolbwyntio ar brofiadau VIAE (Menter y Cymoedd ar gyfer Addysg i Oedolion) yn ystod y 1980au yn y broses o gyfranogaeth gymunedol. Mae'r bennod yn ystyried rhaglenni dysgu a ddatblygwyd ar gyfer y rhai sydd wedi'u rhwystro rhag gwneud penderfyniadau ac i sicrhau eu bod yn cael cyfle i ddadlau a gwaredu rhwystrau sectoraidd a daearyddol. Mae'r rhain yn cynnwys enghreifftiau fel y 'Valleys Women's Roadshow' a arweiniodd at 'Groeso'r Gymuned' (Community Welcome), hynny yw pobl leol yn gweithio ar ddatblygiadau twristiaeth, neu'r seminar 'Byw yn y Cymoedd'.

Mae'r bennod yn edrych ar rai o'r rhwystrau sy'n amharu ar y broses gyfranogi, ac yn annog dulliau newydd o weithio, sgiliau newydd ac, yn fwy na hynny, yr angen am ymwybyddiaeth newydd er mwyn cynnal a datblygu ffynonellau ariannu a pholisïau newydd ar gyfer y mileniwm newydd. Bydd gweithio mewn partneriaeth gan ddefnyddio'r dulliau hyn yn herio strwythurau a chysylltiadau sy'n bodoli eisioes er mwyn sicrhau cynhwysiad.

Y dull a ddefnyddiwyd oedd Hyfforddiant ar gyfer Trawsnewid, model a ddatblygwyd yn y Trydydd Byd yn seiliedig ar feddylfryd Freire. Hyfforddiant yw hwn ar gyfer grwpiau sydd am weithredu i sicrhau newid cadarnhaol yn eu cymunedau.

Valleys Initiative for Adult Education

Since it began more than ten years ago the Valleys Initiative for Adult Education (VIAE) has placed itself at the interface between education and community development as a response to the needs of Valleys communities following the decline of traditional heavy industries. VIAE's founder members had backgrounds in education and saw the need for investing in people as a vital strand in Peter Walker's Valleys Programme (1988). This was a minority view in 1988 when the focus of regeneration was on infrastructure and inward investment; today, however, we see this view emanating from Europe, the National Assembly for Wales, local government, TECs, ELWa and even the WDA. Academics such as Professor Peter Lloyd of Liverpool University, who carried out the evaluation of Britain's first Objective One Programme in Merseyside in 1995, are prepared to assert that without the involvement of local people, especially those most excluded, no lasting regeneration can take place. This chapter will focus on our definition of the critical contribution of learning in the regeneration process and examine how it can support and develop the new opportunities opened up by the National Assembly, the coming of EU Objective One funding to the Valleys of south Wales and the creation of the Coalfields Regeneration Trust by the government. It will also touch on barriers obstructing the process.

VIAE's work began with a desire to open up opportunities for creative public debate to break down geographical and sectoral barriers. From the beginning it created vertical and horizontal partnerships (see Figure 1) which sought to bring all the stake-holders together around the table to focus on issues and on possible solutions. This process has resulted in innovative practice which has directly impacted on the mainstream. For example, the 'Valleys Women's Roadshow' was a VIAE project funded from the Strategic Development Scheme (Welsh Office) and by four local authorities: Gwent, Dyfed, Mid Glamorgan and West Glamorgan which ran from 1993 to 1995. It built partnerships to bring learning information and guidance to women in isolated communities of the south Wales valleys. New courses were developed as a result of it and two of the workers have gone on to play leading roles in local regeneration projects. Women who took up opportunities through the 'Valleys Women's Roadshow' can be found in many different

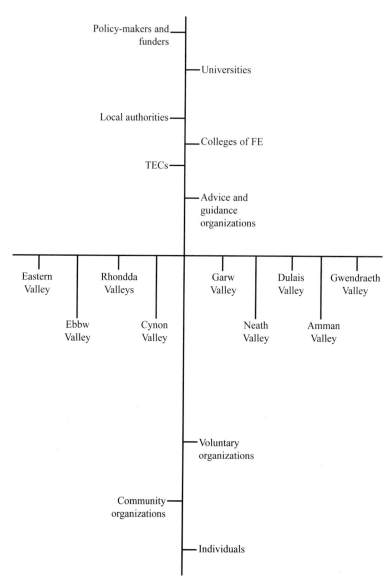

Figure 1: Building horizontal and vertical partnerships in the
south Wales valleys

roles in women's learning (including tutoring). More recently 'Community Welcome' has carried out ground-breaking work in bringing together local groups to work on tourism ideas for the benefit of the community; more than seven projects are now being developed.

The mutual support created by the project has resulted in an outline strategy being developed for community-based tourism in the Valleys. These examples indicate how the cross-Valleys and cross-sectoral approach can yield a special kind of added value.

Challenging attitudinal barriers

Like many other urban and rural areas in Britain, Valleys communities have had to absorb the impact of rapid social change. Loss of local industries, the globalization of the economy and the consequent widening of social divisions have left people in deprived and poverty-stricken communities with a deep sense of powerlessness in the face of an increasingly complex world. The profound discouragement of individuals and whole communities is reflected in the range of social problems which disrupt and destroy the quality of life and concern authorities. Large sums of money have been spent on regeneration agendas but very often they seem to strike wide of the mark so that whilst buildings and streets are given facelifts, crime and vandalism continue to undermine achievements. Listening to the voices of people active in their communities, those voices heard in VIAE's 'Living in the Valleys' seminar in Merthyr in 1997, it is clear that solutions found are still partial, and that people identify a number of barriers still holding back the process. Some of these are rooted in world economic trends, but some are local and regional problems, and some are personal development issues. Remedies for the latter two categories are within our power. Barriers identified included: traditional subservience, red tape, lack of encouragement, unwillingness to share openly, preconceived ideas by partners, the non-participatory nature of the education system, fear, men feeling they have no part to play in the community, poor images reflected in the media, control of community workers, problems of communication, adversarial process in local politics, as well as the most well-acknowledged ones of lack of self-confidence and self-esteem and the need for facilitators to empower communities.

These responses are feeling their way towards a critique of existing relationships and structures, identifying these attitudinal barriers as strong but often unseen or unacknowledged factors that sabotage the best regeneration strategies. No lasting progress will be made until there is a commitment within partnerships to acknowledge the parts we all play in perpetuating negative attitudes. This cannot be achieved without breaking away from old processes, liberating people from the culture of silence and letting the voices of the silenced and excluded be heard. Many organizations and individuals are struggling with new ways of tackling this issue, and from that new processes will emerge. One of these is 'Training for Transformation' which VIAE has been promoting for the last two years. Training for Transformation (Hope and Timmel, 1984) was developed in the Third World over a period of twenty years and draws on Freirean ideas of education, human relations training and concepts of transformation. It seeks to create a level playing-field for participants, where each can become more aware of themselves and of the way they work with others. Training for Transformation is a process-centred training for groups who want to bring about positive change in their communities.

Using Training for Transformation to support partnership

The partnership process begins with the establishment of trust and continues with the opening of dialogue through which partners learn about each other. Goals are agreed and lead to action for the change that people want. In the first place, the establishment of trust is threatened if partners cannot communicate in a common language. As we know, the language employed by professionals is different from that used normally by people in communities – for communication to work there has to be a recognition of this and a commitment to working out a common understanding. Another vital part of this process is establishing how people will get to know information and news. If everyone does not have access, trust will be undermined. People left behind at this point may be present bodily, but they experience exclusion.

When partners begin to express their views, a dialogue is opened. Questions, feelings, worries are all part of this process. If

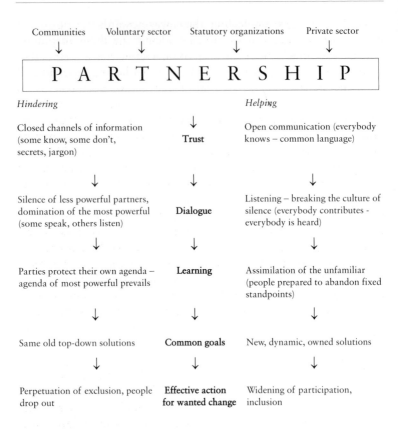

Figure 2: Partnership – a transformative process

the partnership is to be inclusive, everybody needs to be heard. It is not a simple matter to break the culture of silence on which the status quo depends; but change depends on mobilizing the contribution of the silenced. So used are we to this silence we may think there is nothing there – but this is the source of the energy for change and we cannot afford to leave it untapped.

If there is a commitment to listening in the most active and careful manner, this energy will be released and then learning begins to take place. As educators and trainers we know only too well the barriers of fear of the unknown that cause people to draw back from unwelcome or challenging information and experiences, but only when this fear is overcome does learning assume its transformative power. In this process assumptions are challenged, stereotypes exploded and the paraphernalia of status removed. It may be painful; people have to be prepared to 'take into themselves the unfamiliar'.

If, on the other hand, the agenda of the powerful prevails, yet another exclusion takes place and there is little hope of shared ownership of the goals. When action is required to put these goals into practice, if goals are not truly shared, the commitment may be lacking, and at this point criticism is likely to take place. The final seal is set on exclusion and people begin to think of dropping out – the energy of the partnership is drained. If, on the other hand, people have owned goals, thrown themselves into action behind them and succeeded in making changes for the better, the joy of this success is a springboard to further action and becomes its own magnet for drawing in others to work that gives such clear rewards.

At some level I believe all partnerships are struggling with these issues. The pressure of limited time, the extra tasks that working in partnership entail and which are particularly burdensome to volunteer-partners, means that so often the process by which decisions are made is overlooked. Because these are new ways of working which require not only new skills but a new kind of consciousness, it is not surprising that we do not always notice when this happens; or we say to ourselves, there was no other way.

We cannot any longer ignore the need for a holistic vision of regeneration. All the guidelines from EU, national and regional government now ask for community involvement at all levels; it is the ingredient that has been missing, the raising agent as it were, that can produce transformation of the substance. But only if activated correctly can it fulfil its role in the process of change.

New opportunities for lasting, wanted change

The exciting changes introduced by the National Assembly will open up many opportunities to free the old stagnated processes and structures. With the National Assembly for Wales we look forward to a repoliticizing of public life, a more participatory democracy which will open up new avenues for the disadvantaged to articulate their interests. The availability of Objective One funding from 2000 means that vast funds will be available for stimulating economic activity, for

creating new enterprises and kick-starting the Welsh economy. However, it has been clearly spelt out by EU Regional Director of Assistance
and Cohesion, Graham Meadows, that the partnership must include
those who have no resources but only needs, but who have the potential
to contribute to their own regeneration; if this is not done, then not
only will it be impossible to build a programme to spend the money,
but we will fail! National Assembly policies stemming from the central
planning document *Better Wales* (National Assembly, 2000c, pp. 41–2)
emphasize that the partnership must be inclusive and must incorporate
education and training, drawing on the expertise of those who work
effectively within deprived communities.

We also look forward to special funds released by government
for coalfield regeneration: the Coalfields Regeneration Trust which
has been established in response to the work of John Prescott's
Coalfields Task Force in England. The task force emphasized that
communities should be placed at the centre of regeneration
initiatives and should also be equal partners in development. Its
report 'Making a Difference' is subtitled 'Empowering communities to create their own sustainable new start' (CTF, 1998).

The critical contribution of learning to the regeneration of Valleys communities

If these powerful statements are not to remain rhetoric, we must
scrutinize our decision-making processes, acknowledge defici-
encies and make the necessary changes. A vital part of the curriculum for lifelong learning will be to prepare people to work in
partnership to raise awareness of these issues and it is through
programmes like 'Training for Transformation' that capacity can
be built, not only within community organizations, but also within
the statutory and voluntary sectors to meet the demands of
working cross-sectorally in equal partnership.

In the new agenda in Wales the lifelong learning curriculum
must grow to accommodate the new and pressing need for change
(Longworth and Davies, 1996). Participants in the 'Living in the
Valleys' seminar asked for 'education for all', saw 'problems of
communication' and referred time and again to lack of confidence
and lack of self-esteem. To return, then, to the interface between
learning and community economic development, VIAE sees a

relevant and comprehensive programme for supporting regeneration as crucial to its success. Such a programme would draw on all the good practice in the Valleys, Wales, Britain and elsewhere to break down barriers of desperation and isolation, to bring people together for mutual support, to recreate hope by acknowledging issues, to raise the possibility of action for change, to provide skills to enable outreach and responses to community need, to facilitate access to knowledge, information and resources outside the local community; and to extend democracy by giving knowledge of rights, enabling individuals and communities to speak with their own authentic voices, to stimulate a desire and confidence to put the communities' agenda on the table, and to enable input into change and the power to shape that change. The creation of role models, the work within community networks of trust to gain insight into particular local barriers to help create the style and content of local learning programmes, and the tailoring of provision so that the talents, skills and experience of local people are valued must be embedded in regeneration strategies. In this way the capacity of the community and indeed the regeneration partnership can grow through a cycle of learning, action and reflection.

6 Liberation or control in community development work

LYZ JONES

Crynodeb

Mae'r cysylltiad rhwng newid personol a brwydr ar y cyd i wella ein bywydau yn elfen annatod o arfer gwaith cymunedol. Yn y bennod hon, mae'r awdur yn disgrifio ei phroses newid personol hi a'r ffordd y darganfu 'ei llais ei hun' drwy ei phrofiad fel athrawes, gwirfoddolwraig, gweithredwraig dros hawliau menywod, myfyrwraig a gweithwraig gymunedol. Mae'n tynnu sylw at bwysigrwydd addysg feirniadol fel rhan hanfodol o'i gwaith ac yn disgrifio gwerth a dylanwadau rhaglenni datblygu megis Hyfforddiant ar gyfer Trawsnewid a syniadau yr addysgwr o Frasil, Paulo Freire.

Mae'n tynnu sylw at anawsterau ceisio datblygu y math hwn o ymarferiad yng nghyd-destun canlyniadau sy'n dibynnu ar gyllid. Mae'n dadlau'n gryf yn erbyn agwedd orfodol at waith cymunedol ac o blaid dull sy'n galluogi pobl i ddadansoddi eu problemau eu hunain, datblygu eu hatebion eu hunain a chyrchu'r adnoddau a'r gefnogaeth y maent eu hangen.

My motivation for writing this is based on my desire to share my experiences and understanding of work in Valleys communities in south Wales. I want to be an effective community worker and by effective I mean have the ability to support and facilitate those who want to improve their quality of life.

When I ask myself why I want to do this, I am aware that I have to dig deep to find my reasons. My reasons have been slowly emerging over the years as I have become more and more involved in this work. I believe it is my own story of change and growth that leads me into this work. I believe that striving to realize my own potential as a human being and trying to improve my own life has given me some insight into the struggles that we all go through to make some sense of our lives and to give our lives shape, meaning and purpose. I am therefore drawn towards those who are struggling and striving to do the same.

I believe that this desire to improve the quality of our lives is both an individual and a collective struggle. In my efforts to fulfil my own potential, I have followed a path towards community work. I am being up-front here about the realizing of my own needs as a human being. This is my agenda. I wish for all people to have the opportunity to travel on the road towards reaching their full potential. You may think this is arrogant of me to presume that I somehow know that everyone wants to fulfil their potential, but I believe that my potential is bound up with the potential of everyone else and that I will not be able to fulfil my potential unless other people have the choice to fulfil their potential too. So it is not arrogance, it is a kind of survival instinct, but I realize it is definitely my agenda.

So here I am, working alongside people trying, like me, to keep their dignity and reach their potential.

Education for social change

Through my time as a pupil I often asked the questions – Who sets the learning? Why is my knowledge and understanding not listened to? Why am I not asked what I think and feel? How is this learning relevant to my life now? Later, as a teacher in both the primary and secondary sector, I asked the questions – Who owns education? Is it the learner or the educator? What is the role of an educator? Is it to fill the empty vessel or facilitate understanding and knowledge? We do not teach our children to ask 'Why?' only to accept. I believe, from my experiences of learning and teaching, that learning only takes place when we are motivated and that it is based around our desire to gain knowledge and understanding about ourselves and about ourselves in our families, in our communities and in the world. It must be relevant to our lives at that moment if we are to integrate the learning. My experience of stumbling across participatory education and the growth and change that it brought about in my life, are ingredients that I recognize and have experienced at first hand.

I came to understand the idea of education for social change through my involvement as a volunteer with Gwerin-y-coed/The Woodcraft Folk in Wales. The Woodcraft Folk is a co-educational young people's and children's organization based on the principles of cooperation, participatory democracy, internationalism and education for social change. It was developed in the 1920s by a breakaway group of the Labour Party. I was impressed by the young people and the way they were valued within the organization and the way in which these young people found their voices and were encouraged to express their thoughts and understanding of the world they found themselves in – breaking the culture of silence at an early age.

I first came across this way of learning to find my own voice through my involvement in the women's movement and later through attending courses run by the Workers' Education Association.

I understand participatory education as a process in which we are equal participants in the process of learning, and the learning taking place is a two-way process. To me, participatory education is a way of bringing about education for social change as we begin to take control and define for ourselves the knowledge we need to lead a purposeful life and change the people around us who seek to define us too narrowly, restricting our ability to fulfil our potential. In the context of working alongside children, young people and adults I believe two-way learning is fundamental to the process of change (Rogers, A., 1992).

Liberation education

> The role of the educator is to present to the people in challenging form the issues they themselves have raised in confused form. (MaoTse-Tung)

In the process of my learning I have come across *Training for Transformation* (TFT; Hope and Timmel, 1984) developed over the last twenty-three years by community workers practising in Africa. The methodology draws from many sources: social analysis, Christian values, human relations and organizational development. It is based on the ground-breaking literacy programmes developed by Paulo Freire, the Brazilian educationalist.

'Over the years, the thoughts and work of Paulo Freire spread from north-east Brazil to an entire continent, and made a profound impact not only in the field of education but also in the overall struggle for national development' (R. Shaull, in Freire, 1972, p. 9). Paulo Freire developed a critical analysis of the education process through his own experience of poverty. He pioneered a literacy programme which enabled people to come to a new awareness of themselves and begin to look critically at the social situation in which they found themselves, often leading them to take the initiative in acting to transform the society that had denied them this opportunity of participation. Education became a subversive force. He understood education at that time in Brazil to be a form of social control rather than a process of growth and change. He based his literacy programme on his analysis and his understanding of what motivates people to learn:

> His book the *Pedagogy of the Oppressed* (1972) represents the response of a creative mind and a sensitive conscience to the extraordinary misery and suffering of the people around him. Born in 1921 in Recife, the centre of one of the most extreme situations of poverty and underdevelopment in the developing world, he was soon forced to experience that reality directly. As the economic crisis in 1929 in the United States began to affect Brazil, the precarious stability of Freire's middle-class life gave way and he found himself sharing the plight of the 'wretched of the earth'. This had a profound influence on his life as he came to know the gnawing pangs of hunger, and fell behind in school because of the listlessness it produced; it led him to make a vow at the age of eleven, to dedicate his life to the struggle against hunger, so that other children would not have to know the agony he was then experiencing. (Shaull, in Freire, 1972, p. 10)

This experience also led him to the discovery of what he described as the 'culture of silence' of the dispossessed. He came to realize that the ignorance and lethargy he encountered amongst the people of this community were a direct product of the whole situation of economic, social and political domination − and of paternalism − of which they were victims. Rather than being encouraged and equipped to know and respond to the concrete realities of their world, they were kept 'submerged' in a situation in which critical awareness and response were practically impossible.

And it became clear to him that the whole educational system was one of the major instruments for the maintenance of this culture of silence.

The methodology he developed was considered such a threat to the old order that Freire was jailed immediately after the military coup in 1964. He was released seventy days later and left the country for Chile.

He expounded a process of study and reflection set in a historical context in the midst of a struggle to create a new social order and thus represents a new unity of theory and practice. Theory and practice are the benchmarks of his analysis and the resulting techniques that he developed. His techniques are practised all over the world by educationalists. This is the basis of approach and techniques used in Training for Transformation.

Training for Transformation – developing community leadership

I encountered Training for Transformation through the Valleys Initiative for Adult Education and I subsequently attended a two-week residential course in Ireland in 1997 facilitated by 'Partners', an Irish organization that had been responsible for developing Transformation for Training (TFT) practice in Ireland and the UK. They have developed a programme based on their experience of using the techniques of Paulo Freire in the developing world and have been facilitating these courses to develop the skills of Irish community development workers through an experiential pro-gramme of learning. They have also used TFT techniques to undertake community development work themselves – a dynamic process of theory and practice.

Training for Transformation has been developed through the real experience of community workers working with people who are the victims of war and oppressive regimes. The fundamental principle of Training for Transformation is based on working with communities to facilitate their ownership of change and create their theories of society through critical analysis and action. They become the owners of knowledge. In the first instance, this is done through undertaking a listening survey within the community of people and presenting back to them the issues which most concern them and around which there is a strong consensus. This process creates a dynamic and generates energy and motivation for change. Through a process of critical analysis (social and political analysis) of the issues and working within the context of the personal, the community and the wider world, people develop an understanding of their own situation. From this point a plan of action is developed, owned and undertaken by the community of people to bring about change. Running alongside this is a process of group development to support the development of effective teams. The group, the team, is all-important to effect change and is seen as a 'place of forgiveness' and strength. Being the driver of change is key to effecting change.

The programme was built around us – tailor-made. The facilitators met each evening after the activities of the day to reflect on and analyse the sessions and to develop the sessions for the following day. The learning was a two-way process for us and them.

I believe this training has had a profound effect on me. It worked on my intellect and my emotions. For two weeks the twenty participants became the 'community'. Before attending the programme I knew little about this style of working. The process I went through helped me further to develop my own analysis of education and society. I was invited to 'unpack my suitcase' of experience and knowledge and to reorganize it through the process, repacking it and adding in new pieces of learning and throwing out information and knowledge which was no longer useful to me. We were all valued for the experience and knowledge we brought with us and were not treated like empty vessels devoid of the knowledge held only by the experts. The facilitators created opportunities for us to explore, reflect, analyse, develop our own theories and act on them.

This method of breaking through the apathy, discouragement and hopelessness which I and the community groups with which I work often experience as we try to face the hard facts of reality and engage in social analysis, is one which has informed me in my practice and which has made me realize how much I have yet to learn and understand.

Theory and practice

In my experience of working with people to improve the quality of life I have moved from 'doing good works' to the position of working alongside, trying not to impose my agenda. This is not easy as I have strong opinions and my own analysis of the state of the world. It is a developing one because I have a lot to learn, but sometimes I think I have found the answer and I know best what is 'good for people'. Then I become the oppressor.

I can give examples of my work based on my understanding and beliefs but I know I cannot present them to you as being *the* way since I am always learning in the process. However, I can offer them up as *a* way of working, which has brought about change for all of us who have been involved.

I was lucky enough to work with a very experienced community worker on a local authority housing estate in Abergavenny. He taught me to work with people, to help them find their voices, to tell their experiences of life to the people who had control over their lives – namely doctors, social workers, health visitors, midwives and headteachers. I worked alongside them and included them in meetings which discussed plans which would affect their lives. This gave them the opportunity to express their experiences directly to policy-makers and practitioners who often talked about their problems but never asked them what they thought or what they wanted to do about solving these problems. This created an opportunity for them to be listened to, opened lines of communication, improved some of the services and in some cases helped them gain the respect they deserved. It also gave them the confidence to continue to speak out in other situations.

With regard to TFT and my experience of using my new-found knowledge, I have worked with a variety of groups in the Valleys and sometimes it has proved fruitful and sometimes I could have done better. Based on feedback and my own observations, one successful experience was the work with a community regeneration organization based in the Cynon valley. Working alongside two other facilitators, I helped to facilitate a Vision Day for twenty-two volunteers and staff based on their ideas of what they wanted to get out of the day. We developed a programme which helped them to reflect on their history and their achievements, explore their relationships with one another, identify and explore the impact of their positive and negative styles of working with one another, strengthen their effectiveness as a team, create a Vision Statement for the future and develop a set of goals for five years. Following this they developed a five-year business plan that was the basis for a number of successful bids to secure the future work of the organization.

Outcomes, outputs, performance indicators. Who sets the goals?

I am now, after ten years, able to interpret this terminology. I believe that so long as the process of working with communities is part of the methodology, outcomes, outputs and performance indicators are just another way of expressing the changes that communities and individuals want to achieve to improve their quality of life.

Unfortunately, in my experience, the outcomes are defined by the funding expectations and deadlines of the statutory sector and do not take into account the needs of Valleys communities and the process of change that they are undergoing. They are not flexible enough to be able to respond to this change. They are often prescriptive, unrealistic, coercive and more about social control than about social change intended to improve the quality of peoples' lives.

Who owns change?

I would suggest that change comes about when people want and are able to analyse the problems, develop the solutions and access the resources and support they need to make change happen. Change is then owned by them. Change that is uninvited or forced on us – unwelcome change – arouses in us feelings of helplessness, despair, fear, anger, chaos, alienation, refusal and resentment. These are powerful emotions and must be taken into account when working with Valleys communities and in any action that seeks to bring about change in those communities. A coercive approach to change can never be sustainable as it is not integrated into the fabric of the lives and hopes that Valleys communities have for themselves. Institutions that do not take this into account will not be able to serve these communities. Serving these communities is their reason for being in existence. Goals designed and pre-set by those who do not live the lives of people in Valleys communities and goals which do not take into account the ingredients required to enable change to happen or the processes that need to be undertaken to facilitate change are, in my opinion, counter-productive to peoples' desire for change. This lack of responsiveness and a controlling approach is a major barrier to change.

But then, this presupposes that all the parties want change to take place. Those who have the power of decision-making and choice are often unaware of the power they wield. Because of this lack of awareness, when those with little or no choice or decision-making power attempt to be participants in the decision-making process, their attempts often seem threatening, causing the holders of power either to ignore or resist them. At this point the less powerful give up or fight harder, and are therefore labelled either as apathetic or as troublemakers. Ownership of decision-making about their lives is denied to them.

Owning change

Hope and Timmel (1984) repeat again and again the simple truth that there can be no short cut to becoming an effective community worker. There must be sensitivity to the needs of the individuals in our communities and to one another, and instant judgements on what will be helpful at any particular moment can only be developed through constant practice. There must also be complete openness to feedback, critical reflection, analysis and years of experience.

I would like to suggest that this is an approach which may not only improve the effectiveness of community workers and community activists but one which, if taken on board by the statutory sector, could be helpful to the process of serving communities better.

There needs to be a movement towards communities by the statutory sector and a commitment to gaining a better understanding of the process of community development. This calls for community workers and activists to communicate clearly about the process of community development and to work with statutory institutions to create opportunities for this communication to take place.

Is it possible to build a new type of society based on participatory democracy and not bureaucracy? I believe it is. But then maybe I'm just a cock-eyed optimist.

The power of unequal partnerships

Introduction to chapters 7 and 8

There are two essential elements to the process of community work/development. Firstly the worker, the person who intervenes; he or she is usually paid and employed by an external agency. Secondly, the residents or activists (usually unpaid) who choose to engage with the worker in seeking some form of change. Both worker and residents can have different motivations and possess different forms of knowledge and expertise. The opportunities for change emerge when both of these elements combine together around a common goal.

This force can produce its own momentum when activists work collectively for a common purpose. This process can be particularly effective if encouraged and fostered by external agencies. However, if this emerging force is seen as an obstacle to the objectives of powerful external organizations then the potential for conflict is great.

The following case studies from Perthcelyn in the mid-1990s highlight the potential power of the community work/development process. This power is generated when worker and activists initiate a process from current realities and start to build on their existing strengths and experiences. Both accounts challenge the notion that activists are merely passive players in regeneration and merely the objects of agendas set by powerful vested interests. In addition, these accounts highlight the significant gulf that exists between the powerful and the powerless, and the inevitable conflicts that will arise in the absence of a shared understanding and approach to local development in Valleys communities.

7   My story of the 'Lost city'

JILL OWEN

Crynodeb

Yn yr astudiaeth achos hwn, mae'r awdur, preswylwraig a gweithredwraig ar stad Perthcelyn yng nghwm Cynon, yn adrodd stori fywiog am yr ymgyrchu yn y 1990au hwyr. Mae'r awdur wedi byw gydol ei hoes ar y stad ac mae'n disgrifio'r dirywiad cymdeithasol o brofiad personol. Mae'n sôn am sut y daeth yn weithgar gyda Chymdeithas y Tenantiaid a Phreswylwyr ac yn ddiweddarach gyda Grŵp Rheoli Stad Perthcelyn.

Mae'n trafod y berthynas anodd a ddatblygodd gyda'r awdurdod lleol yn sgîl strategaeth gymunedol y stad a sut y trodd sôn am 'bartneriaeth' yn fuan yn deimladau o ddiffyg ymddiriedaeth a gwrthdaro. Mae'n dadlau nad oedd dewis gan Gymdeithas y Tenantiaid a Phreswylwyr ond tynnu'n ôl o strategaeth y stad oherwydd iddi ddatblygu'n 'strategaeth yr awdurdod lleol' yn hytrach na 'strategaeth y preswylwyr'. Daw i'r casgliad bod yn rhaid i breswylwyr, nad oes ganddynt ddewis ond byw ar y stad, barhau i frwydro a datblygu a chyrchu eu hadnoddau eu hunain mewn amgylchedd o ddiffyg cefnogaeth dybryd.

The estate

Over the past five years I have been actively involved in trying to improve the estate where I have lived all my life. This is my own story of how I came to be involved and my personal view of the events that followed.

Perthcelyn is better known as the 'Lost city'. I have lived there for forty years. I was born in the house that my mother still lives in today. I have good memories of growing up in Perthcelyn. Everyone knew everyone. People always stopped and chatted on the streets. Times were hard but what little we had we shared. It was alive.

Even in the long winter nights it was safe to leave your home with the door unlocked. Drugs and house burglaries were never heard of and we never witnessed violence on our streets. Living in Perthcelyn provided a wonderful feeling of contentment. Perthcelyn had it all. Poverty and hardship never stood in the way of people's lives. Even though times were hard, people seemed happy.

After leaving school at the age of sixteen, I found myself a job in a factory. Jobs in those days didn't seem so hard to come by. During the many working years of my life, I lost touch with our community as I spent little time on the estate. However, some years ago I lost my job through ill health. After a short while I began to notice how different Perthcelyn had become. I no longer knew everyone and people no longer seemed to have time to chat and pass the time of day. Something seemed to have changed. Our community seemed lost. I could only see emptiness, loneliness and fear. Drug abuse, theft and harassment had all taken the place of our once contented community.

Crime is now the most serious problem on our estate. People have been burgled while in bed sleeping. It is always the most vulnerable people who seem to suffer. One man, who is disabled, even got burgled at Christmas. It is easy to burgle our houses as the door-locks can be opened in seconds by means of a flat-head screwdriver and the windows can easily be taken out within a matter of minutes. Houses have had to be boarded up in order to prevent vandalism. I have seen racist graffiti such as 'Support the National Front' and swastika signs around the estate. People no longer feel safe in their homes, even with their doors locked. Gangs of youths often hang around street corners harassing people. The telephone box is constantly being vandalized. Some teenagers drink and urinate on the street. Cars are stolen and stripped down at two or three o'clock in the morning and are then dumped or set on fire.

Drug abuse is another major problem. Dirty drug-syringes on our streets are a sign that some people no longer care or are interested in what is going on around them. They begin to withdraw, keeping themselves to themselves. They never really believe that they will become victims of drug abuse. Some teenagers start stealing to feed their habit, without giving a second thought to those from whom they have stolen, people often poorer than themselves. People are afraid to stand up against the drug pushers and criminals for fear of reprisals. The drug pushers and criminals have become the kings and queens of the lost city. They create a climate of fear on the estate, selling their drugs to anyone who cares to buy them. Most of us have become pawns in a game of chess, dominated by these criminals and silenced by intimidation and threat.

Getting involved

Four years ago, I was approached and asked to join the Tenants' and Residents' Association. I decided to give it a go, not really knowing what to expect, or what I was expected to do. All I knew at the time was that it seemed like a good opportunity to try and improve life on the estate. I wanted to see changes on the estate both for myself and for the many good people who live there. I approached the job with determination and commitment and within a short time my fellow-members nominated me chairperson.

At that stage the housing department was very involved with the Tenants' and Residents' Association. We had regular meetings with the housing department over many of the problems I have described and they seemed to me to be concerned about them. The only thing was that, despite all this concern, they never seemed to do anything. For example, despite the existence of a tenancy agreement, they made no real effort to enforce it. When they were challenged about these issues they began to make excuses about legal obligations. We felt that we were constantly banging our heads against a brick wall. However, despite the lack of action by the council, our group went from strength to strength.

Around the same time, the local authority was putting in a bid to the Welsh Office for a regeneration strategy for the estate. The old local authority, Cynon Valley Borough Council, had been working with 'Tops' (the name of a Perthcelyn inter-agency group) to put this plan together. Tops had been formed a few years earlier to involve all of the agencies working on the estate, together with local councillors and estate representatives. However, in practice, there was very little involvement from the local community in the development of the bid. Despite this, the local authority submitted an outline bid to the Welsh Office on behalf of Tops.

At the same time, the Perthcelyn School Action Group had been re-formed with the help of the new Save the Children development worker. The group was campaigning for a new infant and primary school on the estate. They lobbied the education director and councillors and took their campaign to the media. With the help of the Save the Children worker, local people also began to organize together around the issue of crime. The Tenants' and Residents' Association, the School Action Group, the Community Centre committee, Pop-in Women's Group and Neighbourhood Watch all joined together to voice their concerns about crime to the police and the housing department of Cynon Valley Council. We soon began to realize that we as local people had a voice of our own and we had to unite to improve our estate. We would retain our own separate groups and work on our own issues but we would join together and support each other to tackle the issues that affected the estate as a whole. In this way we could best represent the interests of the estate and be a stronger force for change.

Residents' strategy

In January 1996, the Welsh Office announced that they were allocating £25,000 for the purpose of drawing up a strategy for the estate. A plan had to be submitted in six months. Officers from the local authority and Tops asked us to get involved in drawing up such a plan. All of the local groups who had previously worked together decided that they would draft their own plan. We formalized the group by calling ourselves the Perthcelyn Estate Management Group (PEMG).

At this time the local authority seemed to have little interest in the strategy. A worker from the housing department was to act as a liaison worker, and a consultant was taken on to coordinate the plan. The development officer from Save the Children supported the residents. Two other consultants were taken on, one to investig-ate traffic and environment issues and one to examine the community buildings on the estate.

During the six months, the group concentrated on putting the strategy document together. This included regular meetings and 'away days' to ensure that we kept on top of things. We organized a residents' survey to get as much feedback from the estate as possible in the short timescale we had been given. This we did by drawing up a simple survey in order to find out what the people would identify as their priorities. We also conducted surveys for younger children and for teenagers. All three surveys clearly showed us what the needs and problems were. These included crime, drug abuse, violence, high levels of unemployment, lack of play facilities, lack of youth and community facilities and the need for a new school. We then worked to put the entire package together and to ensure that all of these needs were included in the bid, which had to be sent to the Welsh Office via the local authority.

We waited patiently over the next few months, hoping and praying that our bid was going to be one of the successful ones. Everyone had worked so hard and we hoped that a successful bid might lift the spirits of our troubled community. It was about two weeks before Christmas that year (1996) when we received a telephone call saying that the bid had been successful and that Perthcelyn had been awarded £3.5 million from the Welsh Office. Most of what we submitted had been funded, with the exception of an extension on the community centre. I can't explain how I felt. It was fantastic news for our estate. Yet despite all the publicity, many local people refused to believe it and the familiar phrase was still 'I'll believe it when I see it'.

Local authority strategy

As I stated earlier, there was little involvement from the local authority up to this stage. The new authority, Rhondda Cynon Taff (RCT) from the previous April, had replaced the Cynon Valley Borough Council. However, this situation was soon to change. All of a sudden we found ourselves being invaded by representatives of the new local authority. It seemed as if every department in Rhondda Cynon Taff had come to life. A meeting was held between the PEMG and senior officers of the local authority. They kept going on about the need to work in partnership. However, it was very clear that they were completely out of their depth and were not used to working in partnership with local people. The first few meetings stumbled along with each side trying to get to know each other and finding out who was who from which department. From an early stage, it seemed to me that most of the officers at these meetings did not want to be there. I felt they were looking down on us, and if given half a chance would be somewhere else. They often used words and terms we did not understand and seemed to operate as if they were at a council meeting. So we had to keep asking them to explain and requesting them not to use jargon. I also felt unhappy that we were usually outnumbered by two to one by local authority officers. Problems began when officers began making decisions without discussing them first with the PEMG.

Local authority officers then organized a joint planning day at a local hotel, facilitated by an external consultant. RCT officers proposed a complicated series of sub-groups all feeding into the decision-making committees of the local authority. A handbook was to be produced which would set out the ways of working together. However, despite this day, the sub-groups, and the handbook, the problems continued to arise. A PEMG meeting was called, as the group had become unhappy with the way the local authority was working on the strategy. The problems continued and the relationship soon grew into a case of 'THEM AND US', rather than the working relationship we had hoped would emerge.

The next blow from Rhondda Cynon Taff was directed at the Save the Children development officer. It was very clear from early on that RCT officers did not want our group to receive support from the SCF worker. They did not want a strong residents' group who could understand what was going on and could negotiate effectively with RCT officers. They did not want a worker whom they could not control and who saw his job as empowering and strengthening the PEMG. To this end, they made every effort to exclude him from the strategy. To make matters worse, the Save the Children project in Cynon valley was also being cut back around the same time. Save the Children as an organization was no longer going to be doing community development or providing childcare services. They were going to concentrate on working for the rights of children and young people and would have a much reduced workforce in the valley. As a result the development worker's role on the estate ended in July 1997.

From the very beginning, I was constantly in the firing line. I had stood up to the officers of RCT a number of times and I felt they did not like it. I felt they did not like me and would use any opportunity to undermine me. However, I could clearly see what was going on but I was not going to be put off by what I saw as their bullying tactics. I remember being in one meeting of the Traffic and Environment sub-group. Every time I spoke, two of the officers present from RCT constantly 'tutted'. I felt this childish tactic was to try and undermine my confidence and make me feel stupid. However, I challenged this behaviour by putting my pen down and addressing the two officers and saying that if they had something to say to me would they please speak out. This was an example of the kind of behaviour I experienced from RCT officers. I felt it was a deliberate tactic to isolate people who would not go along with *their* agenda and who dared to challenge *their* way of doing things.

By this stage I felt the strategy had become a local authority strategy and not a residents' strategy. I was beginning to lose heart, and the issue that was the last straw for me was in relation to the placing of security cameras on the estate. Money had been allocated from the bid to position five security cameras on the estate: one by the new play area, one between the old school and the community centre, one watching over the new school and two further up the main road. My concern was that the cameras were being used only to monitor the council's buildings and facilities and not to secure people's houses or the areas where people needed to feel safer. This was the end of the strategy for me. It seemed to me that RCT were doing what they wanted and not what was best for our community. The Tenants' and Residents' Association decided to pull out of the strategy altogether.

However, this was not the end of our problems. The Tenants' and Residents' Association worked from a flat on the estate where people could come and report any problems, for instance with repairs. The flat is open to the public five working days a week. We found that people came to us with housing and often deep-rooted personal problems. Despite the fact that we were all volunteers and we had no worker to support us, we never turned anybody away. We invited people to stay and chat over a cup of tea. That's how we got most of our members. We have had education classes on drugs for children and young people; we are trying to get a support group together in the hope of helping people with personal problems; and we have held 'fun days' for the children and a very successful Santa's grotto. Soon after we left the community strategy in 1997, our grant from the local authority for running our service to the tenants was withheld. When we asked for the reasons, we were told that they (housing department officers) felt we were not working to the rules set out in the participation agreement. We had several meetings to discuss our funding without any success. The reason they gave for the withholding of our funds changed frequently. By 1998, we had been without funding for almost a year. We had been left with outstanding bills and, as we could not pay the bills without grant aid, we were forced to shut down the flat.

What I have learned from getting involved

(1) I have learned that many local authority officers and councillors do not make enough effort to listen to residents who live on estates like Perthcelyn. They don't seem to care. Maybe it is because they do not have to live with the problems day and night and as a result do not understand the strain on residents who have no choice but to live in these situations.

(2) I have learned that most local authority officers and councillors seem to want to control things. They seem to be afraid to allow the residents to have the power or to take the necessary action to improve estates like Perthcelyn.

(3) I have learned that there is very little support for local people to help us carry out our roles in local groups. I also learned how difficult it can be to get people involved because of all of the things that are happening in and around this estate. As a result, we can easily get burnt out by increasing demands that come from within the estate and from the local authority.

(4) I have learned that community development workers who are employed by local authorities are not free to work for the benefit of local residents.

(5) I have learned many things about the estate and the people who live here. I have learned how some of them feel and how they cope with everyday life. I have seen how grateful and supportive many of them have been towards the Tenants' and Residents' Association.

(6) Despite all the difficulties and barriers we face, I have learned that we need to continue to support and help people on our estate to the best of our ability and to continue our fight against crime and drug abuse.

8   Local action for participation and change

MARTIN HOBAN

Crynodeb

Agorwyd Ysgol Gynradd Gymunedol Perthcelyn yn rhan isaf cwm Cynon yn swyddogol ym mis Rhagfyr 1999. Yn yr astudiaeth achos hwn, mae'r awdur yn disgrifio'r frwydr leol i sicrhau hynny. Mae'r awdur yn olrhain y gweithredu o'r cyfnod pan ddechreuodd weithio ar y stad ym 1995 gan ddisgrifio gwaith ymgyrchu Grŵp Gweithredu'r Ysgol; datblygiad Grŵp Rheoli Stad Perthcelyn dan arweiniad preswylwyr; a'r ymgyrch i sicrhau adnoddau sylweddol ar gyfer y stad.

Mae'r awdur yn dadlau i breswylwyr Perthcelyn dderbyn y pŵer pan gawsant y grym a'r gefnogaeth i wneud hynny. Penderfyniad ac egni pobl leol, menywod yn bennaf, a sicrhaodd hynny. Dadleuodd fod ei rôl ef yn hanfodol i sicrhau grymuster a chyfranogiad preswylwyr, a bod hynny yn hollol ar wahân i'r gwaith o gydlynu a rheoli strategaeth y stad. Daw i'r casgliad fod y rôl rymuso hon yn bosibl gan iddo gael ei gyflogi gan asiantaeth gefnogol allanol (Achub y Plant) yn hytrach na chan yr awdurdod lleol.

Introduction

On 3 December 1999, Neil Jenkins, the Welsh international rugby player, officially opened the Perthcelyn Community Primary School. The opening marked the beginning of primary school education on the Perthcelyn estate. Returning to the estate after an absence of two years, I began to reflect on the campaign that had brought it about – a campaign that not only led to the provision of a new school but also to a wide range of benefits for residents. As the Save the Children development officer on Perthcelyn at the time, I was lucky to have been part of that experience. It is an important story that should be told. It is about local people on a housing estate in the Cynon valley and *their* collective efforts to improve *their* living conditions. Above all, it is about *their* struggle to be heard and to have *their* say in decisions that affect *their* lives.

To recall and to write about all the events that happened during the period from September 1995 until December 1996 would require more extensive research and would probably fill a book. All I can do in this chapter is trace my own role as a worker in this campaign and relate the key events that led to local activists taking the power that led to *their* achievements. For this purpose, I will rely on my own memory and personal fieldnotes.

The background

Perthcelyn is a small council estate. It contains about 400 houses and flats. It is perched high up on the hillside overlooking the town of Mountain Ash and the village of Penrhiw-ceibr in the lower Cynon valley. A main road runs through the estate connecting Mountain Ash with the lower end of the valley. The estate has a post office, two shops and a private residential centre for the elderly. Local facilities include a flat on the main road that is used by the Perthcelyn Tenants' and Residents' Association. At the bottom of the hill, stands the community centre. Adjacent to the centre is the new Perthcelyn Primary School.

In July 1995, I started work on the estate with the Cynon Valley Project, or Save the Children (SCF) as it was more commonly known in the area. The project had been set up in 1991 to work on two estates in the lower Cynon valley, Perthcelyn and Fernhill. The project was funded jointly by SCF and the Dutch-based Bernard van Leer Foundation. My main role was to provide development support on Perthcelyn. The project ran childcare sessions and a playgroup on the estate. Grant aid was also provided to the community centre. The main aim of the project was to develop family and childcare services on the estate. SCF hoped to achieve their objective by involving parents in developing and delivering childcare services. In doing this work, the project was anxious to work in partnership with residents, the local authority and other agencies. There had been two SCF development officers on the estate before me. Each worker stayed for approximately two years.

As I was new to south Wales and the Valleys, I spent a short period trying to assess the local scene. I spoke first with local people from the estate. I then met with officers of the local authority and workers from voluntary agencies who had regular contact with local people.

The activists

The main activists, all of whom were local people, were active as part of the community centre committee. This group was the longest-serving committee on the estate. They managed the centre and organized a range of activities for different age groups. Childcare was provided at the centre by SCF. Parents using this service had formed a 'Pop-in' group. All of its members were women. During the childcare sessions, they participated in different forms of training organized by external agencies. This group had also been involved in a number of local campaigns. There was also a Tenants' and Residents' Association on the estate. This group comprised a small group of activists who were concerned with housing issues. At the time of my arrival, they appeared to be struggling as their chairperson had recently resigned.

From discussions with this small group of activists, it was clear that they had little time for outside agencies, councillors and especially the police. There were concerns over vandalism, young people and the general lack of facilities on the estate such as play areas for younger children. The central issue to emerge from these discussions was the need for a new school. The previous year, four activists from local groups had formed the Perthcelyn School Action Group (PSAG) with the help of SCF. They wanted a new school built on the estate. The then infants' school had been built in 1950 as a temporary construction. They were concerned that the facilities at the school were inadequate. There was no assembly hall and the children had to eat their dinners in three cramped classrooms. There was no space to do physical education which in effect meant that the full national curriculum could not be implemented. Assemblies, concerts or other social activities were not possible within the existing space. In addition, the building was in a bad state of repair with constant problems from a leaking roof. At the age of seven, children from Perthcelyn had to transfer to the Penrhiw-ceibr junior school located in the next village further down the hillside. Parents had many concerns about the route that their children had to travel to the junior school. They felt the narrow and steep road was unsafe and were very concerned about their children's safety. Parents also felt that having to transfer to another school at a crucial age affected their children's educational development. There was a strong sense among many of the parents that Perthcelyn children were losing out. They felt that a new infants' and primary school on the estate was essential for the educational and psychological development of their children. They were supported in these demands by the local headteacher of the infants' school.

The previous year, in 1994, the Action Group had met with the director of education of Mid Glamorgan County Council to make their case. However, he made no firm response to their request. As a result, the group proceeded to organize a boycott and demonstration at the school to highlight the issue. They contacted the media and received high-profile coverage on television and in the local newspapers. Despite all of this effort, they felt that, while they had achieved a great deal of publicity, their campaign had not moved forward.

The local authority

At the time, the local district authority for the area was the Cynon Valley Borough Council (CVBC), which was responsible for housing, recreation, local planning and environmental health. Mid Glamorgan County Council was responsible for social services and education, as well as structural planning. However, following local government reorganization in April 1996, the borough was to become part of a new unitary authority of Rhondda Cynon Taff. The political ward links Perthcelyn with Penrhiw-ceibr in the next village. Penrhiw-ceibr is an area of traditional terraced housing. In 1995, the ward had two councillors, one from the Labour Party and one from Plaid Cymru. There was also a Plaid county councillor. None of the councillors lived on the Perthcelyn estate. Local authority officers tended to perceive the area as a 'problem estate'. Following some disturbances involving young people on the estate in 1989, an inter-agency group was formed which later became known as the 'Tops'. While some local activists attended the Tops meetings, they were mainly attended by agency representatives. Shortly after I arrived, officers from CVBC were pushing for an estate strategy through the Tops. In this process, they had been supported by other agencies and particularly by SCF.

My approach

From my initial analysis of the area and my discussions with activists, it was clear that the existing agencies had failed to involve local activists to any significant extent in local projects or initiatives. The aims of SCF were laudable but I soon realized that local activists were clearly not concerned with providing childcare services. By providing this service, SCF played an important role in providing quality childcare for pre-school children and by allowing parents the space and time to engage in training and other activities. SCF had created the conditions for change to happen. The question now was how could residents extend their participation to achieve the changes they wanted. On the basis of my own analysis, I believed that their increased participation could be enabled in the following ways.

Firstly, by building on their existing capacity for local direct action. Many of the existing activists involved with the Pop-in group were women with young children. Many had a strong history of taking direct action to resolve grievances. They had been involved in direct action for a new school and in a local campaign over school uniforms. In 1993, they had organized a roadblock to protest against speeding cars through the estate. It was clear from these campaigns that action for children was their main motivating force. In fact, the main focus of all the campaigns arose from the need to improve the quality of life for children on the estate. They were advocates for their children, rather than service providers. For me, this direct form of engagement, which sprang from their immediate concerns about their own children, was a very positive force. I believed this form of involvement should be supported and developed.

Secondly, by standing alongside and negotiating my role with local activists, I could help them achieve what was important for them in their own lives. My role could be to act as a resource for advice and to support *their* participation to achieve *their* aims. It was clear that I could only successfully adopt this role if I could build the trust of local people and establish an honest working relationship. I was also clear that by adopting this role there was potential for conflict, particularly with the local authority

The story

Very soon after I started in post, I was asked by SCF to assist the local authority officers to draw up the outline bid for an estate strategy. This was a worthy objective, but I soon realized that there was no resident involvement in this process. While I helped to develop the bid, I emphasized at the Tops meetings and to agency workers that any bid for money on the estate needed to involve local activists if the strategy was to have any chance of success. The danger was that a top-down approach could lead to the domination of the strategy by the local authority. Officers and professionals would have most to gain and residents would merely be spectators. I had learned from previous estate strategies, while employed as a local authority community worker, that funding-led developments were doomed to failure if they did not have the support and involvement of local residents. Officers of the local authorities that preceded Rhondda Cynon Taff Borough Council (RCT) submitted the outline bid in September 1995. The bid did not seek money for projects but sought a small amount of revenue funding to develop a detailed plan for the estate. Such a bid would allow time to seek the involvement of residents. I saw the estate strategy as a possible opportunity for residents to achieve what they wanted. However, at this stage it was still very much a local authority and agency-led initiative. Activists were not really interested, as they had not been involved in shaping it. The real question was how might this participation be developed.

I soon got a chance to start developing a working relationship with activists. The School Action Group asked for my help and expressed an interest in trying to resurrect their campaign. In November, I suggested a letter be sent to the new director of education outlining the case for the school and seeking a direct meeting between the director and local people. To everyone's surprise, the director responded and offered to meet. The School Action Group responded to this development by holding a preliminary meeting and asked me to attend. I helped the group to plan and organize the meeting. The group decided to make a presentation, to give the director a tour of the route to Penrhiwceibr, to organize a visit to the old school and to identify certain supporters to attend. Most importantly the group decided to run the meeting themselves and not to rely on professionals or councillors. The chairperson of the community centre, a woman with long experience of involvement on the estate, volunteered to chair the meeting.

While activists prepared for their meeting with the director of education, another opportunity arose in December for further work with a broader group of activists. Some residents began to be concerned about crime on the estate. There had been a number of burglaries and a local Neighbourhood Watch group had been formed. The activists from different groups decided to hold a meeting about the problems of increasing crime. These activists included people from the community centre, the Tenants' and Residents' Association, the School Action Group, the Pop-in group and the newly formed Neighbourhood Watch. The shared problem of crime brought the activists together for the first time. I helped them to prepare and plan for a meeting with senior housing officials and senior police officers. The chairperson of the community centre again chaired this meeting. The activists controlled the meeting by firstly allowing residents to have their say and then asking the agency representatives to respond. My role at the meeting was to support the chairperson and to enable activists and residents to participate. This meeting was a turning point in that activists from different groups were now starting to work together.

In January 1996, the Welsh Office responded to the bid submitted by the local authority and gave approval for a community strategy bid to be developed for the estate. Perthcelyn was chosen as one of a number of areas throughout Wales. Each of these strategies was to be awarded a sum of money (Perthcelyn was granted £25,000). Completed area strategies would then be submitted to the Welsh Office by the end of August 1996. It was expected that at least some of the strategies would receive long-term funding under the Strategic Development Scheme (SDS). Following this decision, at a meeting with local authority officers and key activists, I was asked to coordinate the development of the plan. A representative of the Bernard van Leer Foundation who was visiting the SCF project at the time also felt I should take on this role. However, I declined as I argued that this role was distinct from supporting the participation of residents and activists in devising the plan. It would also have to involve some kind of secondment arrangement with the local authority. If I accepted this role, I would have to act as broker between activists and the local authority. I was not prepared to take on this role. While coordination was important and necessary, I believed it was more important to support the process of participation that had started.

Also in January, the arranged meeting went ahead between the School Action Group and the director of education at the community centre. The activists from the School Action Group made an excellent presentation and used personal experiences to state their arguments for a new school. The meeting was supported by activists from other groups on the estate, and by some local authority officers. The director was taken on a tour of the route to Penrhiw-ceibr school and was shown around the infants' school. The director responded positively and indicated his support. Once again the activists had carried this off themselves. Activists from the different groups supported each other and they controlled the meeting throughout. Again my role was to support the chairperson and activists to make their case. As the meeting was held during school hours, SCF provided childcare workers to enable activists to attend.

Four days later, the School Action Group was to face another challenge. Perthcelyn parents of junior school children, who attended Penrhiw-ceibr school, received letters asking them to attend a meeting on 22 January 1996. Apparently there were problems of subsidence at the junior school. At the Penrhiw-ceibr school meeting, there was an announcement that the school was to be closed due to these problems. The children were to be transferred on a temporary basis to an old school further down the valley. A new school would now become an issue for Penrhiw-ceibr residents. Perthcelyn activists were fearful at this stage that the sudden closure of Penrhiw-ceibr junior school would affect their chances of getting a new school at Perthcelyn. However, School Action Group activists responded by calling another meeting of Perthcelyn residents who decided to step up the campaign. I helped the group to plan the next steps. They decided on the following tactics.

- to continue to campaign for a school on the estate, a school that is open to all children from the areas of Perthcelyn and Penrhiw-ceibr;
- to seek an urgent meeting with the chair of the RCT education committee;
- to send letters to RCT councillors asking for support;
- to write to William Hague, then secretary of state for Wales;
- to seek legal advice;
- to issue a press release;
- to prepare for a lobby of the education committee.

My role at this stage was to help the group to plan the ongoing campaign, carry out tasks such as helping with letter writing and press releases, and to be available and accessible for advice to key activists. Planning was done in a full meeting of the group and specific tasks were carried out with individuals or small groups. Leaflets were distributed to ensure that all residents on the estate were kept informed of the progress of the campaign. The threat of legal action got the desired response from the media, and PSAG activists were interviewed on BBC Wales *Today*. At the same time, the activists prepared for a lobby of the RCT education committee. A coach was organized by activists to travel to Clydach Vale, the headquarters of RCT and a large group of local parents were mobilized for the lobby. All of these were women, except for one man who came from the Fernhill estate to support the campaign. The group made its own banner in the morning, prepared placards and prepared a leaflet for distribution to councillors. An SCF project worker helped to type and photocopy leaflets. While residents attended the lobby, SCF workers and I stayed behind and looked after their children. Two months later, RCT took over responsibility for education from CVBC and the old Mid-Glamorgan County Council: £100,000 was allocated for site investigations for a school on the Perthcelyn site. The tide was beginning to turn.

By now, activists from the different groups had experience of working together on the problem of crime and with the campaign for the new school. They had also agreed to work with the local authority to develop a plan for the estate. They now began to see that the strategy was a possible way of helping *them* to achieve *their* aims. The £25,000 from the Welsh Office was used to recruit a number of consultants to put the bid together. I was to continue to support the participation of activists and to organize and facilitate the wider participation of residents in drawing up the estate plan. The group was now sufficiently united to decide to give itself the title Perthcelyn Estate Management Group (PEMG). This group was made up entirely of activists from the estate groups. They elected their own officers and began to organize a series of 'away-days' to start drawing up their plan. The activists *themselves* conducted surveys on the estate of adults, children and young people. They compiled the findings and identified the key priorities to be included in their plan. In addition to a new community school, the plan included new play areas, new playing fields, new fencing, traffic calming and an extension to the community centre. The group then held a final consultation and fun-day for estate residents in July 1996.

However, while the PEMG activists had finalized their plan, William Hague and the Welsh Office had other ideas. In August 1996, it was announced that the Community Strategy scheme was to end. The scheme was replaced by Welsh Capital Challenge for capital projects linked to regeneration. PEMG activists were very angry. They had been led to believe they could bid for this scheme. Estate activists had pinned their hopes on a strategy that would attract funding for up to seven years. Expectations had been raised and activists had given large amounts of free time and commitment over a period of eight months. PEMG activists decided to issue a press statement calling on the Welsh Office to honour their commitment. The issue received good coverage on BBC Wales *Today* and in local newspapers. However, RCT senior officers were not happy with the fact that the PEMG had gone to the media. The Welsh Office was obviously not happy with RCT. They probably assumed that the local authority was running the strategy and not the PEMG. The PEMG was the only community group in Wales to register a public protest over the ending of the Community Strategy scheme.

Within days of the media coverage, senior RCT officers came to the estate. They offered to submit the capital costs of the estate plan for Capital Challenge. In addition, they offered revenue funding for new workers from the Strategic Development Scheme. PEMG accepted this proposal as the school and other elements of their plan could be included in the final bid. A bid for Capital Challenge funding was submitted. In December 1996, the Welsh Office announced that the bid was successful. A total of £3.5 million, the largest in Wales was awarded to Perthcelyn. The PEMG had got everything it had campaigned for except for the extension to the community centre.

What did I learn?

What did I learn from this experience of working on Perthcelyn?

(1) That residents in the Valleys can still fight back. It was only when local people took control of the campaign that things began to change. When they were supported and encouraged to fight back, they did so with amazing gusto and determination. They were not afraid to stage a road protest, to lobby councillors, to appear on television or to confront officers and politicians. They got things done by cutting through the intermediaries and going straight to those with power. They were angry and they wanted action. Most of all, they wanted action for their children.

Apart from a small number of men, all of the activists were women. This showed that women were the main driving force on the estate. They were the ones who clearly saw the issues affecting their children and who had the organizational skills to do something about it. They organized meetings, demonstrations, lobbies, buses, and wrote letters. They did all of these things with determination and persistence, but with a sense of fun and good humour. While they knew it was a serious business, 'you had to have a laugh'.

(2) That the media was a crucial and powerful vehicle in this campaign. Having a good case, activists demonstrated how they could use the media to their benefit. One of the key factors throughout the campaign was their ability to gain persistent and supportive media attention. They achieved this coverage by developing good relationships with people in the media over a

number of years. As a result, journalists were anxious to follow the progress of the campaign from start to finish. The Welsh Office and RCT were left in no doubt that in the event of Perthcelyn not gaining the resources, there would be one hell of a public row.

(3) I confirmed my belief that local activists can take power when they are enabled and supported to do so. As they became more involved, they became more confident. As the campaign progressed, they insisted on a greater say in decision-making. However, those who hold power do not give it up easily. It was inevitable that Perthcelyn activists would have to fight every step of the way. Local authority officers were unwilling or unable to deal with an empowered group of local people. Their response was to seek to control a process rather than to try and understand it and work to the agenda of local activists. This response was to lead to serious conflicts over a whole range of issues as activists struggled for a greater say in the regeneration of their estate.

(4) I learned that choosing to stand alongside local people in the Valleys is a challenging role. I got the distinct impression that community workers who work in the Valleys are still expected to act as 'brokers' and 'gatekeepers' between the power-holders and residents. The fact that I was employed by SCF and not the local authority meant that I was able to stand *with* local people. Of course, by adopting this role I was not very popular with certain local authority officers. After the strategy-bid was successful, senior officers and councillors of the local authority made it very clear that they saw me as the problem. Of course, it is a well-known tactic to blame community workers when local people become too empowered for officers to handle. It must be the community worker's fault. The power-holders are unable (or unwilling) to comprehend that local people can empower themselves. Local authority officers then went on to devise a complicated process to integrate the PEMG into the decision-making structures of the authority. In my opinion, this was the wrong response. The most significant aspect of the strategy up to that point was the growing participation of local people. That process could have been supported and developed in a variety of ways. As I continued to resist this integration, I was further excluded from the process. While SCF management in Wales

understood what was happening and were supportive, they were limited in what they could do. Unfortunately, while all this was going on, a global policy-shift within the organization meant that SCF were moving towards a different model of working. They were moving away from localized community development in poor neighbourhoods to a focus on the rights of children and young people on an all-Wales basis.

(5) Finally, my experience also questions to what extent development/community workers can seriously promote participation of local people within top-down initiatives. While top-down initiatives can achieve real gains for estates they can often limit the participation of local people. Any attempt to involve local people within a top-down model would require, at a minimum, highly skilled workers, supported by 'independent' agencies (outside the official strategy) committed to long-term generic and participatory work. Above all, if top-down initiatives are to have any chance of success, local authority officers will have seriously to address the issue of the participation and empowerment of local people. This will require a significant shift in traditional attitudes and methods of working.

The struggle goes on

What happened after I left is somebody else's story. All I know is that for a short time on an estate in the Cynon valley, local activists made an impact. They took control and achieved real concrete gains for their estate. I was glad to have been there and to have played a small part. In the meantime, local activists will know that securing a school and other resources for their estate is just the beginning. The work continues to ensure that these resources are managed effectively and used for the benefit of all the residents. In this sense, their struggle goes on.

9 The South Riverside Community Development Centre: a legacy of a concerned and active community*

STEVE CLARKE

Crynodeb

Mae Canolfan 'South Riverside' wedi bod yn rhan barhaol o'r gymuned ers yn agos i 30 mlynedd. Bu'n gweithredu fel canolbwynt i drigolion sydd â diddordeb mewn gweithgaredd cymunedol. Bu'n darparu ystod eang o wasanaethau sylfaenol ac yn gweithredu fel sianel ar gyfer asiantaethau gwasanaethau allanol i ddod i mewn i'r gymuned gyda'u hadnoddau eu hunain. Riverside yw un o gymunedau mwyaf amrywiol Cymru ac mae'n gynrychioliadol o'r gwahanol donnau o fewnfudo yr ydym wedi eu profi. O fewn yr amrywiaeth hwn, mae'r Ganolfan wedi creu ysbryd cymunedol deinamig sydd wedi goresgyn yr enwadol a'r plwyfol a grymoedd eraill sy'n dueddol o rwygo cymunedau. Bu rhai personoliaethau ymroddgar yn y broses hon o ddatblygu, ac ni allwn ond dychmygu beth fyddai tynged y Ganolfan heb gyfraniad y bobl hyn. Ystyriwn y ganolfan hon fel enghraifft ardderchog o gynllunio cymdeithasol dros gyfnod ystyrlon o amser ac fel model o fuddsoddiad mewn bywyd cymunedol.

*The material for this chapter has been gathered through interviews with some key personnel who have been connected with the South Riverside Community Development Centre since its opening and even before that. This is not a comprehensive history, and is written sympathetically in order to make some important points about community life. When the significance of this Centre is assessed, the role which community development plays over time becomes clear: to underpin a community with resources and features that become part of the lives of all the residents. We make no apologies for omissions, and hope that we have not made too many mistakes of fact. We are responsible for the emphases that we have placed on certain aspects of the work of this Centre, to the detriment of the rest. We know how all the work over the years has been valued, and it is a tribute to the Centre that we are able to write so much about it, and learn so much from it all. We apologize for anything that we have not said, and hope that in our next volume someone will come forward and set the record straight.

The South Riverside Community Development Centre is one of those community institutions that defy history and the normal forces that make up community life in the twenty-first century. In one of Cardiff's most diverse and complex community settings, this essential building and the services that it provides have endured the most traumatic events, and it stands today as a symbol of community determination to sustain it. Over the years, the Centre has continued to be an institution that truly meets community needs. Visit the Centre at any time on any day when it is open, and there will be a steady stream of visitors – enquiries, leaders of activities, members of community groups and organizations, activists seeking support and expertise for their work. Whatever the politics or difficulties of running such a service, the momentum of the place holds it all together. This fact demonstrates that community is greater than the sum of its parts. Mere individuals, and even public authorities, cannot put it out of action.

The Centre actually forms part of a chain of similar buildings which, over time, and in themselves, constitute a major factor in the development and sustaining of our national community life. Activities may come and go. Personnel may change with incomprehensible rapidity, and the management control may appear to waver, go under or change the character of the whole institution, but still its effects endure (Taylor, 1980 and 1983). 'A resource centre is essentially a long-term concept. The essence of the centre's work [is to] provide a consistent, reliable service that otherwise independent groups can call on' (Taylor, 1980, p. 171). Riverside is one such factor in the lives of all the people in and around Riverside. It is run by the people, managed by the people, and accountable to . . . well, whoever. It is a latter-day replacement of the community settlement, which heralded the beginnings of community development in the latter days of Queen Victoria's reign.

In those days, it was the 'ruling class' who decided to set an example to working-class folk by going and living among them – 'settlements'. Over the years, this activity changed in both form and content to become an anchor of the local community. These settlements now provide services (such as advice and support for local activities), premises for local events and expertise in the matter of community change and survival issues (Kennedy, 1980; Lees and Mayo, 1984; Kelleher and Whelan, 1992; Walsh et al., 1998). Today they are still the inspiration for much of the innovation that goes on in their part of the cities (especially London, Birmingham, Manchester and Liverpool), and they have not only survived for over one hundred years but have also provided good role models.

In keeping with this tradition, but with a completely opposite class origin, the South Riverside Community Development Centre provides all the above facilities and services to the people of Riverside. It also acts as the agent for the community in accessing funding from outside the community. This standing in the wider community allows it to act as surety and custodian for many local enterprises until they can establish a reputation and track record of probity to manage public funds for themselves.

The movement that inspired this centre began 'over the road' in Canton, where local residents and activists campaigned to save streets from redevelopment and arbitrary council interference. The organization was called CRAG – the Canton and Riverside Action Group. By the mid-1970s, the activities and insight that had been obtained into the area, enabled CRAG (now renamed Action for Riverside and Canton) to put forward the idea of a community centre for public funding through the Urban Programme. Enough money was obtained to purchase the redundant church building, which still houses the Centre.

The most urgent priority in those days was the provision of play space and supervised activities for the young of the area. There was also a need for information concerning the structural issues in people's lives: benefits, housing fitness, landlord and tenant matters, leasehold reform, environmental problems (such as heavy traffic), and so on. The tenants and residents had been active for some time, but it was the infusion of professional activists that got the project up and running. Fresh from their exploits in challenging the Cardiff Council over the infamous Hook Road scheme and the partial demolition of the Canton area, the activists maintained their interest in the fundamentals of democratic life. Their concentration moved to areas where there was no imminent danger to the material or physical structure of the community. Instead, the focus for their talents became those populations where there was danger of social decay and fragmentation. The Urban Programme provided the means to make a direct investment in the fabric of the community with the provision of public funds, while still maintaining local control over the facility.

Obtaining equity in their community facilities was seen as a necessary step towards sustaining responsibility for the shape of community life. This underpinned their capacity to provide services for all on a communal basis. The Centre was activated without, necessarily, any direct promotion of organization-building. In the case of another area of Cardiff, Adamsdown, the provision of a neighbourhood Law and Advice Centre contained a professional community development component. In the case of Riverside, where there was not to be any direct income-earning capabilities (as in the Law Centre), the Centre aimed to provide direct services.

A pattern developed from the start that is being followed to this day. Whenever a new service was deemed to be required, a case was made to a relevant public grant-making organization, and the service then got underway. Insofar as promoting service-provision within the community on a self-help basis, the Centre provided support to all who asked, but the Centre itself did not interfere in the pattern of community services in a typical community development manner. The reason for this lies in the composition of the local community. There are significant sub-communities of Sikhs, Bengali- and Sylheti-speaking Bangladeshis, Pakistanis, Chinese, Kosovans, Albanians, Croatians, Italians, Anglo-Welsh, Irish and all the 'company of heaven'. Most of these sub-communities have preoccupations of their own – a Catholic church for some, a gurdwara for another group, a mosque for a third. In their own way, these sub-communities stabilized their own settlement into the area and, through this settlement, they developed the capacity to integrate and play their part in some of the less parochial activities. The Riverside Community Festival reflects the vibrant make-up of the community, with all of the activity groups, community associations and sub-community organizations making their contribution. The Centre has enabled all facets of community life to see, experience and come to understand the diversity and differences that coexist in the area. Religious festivals, high days and holidays are celebrated, and all non-participants are included by association with the Centre. Over the years, Riverside has become synonymous with cosmopolitanism and a richness of cultural and ethnic resources. One look at the list of community organizations that use the Centre reveals that the place thrives on the differences within the community. It is hard to believe that this is the same district of Cardiff that witnessed Wales's (and Britain's) first race-murder in 1919 (Fryer, 1984).

The Centre became the launch pad for a succession of community-based welfare, health and education projects over the years. In 1983, an 'English for Pregnancy' scheme was developed to target the many women from the Asian sub-continent who were living in relative isolation and, in some cases, semi-purdah. Bereft of English, these women were cut off from the neighbouring culture and the normal expectations of midwifery and the National Health Service. These women missed out on the bulk of health services and faced a frightening and traumatic time in the event of a complicated pregnancy. Providing basic linguistic skills and interpreters for the women of (especially) the Bangladeshi community in this way helped to raise the whole profile of social awareness of minority cultures (Baruah, 1997). It highlighted the way in which traditional provisions for health and welfare in south Wales had completely failed to adjust to the obvious changes in the real world outside.

The English for Pregnancy project prompted a succession of related schemes, which drew money into the Riverside area and which targeted the situation of Asian women and their relationships with the wider community. The importance of the Riverside experiment in this direction has been influential in another quarter. In the 1990s, Barnardos opened their Multi-Cultural Resource Centre nearby, on Neville Street, Riverside. This centre still provides professional and self-help activities, and draws in a multitude of minority interests within a culturally acceptable and physically safe environment. It also diversified to provide a drop-in service for the South Riverside Centre. This provided much-needed training and educational programmes for local women, and it was able to expoit the reputation of the Multi-Cultural Resource Centre in the process.

Another major project for Riverside was the installation of an advice service which was responsive to the diverse ethnic composition of the community. Riverside had become the main area for Punjabi settlement in Cardiff, with a strong Sikh religious and cultural organization at its heart. In a community such as this, there are obviously many factors which contribute to its prosperity, but the Riverside Centre took an imaginative step in 1979 to appoint a Sikh as its main advice worker. This ensured that minority languages received aware and sensitive acceptance in the Centre. It meant that minority community interests were reflected in the dynamics of Centre management and planning, and that the future development of the Centre would remain responsive to a significant sector of the community.

In 1979, the Centre appointed Jaswant Singh (Jas) to the post of community advice worker. His job was to provide straightforward advice service to enquirers, but it set in train a significant process which helped anchor the Centre in the community. In addition to being a qualified social worker, Jas Singh was also a community leader in the Sikh community. Over the years, he occupied all the important posts within the religious and cultural aspects of Sikh society, and this blended in with his role as intercessor for the community on welfare issues. Jas has outlined the essential differences in social outlook between an Asian community and the native south Walians. Asian traditions are directed towards consolidating and protecting their own family, community and interests ahead of extraneous issues. In the case of migrants seeking to survive and settle in a new land, this aspect receives heightened priority. This leads to the community (for instance, Sikh) concentrating its efforts on establishing its own support structure ahead of 'mucking in' with the local voluntary or community activities (Ellis, 1989). Jas Singh occupied the post of community advice worker for ten years, during which time he established a reputation for being a grandee of community service in Cardiff. It is for this reason that the longer he was at the Centre, the more he was drawn into community and city-wide activities. He had to fight the insidiousness of tokenism, as his face began to crop up everywhere. 'Once you spend your whole time attending meetings, you lose touch with what you are supposed to be doing', he said. Jas's insights gained in the Centre allowed him to make a positive contribution to the city as a whole and to its understanding of some of the most basic health and welfare needs of the population. In his 'second career' with Barnardos, he became responsible for opening up services in mental health to Asian and other minority groups. Now he is back in the community full-time, acting as an unofficial resource for the Sikh community, within which he is a chosen leader.

The Centre became a magnet for community organizations and, in 1992, the Centre was able to revive its own interest in the wider community. A Community Renewal and Development Project was established with the equivalent of a full-time community development appointment. The general repair and refurbishment of the South Riverside area was a major initiative of the Cardiff City Council. The community development workers set about generating community interest in the programme and also establishing the full nature of community resources, as represented by the community organizations and population groups. In addition to assessing the resources of the community, a community profile also assessed the felt needs of the community, and gave it a lever with which to approach the city council for appropriate resources and services. This direct involvement in assisting in the restructuring of the community had been an 'on-off' activity since the late 1970s, but now the renewal scheme gave it a firm underpinning.

Riverside has always been an area where the ripples of national forces have greater effects than in more prosperous areas. This has resulted in the Centre having a natural orientation towards assisting community members to gain skills that will help them in the market place. It also has a direct interest in the local economy through its sponsorship of the credit union activities in the area, and the establishment of a community market. The South Riverside Regeneration Programme has introduced the services of the Training and Enterprise Council (TEC) into the consciousness of local people, and the TEC has been able to tailor its own input to suit the needs of local residents.

There is one feature of all community centres, settlements and community buildings that represents a physical expression of community vitality, and that is the efficiency with which the organization is run. The South Riverside Centre was gutted by fire in 1989, and it is a credit to the management committee and the exceptionally loyal band of supporters, some of whom actually rebuilt part of the place themselves, that the survival of the Centre was assured. The history of community-based schemes, projects, 'initiatives' and the like, has been fraught with the problems of short-term funding and shifting definitions of need (as defined by the funders). The Urban Programme provided a false hope from the start since, in those days, three years' funding seemed as if it would last forever. Today, three years' stability seems like a miracle, with most contracts being negotiated on an annual basis. Workers come and go, skills are learned and then lost to the community.

Credibility has to be regained each time. That is progress in community development.

Another 'personality' in Riverside is one whose presence is felt more than it is seen. This is Ken Barker, who was 'in at the start', or nearly at the start, as he was a member of CRAG in the early 1970s. Ken is the administrator. He has been in this job since 1987, and has the responsibility, amongst others, for monitoring the flow of funds through the Centre. He has to ensure that management is prepared to take the Centre through all the hoops and over all the obstacles to obtain continuity of funding. This means opportunistically anticipating changes in government and council priorities for distributing funds to the 'independent sector'. Once information is gathered, the programme of the Centre has to be assessed for eligibility and refashioned to comply with new guidelines, or new schemes planned to take advantage of every twist and turn in focus. Only someone with exceptional knowledge of the system can achieve the success that Ken Barker has over the years. The Centre's finances are never secure, but the obvious vitality of the Centre is a testimony to the application of considerable skill in this department.

The Centre has been able to use its position to ensure that it influences initiatives that originate outside the community. National welfare organizations find it convenient to enter into relationships with the Centre when seeking to provide services or outlets for their work. In turn, this puts the Centre within the view of institutions with larger agendas, such as the European Union, and national government. As the local communities become more and more prominent as forces for social change in their own right, so the standing of the whole area, and the Centre, benefits.

Where does one start to analyse the function of a community development process within this structure? The personalities, the projects and the history of the area have all had their own influence, and there has been no grand design. Nevertheless, there was a vision in the 1970s, and it has come to fruition in the most enduring and enterprising of ways. Was it because of the difficulties that this scarce resource became all the more valued and therefore a irreplaceable feature of community life? If a benign person had endowed the area with this Centre, and community development workers had been able to work without the tensions of never knowing where their next meal was coming from – would it have turned out better? Or is time of the essence in community development? Is a generation without support a generation permanently deprived? If this is the case, then community resource centres should be a feature of any progressive local authority. This would be a simple step in opening up whole communities to the processes of social planning, promoting social harmony, enabling local responsibility and ensuring that local needs were identified. On a day-by-day basis, a community centre is taken for granted. Over the years, its value cannot be overestimated.

Capacity-building

Introduction to chapters 10 and 11

Capacity-building is the vital component of locality development. It marks the beginning of the community-building process and the promotion of local understanding of the complexities of change. It links directly with social capital, and the long-term sustainability of communities at both the social and political levels. There is, presently, a desperate shortage of workers who are trained to build communities, especially those that become capable of participating in the planning of change and development. Local leadership is often targeted by outsiders intent on developing local participation as a short cut to engaging the whole community. This often happens when initiatives are planned outside communities. This tactic will result in the mass of the population becoming more dependent and excluded, since local leaders, even more than professional community development workers, lack the time and space to transfer their skills further down the line. An allowance for community development workers to spend time in strengthening the skills base of an entire community is often just not planned into policy development. This process requires considerable expertise, insight and patience (Day et al., 1998), and these two chapters give us a brief glimpse of what goes on.

10   Profi menter

DERITH POWELL

Summary

This chapter discusses the Valleys Initiative Programme which was designed to improve prosperity, increase confidence and change public perceptions as regards the potential for investment in the Valleys. This huge task still remains unfinished with current pressures as great as, if not greater than, during the time of writing. The Under-5s Project was one small outcome of this initiative. Even with the numerous obstacles and barriers to overcome, the project proved that capacity-building even in the most deprived and disadvantaged communities can bear fruit: the process of community development must never be undervalued, and small grassroots initiatives can 'make a difference'.

Cyflwyniad

Mae gan gymoedd de Cymru hanes o radicaliaeth a brwydrau ar lefel bersonol a chymunedol. Roedd dirywiad hir a phoenus y diwydiannau glo a metel a diwydiannau cysylltiedig wedi dechrau erbyn diwedd y Rhyfel Byd Cyntaf. Yn y blynyddoedd nesaf, gwelwyd nifer o ddatblygiadau a mentrau wedi eu hanelu at adfywio cymunedau. Ymdrechwyd a methwyd i ailafael yn y grym cymdeithasol ac economaidd a oedd unwaith yn dynodi'r 'Cymoedd'.

Yn ystod f'oes i, bûm yn dyst i ddigwyddiadau symbolaidd anferth megis dwy streic y glowyr yn y 1970au a'r 1980au, cau'r pyllau dwfn lleol i gyd, a rhaglen gau Heseltine. Gwelwyd y digwyddiadau hyn yn bennaf drwy lygaid teulu glofaol a oedd â'i enghreifftiau ei hun o berygl a chaledi diwydiant a oedd unwaith wedi cynnal cymunedau lleol. Cafodd effeithiau cymdeithasol polisïau economaidd Thatcher eu hamlygu fwyaf mewn ardaloedd fel y Cymoedd. Nid yw'n hawdd cael gwared ar amddifadedd cymdeithasol ac economaidd ar y raddfa hon ac mae llawer o'r rhai sy'n dioddef anfantais gymdeithasol yn methu defnyddio'u hawliau sylfaenol hyd yn oed.

Erbyn i mi ddechrau ar fy ngwaith ymarferol yn y gymuned roedd yr ardal hon yn ei chael yn anodd a doedd dim i symbylu'r boblogaeth leol mewn economi o gyflogau isel, gyda nifer y rhai a oedd yn byw o dan y llinell dlodi gydnabyddedig ar gynnydd. Cymunedau oedd y rhain a oedd yn teimlo eu bod wedi cael eu hamddifadu a bod gwleidyddiaeth amherthnasol ac 'adfywiad' pell i ffwrdd wedi anghofio amdanynt. Yr ansoddeiriau sy'n dod i'r cof o'r cyfnod yw'r teimladau hynny o fod yn ynysig, o fod wedi ein gwahanu'n gymdeithasol – apathi ac iselder. Roedd y pwysau ar gymunedau bron yn eu torri a'r strwythurau teuluol traddodiadol yn datod.

Roedd sefydliadau'r gymuned megis addysg y gweithwyr, cyrff lles a chyrff cynulleidfaol crefyddol hefyd ar drai. Roedd dewisiadau cyfyngedig a diffyg mynediad i adnoddau yn ennyn teimladau o rwystredigaeth, diffyg grym a gwendid. Yn erbyn y cefndir hwn y cyflwynodd Peter Walker ei fenter an-Thatcheraidd o adfywio'r Cymoedd gan ddarparu arian ar gyfer y prosiect y byddaf yn ei ddisgrifio maes o law.

Wrth ysgrifennu'r darn hwn, rydym mewn cyfnod ôl-Thatcheraidd – cyfnod pan fo strwythurau democrataidd Cymru (y Cynulliad Cenedlaethol ac ad-drefnu llywodraeth leol) yn hollol wahanol i'r rhai a oedd mewn grym ar y pryd; cyfnod pan fo cyfle am arian Ewropeaidd Amcan Un yn cynnig gobaith am un siawns olaf am fuddsoddiad ariannol cyn i'r Undeb Ewropeaidd droi ei olygon ailddatblygu at ganolbarth a chyrion dwyreiniol Ewrop.

Diben ailymweld â Menter y Cymoedd yw fy mod yn credu bod llawer o'r ymarferiad sy'n seiliedig ar y gymuned yn berthnasol ac yn gallu bod yn sail i'r strwythurau a'r mentrau newydd os ydynt i lwyddo lle mae cymaint wedi methu o'u blaen. Wrth weithio o fewn y cymunedau hyn, fe welais i a'm cyd-weithwyr y cyfle, y potensial a'r grym sydd i waith cymunedol yn y Cymoedd.

Prosiect Plant Dan-5 y Cymoedd

Cynlluniwyd Menter y Cymoedd 1989–93 i wella llewyrch, cynyddu hyder a newid y ffordd yr edrychai'r cyhoedd ar y Cymoedd fel ardaloedd ac iddynt botensial ar gyfer buddsoddi. Un o ganlyniadau'r fenter oedd ceisio gwella'r ddarpariaeth cyn-ysgol trwy ddarparu Prosiect Dan-5 y Cymoedd, a oedd yn weithredol mewn tair sir ac ar waith mewn 22 o bentrefi yng Ngorllewin Morgannwg, fy sir i. Nodweddwyd yr angen am y prosiect gan y canlynol:

- diffyg cyffredinol o ran darpariaeth a chydlynu gwasanaethau;
- diffyg deialog ac ymgynghori yn y prosesau gwneud penderfyniadau;
- cefnogaeth ac anogaeth annigonol i blant ifainc a'u teuluoedd;
- lefelau dealltwriaeth a gwybodaeth isel am ofal plant ac, o ganlyniad, dealltwriaeth gyfyngedig o'u hanghenion.

Nodwyd mai amcanion y prosiect oedd:
- tynnu sylw at y diffyg darpariaeth;
- gwella ansawdd a chynyddu nifer y gwasanaethau;
- cymell gweithredu cymunedol a hunangymorth;
- datblygu partneriaethau rhwng gwasanaethau gwirfoddol a statudol.

Roedd yr amcanion yn cynnwys:
- cynnydd mewn darpariaeth i rai dan bump oed a'u teuluoedd drwy ddatblygu mentrau newydd;
- mwy o ddeialog, cydlynu rhwng unigolion, grwpiau ac asiantaethau;
- asesu'r bylchau a nodi'r angen er mwyn datblygu mentrau addas;
- tynnu sylw at gryfderau ac adeiladu ar y potensial sy'n bodoli yno'n barod.

Yr egwyddorion sylfaenol a ystyriwyd yn gyson gan y prosiect oedd gweithio ochr yn ochr â phobl leol, gan wrando, galluogi ac ymateb i'w hanghenion. Ariannwyd y prosiect gan grant y Swyddfa

Gymreig gwerth tua £126,000 dros gyfnod o dair blynedd, a gweinyddwyd yr arian gan dri Chyngor Gwasanaethau Gwirfoddol. Roedd fy ngwaith i'n cynnwys dod ag unigolion ynghyd i ddechrau datblygiadau amrywiol a nodwyd ganddynt o fewn eu cymunedau. Yn dilyn cyfnod o ymgynghori gyda'r cymunedau, y prif dasgau a ddaeth i'r amlwg oedd:

- cydlynu a datblygu gwasanaethau drwy gyngor cyllido, benthyg offer, hyfforddi, recriwtio gwirfoddolwyr, cyhoeddusrwydd, a chymorth a chyngor cyffredinol;
- tynnu mudiadau ac unigolion ynghyd fesul ardal, cyfnewid gwybodaeth, osgoi dyblygu gwaith ac ymgymryd â mentrau a phrosiectau ar y cyd;
- cysylltu ag awdurdodau statudol, darparu fforwm i drafod materion perthnasol a phryderon, nodi a thrafod syniadau a safbwyntiau'r sector gwirfoddol; cynorthwyo gyda'r gwaith o gynllunio a gweithredu datblygiadau newydd;
- ymchwilio a nodi anghenion, gan dynnu pobl ynghyd i drafod ffyrdd o fynd i'r afael ag angen, cydweithio i lunio amcanion cyraeddadwy a sicrhau dealltwriaeth ehangach o'r angen;
- cefnogi a chynorthwyo gyda'r gwaith o gynllunio a gweithredu menter; helpu i osod amcanion tymor hir a chynnal y fenter; gwerthuso perfformiad yn erbyn yr amcanion gwreiddiol;
- darparu adroddiadau cynnydd rheolaidd, mynychu cyfarfodydd perthnasol.

Y Cymoedd – proffil

Lleolir cymunedau cymoedd Gorllewin Morgannwg yng nghymoedd Nedd/Dulais, Lliw ac Afan, ac fe'u canolir yn bennaf ar y pentrefi yn nhabl 1. Mae tua 31 o bentrefi yn yr ardal hon. Roedd y prosiect ar waith mewn gwahanol ddulliau yn 22 o'r pentrefi hyn. Sefydlwyd a thyfodd y cymunedau hyn yn sgîl datblygiad diwydiannol yr ardal, a oedd yn seiliedig ar y diwydiant glo a diwydiannau sylfaenol cysylltiedig. Mae hanes y Cymoedd a'u pobl yn adlewyrchu eu hynt economaidd. Mae'r hanes hwn, sy'n chwarae rhan amlwg yn llên gwerin y genedl, yn ffurfio etifeddiaeth cenedlaethau presennol y Cymoedd. Mae nodweddion daearyddol wedi cyfrannu at anawsterau cyfathrebu, ac mae

Tabl 1

Nedd/Dulais	Lliw	Afan
Aberdulais	Brynaman Isaf*	Abercregan*
Blaendulais*	Cilmaengwyn	Aberdulais
Blaengwrach/Cwmgwrach*	Cwmgors	Abergwynfi*
Caewern*	Cwmllynfell	Blaengwynfi*
Creunant	Cwmtwrch*	Croeserw*
Glyn-nedd*	Garnswllt*	Cwmafan*
Onllwyn/Banwen*	Godre'r Graig	Cymer*
Pontrhydyfen*	Rhiwfawr*	Dyffryn Rhondda*
Resolfen	Tairgwaith*	Glyncorrwg
Tonmawr*	Ystalyfera	Trecynon
Y Clun		

* Pentrefi lle bu'r prosiect ar waith.

pentrefi yn aml, er yn gymharol agos at ei gilydd yn ddaearyddol, yn gymunedau anghysbell. Nid ydynt bellach yn meddu ar yr adnoddau i fod yn hunangynhaliol nac i gwrdd ag anghenion cenedlaethau newydd.

Datblygwyd darpariaethau newydd yn yr ardaloedd canlynol: Blaendulais, Blaengwrach/Cwmgwrach, Caewern, Cwmafan, Cwmllynfell, Dyffryn Rhondda, Onllwyn/Banwen, Pontrhydyfen, Rhiwfawr, Tairgwaith, Tonmawr, Tonna. Ar gyfartaledd, mynychodd 20 o blant dan 5 y darpariaethau. Y grŵp lleiaf oedd 8 o blant dan 5. Y grŵp mwyaf oedd 30 o blant dan 5.

Diwrnodau hwyl
Trefnwyd y diwrnodau hwyl yn Onllwyn, Banwen, Blaendulais, Rhiwfawr a Chroeserw. Yng nghyd-destun cymunedau anghysbell, gyda lefelau isel o adnoddau a chyfleusterau, profodd y diwrnodau hwyl i fod yn ddull o ddatblygu ysbryd cymunedol.

Hyfforddi
Datblygwyd nifer o sesiynau hyfforddi anffurfiol a gweithdai gwybodaeth yn ymwneud â materion megis hawliau plant. Darparwyd nifer o sesiynau hyfforddi i hyrwyddo sgiliau bod yn rhieni positif.

Yn ogystal, adeiladodd a chysylltodd y gwaith hwn â sectorau perthnasol eraill, fel ymweliadau iechyd a darpariaethau gwasanaethau cymdeithasol. Sefydlwyd nifer o grwpiau hunangymorth a fforymau rhieni. Yn ogystal, sefydlwyd mentrau newydd fel grwpiau rhieni a phlant bach a grwpiau cefnogi rhieni/gofalwyr.

Gweithio gyda phlant ifainc

Tarddodd dau brosiect yn uniongyrchol o ganlyniad i'r gwaith hwn, prosiectau sy'n parhau hyd heddiw. Yn gyntaf, cwrs 'Gweithio gyda Phlant Ifainc' – cwrs a achredir. Nododd y Prosiect Dan-5 y diffyg hyfforddiant gofal-plant addas, perthnasol a hygyrch ar gyfer unrhyw un a oedd am gynyddu eu gwybodaeth a'u dealltwriaeth o faterion yn ymwneud â'r pwnc hwn. Ymddangosai'n briodol felly i ddatblygu cwrs gyda mewnbwn sylweddol gan gyfranogwyr ynghylch cynnwys a chyflwyniad – cwrs a allai weithredu heb rwystrau i fynediad, gyda chefnogaeth gofal-plant ddigonol a chynlleied o broblemau teithio 'o fewn y gymuned' â phosibl. Mae'r cwrs blwyddyn cynhwysfawr hwn yn parhau i roi gwybodaeth i rieni ac mae mor boblogaidd ag y bu erioed. Rwy'n credu ei fod yn llwyddiannus a bod galw amdano o hyd am ei fod yn gwerthfawrogi profiad bywyd y cyfranogwyr ac yn cydnabod yr amryfal sgiliau sydd eisoes gan y sawl sy'n gofalu am blant ifainc, a'i nod yw adeiladu ar y rhain.

Prosiect y Plentyn Iach

Yn ail, datblygwyd Prosiect y Plentyn Iach hefyd o ganlyniad uniongyrchol i'r gwaith ar y Prosiect Dan-5. O weithio gyda rhieni ar y lefel sylfaenol, daeth yn amlwg fod angen dirfawr am becyn o ddeunyddiau hylaw yn ymwneud ag iechyd. Byddai'r rhain yn cael eu defnyddio i ddarparu gwybodaeth hanfodol, er mwyn hyrwyddo ffordd iachach o fyw. Cefnogwyd y gwaith gan ymwelwyr iechyd lleol a oedd yn gweld bod y prosiect yn ategu eu gwasanaethau hwy.

Nodau ac amcanion y prosiect oedd:

- hyrwyddo ffordd iachach o fyw i blant ifainc a'u teuluoedd;
- hyrwyddo sgiliau iechyd drwy gynorthwyo rhieni i fagu gwybodaeth, dealltwriaeth a hyder;

- cynnig deunyddiau hyfforddi i'r rhai sy'n gweithio gyda phlant ifainc a'u teuluoedd i hyrwyddo ffordd iachach o fyw a sgiliau iechyd, a thrwy hynny wella safon eu bywydau.

Sicrhawyd arian dros gyfnod o dair blynedd gan y Swyddfa Gymreig i gyflogi gweithiwr datblygu cymunedol i gynhyrchu deunyddiau hyfforddi ar y cyd â rhieni lleol. Gellid wedyn ddefnyddio'r rhain mewn amgylchiadau addas. Defnyddir y deunyddiau hyn hyd heddiw.

Mae'n anodd mesur yn union faint o unigolion a'u teuluoedd a gymerodd ran yn y prosiect hwn ac a gafodd fudd ohono. Fodd bynnag, mae digon o ddata o safon ar gael i gefnogi fy marn fod modd cyflawni pob math o bethau yn sgîl gweithgaredd sy'n digwydd yn y gymuned.

Casgliad

Rhoddodd y Prosiect Dan-5 hyder ac anogaeth o fewn amgylchfyd llwm yn ddaearyddol, yn emosiynol ac yn feddyliol. Roedd datblygu gofal-plant cymunedol yn fan cychwyn i bobl gymryd rhan mewn gweithgaredd cymunedol. Galluogai unigolion i reoli eu bywydau i ryw raddau trwy nodi anghenion gofal-plant a sefydlu mentrau bychain yn lleol. Roedd galluogi unigolion i ddefnyddio'u sgiliau a'u cryfderau ar y cyd yn agwedd amlwg o'r prosiect. Agwedd arall arwyddocaol oedd cydweithio ac adeiladu pontydd.

Sbardunodd y prosiect unigolion a grwpiau i leisio eu barn wrth ddatblygu gwasanaethau newydd a dylanwadu ar farn trwy gael gwared ar y rhwystrau a oedd yn eu llesteirio rhag cyfranogi. Cysylltodd y prosiect â phobl ar y cyrion a oedd yn wynebu rhwystrau rhag cymryd rhan. Gweithredodd trwy weithio ar y cyd o'r gwaelod i fyny ac fel tîm. Creodd y prosiect deimlad o hunan-barch ac agweddau positif ymhlith pobl, gan godi ymwybyddiaeth a meithrin brwdfrydedd a galluoedd. Daeth y profiad o weithio yn y dull hwn â materion megis amddifadedd i'r amlwg, ond amlygodd hefyd yr ysgogiad a ddaw yn sgîl grwpiau bach yn dod at ei gilydd i drafod materion o gonsýrn cyffredinol. At hyn, roedd y teimlad o lwyddiant, hyd yn oed llwyddiannau bach iawn, yn hollbwysig wrth herio'r rhwystrau niferus roedd pobl leol yn eu hwynebu. Y prif rwystr oedd morâl isel a hynny'n bennaf wrth i bobl wynebu dyfodol wedi ei gyfyngu gan amgylchiadau a diffyg dewis.

Roedd diffyg hyder yn nodweddu llawer, ac roedd angen llawer o anogaeth ar eraill, ond datblygwyd hunanhyder trwy godi ymwybyddiaeth a thrwy'r profiad o gyfranogi. Deuthum i gredu mai gweithgareddau'n seiliedig yn y gymuned yn aml oedd yr unig bont effeithiol rhwng cymunedau wedi'u heithrio a'r byd y tu allan. Roedd meithrin sgiliau ymwybyddiaeth beirniadol, a'r gallu neu'r bodlonrwydd i herio tybiaethau a chredoau, yn rhan annatod o'r gwaith yma. Credaf i hyn rywsut arwain at ryw fath o newid, gyda'r newidiadau hyn yn rhai tymor-hir mewn rhai achosion.

Daeth y prosiect hwn i ben yn y ffordd arferol, sef ar ddiwedd y cyfnod ariannu, yn ôl yn 1992. Fodd bynnag, gellir synhwyro yn bendant i'r gwaith adael ei ôl, trwy greu rhywfaint o newid personol mewn pobl, a thrwy greu ffyrdd i alluogi pobl i ymdrin â materion a mynd i'r afael â phryderon. Ni ddaeth y gwaith i gyd i ben ar ddiwedd y prosiect. Mae rhai elfennau'n parhau yn eu lle. Fe'm hatgoffir felly o'r potensial, y galluoedd a'r grym sy'n bodoli o fewn ein cymunedau, ac mai'r bobl yw'r arbenigwyr wrth lunio hanes eu bywydau eu hunain. Pan ystyriwn adeiladu galluoedd fel dull, mae'n rhaid i ni gofio bod nifer o grwpiau'n sefydlu eu hunain heb gymaint â hynny o gefnogaeth gan wasanaethau allanol, fel y digwyddodd yn achos y prosiect hwn. Weithiau, mae'n rhaid atgoffa asiantaethau a gweithwyr cymunedol proffesiynol am hyn. Ffolineb yw meddwl nad oes potensial mewn cymunedau sydd 'dan anfantais'. Hyderaf fod Prosiect Dan-5 y Cymoedd wedi profi bod rhyddhau potensial o fewn gwaith datblygu cymunedol yn gwneud newid parhaol a phositif yn bosibl.

11 Regeneration strategies – a personal to political perspective

ANTONINA MENDOLA BYATT

Crynodeb

Mae'r bennod hon yn adlewyrchiad personol o'r dulliau a ddefnyddiwyd i adnewyddu stadau tai yn ne Cymru yn y 1990au. Mae'n canolbwyntio ar enghraifft o Stad y Gurnos, Merthyr Tudful, a chynllun garddio cyd-weithredol a ffurfiodd sail i strategaeth adnewyddu ehangach. Mae'r bennod yn rhoi gwybodaeth gam wrth gam o'r broses o weithio gan grwpiau cymunedol tuag at amgylchedd sy'n fwy cynaliadwy. Mae'n cyfeirio at sut y cafodd cyfranogaeth, perchenogaeth, cystadleuaeth rhwng grwpiau, a phartneriaeth eu rheoli. Mae'n dadansoddi'r canlyniadau tymor-byr a'r canlyniadau tymor-hir er 1999 a sut y llwyddwyd i sbarduno newid arwyddocaol.

Mae'n tanlinellu pwysigrwydd rôl y gweithiwr cymunedol er mwyn ymrwymo pobl ar eu termau eu hunain ac i greu cyfle i'r rhai sy'n draddodiadol wedi'u heithrio rhag cyfrannu. Mae'n pwysleisio sut mae agenda unigol pob cymdeithas sy'n seiliedig ar ganlyniadau yn rhwystro cyfranogaeth drwy greu brwydrau grym a difreintio grwpiau cymunedol ymhellach. Mae'n gofyn i gymdeithasau sy'n gweithio mewn partneriaeth â'i gilydd i beidio â cholli golwg ar y darnau bach o waith sy'n angenrheidiol i adeiladu cynhwysiad tu fewn i'r gymuned. Bu'r gwaith hwn yn sylfaen i greu dinasyddion gweithgar ac ymdeimlad o berchenogaeth tuag at y gymdeithas. Mae'n canolbwyntio ar bwysigrwydd y gallu i weithio ar bob lefel, yn strategol yn ogystal â chymunedol. Mae'n galw am symud i ffwrdd o raglenni adnewyddu cyfoes sy'n canolbwyntio ar un pegwn o'r sbectrwm yn unig, ac sy'n gwneud gwaith y gweithiwr cymunedol yn amhosibl ac yn ddiystyr i'r gymuned.

Introduction

This chapter aims to share some of the experiences and knowledge I have gained from working on 'regeneration projects' on south Wales housing estates throughout the 1990s. I have been engaged in paid community work for ten years and have had a key part to play in devising and implementing a number of regeneration strategies. In this time I have developed an approach to working within environments where people feel disenfranchised, and apathy rules OK! In this context, and as far back as the 1950s, it is recognized that community development is a

> movement designed to promote better living for the whole community with the active participation, and if possible on the initiative of the community, but if this initiative is not forthcoming spontaneously, by the use of techniques for arousing and stimulating it. (Colonial Office, 1958)

The example I will be focusing on is a case study in which I hope to analyse some of the methods and lessons learnt in this time. The work took place on the New Gurnos Estate (part of the infamous Gurnos Estate), Merthyr Tydfil, whilst working for an environmental charity. The charity aims to 'bring about sustainable improvements to the local environment through partnerships and to contribute to economic and social regeneration' within the Merthyr and Cynon valleys (Groundwork Merthyr and Cynon Ten-Year Review and Annual Report, 1996). I was a member of a team of workers running a community development programme, which underpinned physical as well as educational environmental activities. My role was to plan interventions in targeted housing-estate communities within our geographical area of operation, to implement projects based on needs identified and to build on these. Having undertaken an extensive community consultation exercise, in which residents were invited to identify problems and prioritize solutions, a number of pilot projects were developed.

The project I will be discussing was one of these pilots, undertaken from 1994 to 1996, which formed the basis of the New Gurnos Environmental Strategy 1996, precursor to the now Gurnos and Galon Uchaf Regeneration Partnership set up in 1997. Between 1991 and 1994 I had played a major role in developing a series of community-gardens schemes on the Fernhill Estate, Cynon valley (Groundwork Foundation, 1993). It was on this basis that my co-worker, a landscape architect, and I decided to pilot a similar, small, non-contentious scheme on New Gurnos (Groundwork Merthyr and Cynon, 1995).

The aim

The aim was to encourage participation and engender a sense of ownership, belonging and neighbourliness. Underlying this was my own strategy – that the process in the long term would lead to active participation of individuals/groups in the decision-making structures (or political decisions) which affected their lives. Holman's observation that 'participation is often at worst token-ism and at best, mere consultation' (1997, p. 41), is something that I personally wanted to turn around. I believed that many of the agencies working the patch were being tokenistic towards the community and I wanted our intervention to have more substance.

The case study

At the consultation days we had picked up on requests for more flowers and trees in more areas of 'personal space' (for instance, the immediate area surrounding a person's home) as well as in public spaces. Our previous work on Fernhill had concentrated on public spaces such as large, grassed and open areas, which were not cared for or used to their full capacity. Even though public spaces were still targeted as part of our pilot programme, we decided to act on the requests and take the project one stage further by concentrating on front garden areas. Although the local authority maintained these, we wanted to see if residents would take up the feeling of 'ownership' of their 'defensible space' (Ardrey, 1966, pp. 208–10). We targeted three households in the middle of a row, members of which were already keen gardeners and had lived in a quasi-cul-de-sac area for a number of years. Our previous experi-ence had proved that there are pockets within estates where high levels of transience occur. These problems are mainly to do with the type of housing stock and local housing allocation policy. This then creates the problem that people do not tend to take care of their homes, let alone gardens, as they will only be staying for a short period. We therefore decided to find an area where people were less likely to move on and where a simple idea might encourage others to follow – the 'Well, if he/she can do it, so can I' scenario. Our method was to work with the residents in designing their front garden areas, thereby ensuring that the residents owned the ideas from the outset. We devised an agreement between the residents, the housing department (or landlord) and ourselves. This stated that our agency would fund plants, trees and shrubs from our grant and support residents in greening their front garden areas. However, the long-term maintenance would be transferred from the local authority to the residents. We set out to give people the feeling that the 'defensible space' around the home was theirs by creating stakeholders in their own environment. The housing department also agreed to ensure that, if any of the residents were to move, future tenants would take on the maintenance agreement. We tried to cover all angles so as not create dependency on or expectation of the local authority to maintain the gardens thereafter, which can often occur, thereby increasing the chances of successful sustainability.

We set up a series of house meetings with the target residents. (We will refer to them as Row 1.) The meetings went well and often occurred in alternate homes, bringing together the three households. There appeared to an excited buzz when we turned up, each household having differing priorities, likes and dislikes, such as prickly plants to discourage vandalism, colour, hedging etc. At this point low-level walls were an option for enclosing each garden. However, the residents seemed happy to try hedging first with a plan to review the whole idea if it did not work.

On 'D-Day' my co-worker and I arrived to inspect the plant delivery. All hell had broken loose between Row 1 residents who had begun planting and those who lived on the opposite side of the street. (We will refer to them as Row 2.) We recognized the small group of women shouting abuse from an open front door, from the consultation exercise. We went over to deal with the problem and they explained they felt robbed because they had taken the time to come to the consultation exercise and we had favoured Row 1 by giving them free plants and they would like some. The three households had added to our problems by having distributed some of their plants to friends – in four houses in Row 1 and one house in Row 2. We explained this was one of our pilot projects for the first year. However, if they also wanted to become involved they would have to abide by the same rules as Row 1, and we explained the agreement. They were interested, but we wanted to ensure that they were serious and not perceiving us as an easy 'hand-out' type organization (which I had experienced in the past). We also knew that if this were to be the case, the residents would not value the project. Therefore we made the group wait over a month to ensure they were serious and prepared to fulfil their end of the bargain. There had also been interest shown on other parts of the estate, and at this point we had to create a waiting list. Our 'I can if he/she can' had most definitely worked. However, we had not expected to have been the cause of starting a neighbourhood dispute . . .

The pilot scheme now implemented, we undertook some follow-up work with Row 1 residents. We found out the dispute had not been a one-off, but part of a longer-standing feud, which existed with the older, long-standing residents and two households with young children from Row 2. In fact it had come to blows on one occasion! It was a 'them and us' situation with little tolerance between the two camps. It was apparent that we had not done our homework! Phase 2 of our plan had commenced earlier than we had anticipated but we decided to use the added impetus by calling new house meetings one month later with a view to physical work commencing by the end of 1995. This was not implemented until March 1996. Another request had also come from residents living in the row between the warring streets. (We will refer to them as Row 3.) We had decided to incorporate Row 3 with Row 2, as the idea had most definitely snowballed in this one small area. We set about asking for one person to be our main contact from Rows 2 and 3. This meant that they would be responsible for arranging meetings with us and for organizing/liasing with their neighbours. This was done for the sake of expediency, so that we did not have to ring every neighbour, since seventeen households were involved, but also to create some kind of organization within the community. Every time a meeting was called, the neighbours would go to the contact's home. The process enabled people to come together towards a common aim. This worked well, as the contacts made the meetings a small event in itself, getting out the best china and buying special biscuits. This was exciting, as some had never previously been invited into each other's houses. The meetings would mainly be about discussing the type of plants or problems people encountered, and lists of plants and books would be passed around. Then other issues about the estate would be discussed – relationships, problems, and sometimes individuals would confide in us regarding personal issues: where feuds were ongoing, who were the gangs, where the children played, who key individuals were. This is important knowledge to have, especially when negotiating with the local authority or other agencies towards other developments.

The whole time this was going on we would drop in to see Row 1 residents regularly. A good working relationship had been established. We also believed they were proud to have started the ball rolling not just in their area but on the estate. This process of balancing the task and maintenance of a group is illustrated by Kindred who states 'although the degree to which either is attended to at any given time will vary, they should always be complementary the one to the other' (1991, p. 35).

This next phase of our project threw up different needs from those of the pilot homes in Row 1. The group of women from Row 2 had homes with large, sloping garden frontages and there were concerns about the safety of their children playing. We gave the women a number of options for boundaries and they decided on brick walls. Row 3, who had originally decided on wooden fencing, changed their minds when they saw the wall designs. Our architect had set about designing something which was not the standard 'housing-estate' style, but gave a private-estate flavour. After a few redrafts of ideas we set about letting the contract to have the walls built. We were in constant liaison with the local authority and they seemed pleased to see so much progress, but also particularly to see the money, which they did not have to spend, being put to good use. This is not always the case with housing departments, as some are more guarded about allowing new approaches and have a number of bureaucratic systems which are used to cover themselves. However, this department appeared open, and we established a good rapport. It is worth noting that the local community worker employed by the housing department enabled this good working relationship as she was supportive of what we were trying to do and acted as go-between.

Everything was going well until the day the walls started to be built. We received some angry calls and found out that the contractors had started preparing the ground on the wrong houses – Row 1. When we went to have a look we had to explain to Row 1 that this had been a mistake. Row 2 was also angry, as work had not commenced on their walls as planned. We realized this could result in fuelling the animosity which already existed. Row 1 complained of the consistent abuse they were experiencing from Row 2 children and they felt that the women over the road were having the last laugh. However, we went over our original agreement and although they still felt hard-done-by, they agreed to wait until their plants had matured. We could not at this stage have budgeted them in to phase 2 and it was in September 1996 when they finally had their walls built, a month after I left the charity.

The outcomes

Although bridges were never built between the two warring sides of the street, and have not been to this day, some interesting outcomes did occur relatively quickly.

Short-term outcomes
(1) One Row 3 resident told us she had enjoyed working on her front garden so much that she started work on her back garden. This had not been touched for eighteen years!
(2) We had left a gap in the walls for each resident to put in their own gates, not thinking that this would occur straight away. However, within days one resident had ordered a wrought-iron gate from a relation and arranged a knock-down price for the others. Within a short space of time everyone had brand-new gates.
(3) Residents of Rows 2 and 3 had started to swap cuttings, seeds and garden tips.
(4) The process had generated such an interest in people's own personal space and a sense of ownership, that this culminated in talk of street parties and of organizing tree-planting days in public areas.
(5) This had proved to be such a success that the list of requests for enclosing people's private space with walling and plants snowballed to other areas and is still a part of the charity's ongoing work (author's recording, 29 January 1999).

Long-term outcomes

(1) In January 1999, nearly three years later, I revisited the estate and was surprised to see no vandalism, the scheme well-maintained and the shrubs, trees and flowers well-established.

(2) I was able to interview a Row 2 resident and these are some of her impressions. She stated that in the twenty-three years she had lived in the row 'people had not passed the time of day with each other'. She believed that even though there had been some negative outcomes at the time, the positive results out-weighed these in the longer term. 'People are more neighbourly . . . help and look after each other more . . . are more interested in each other.'

(3) She explained that not one plant or garden ornament had been stolen and believed that this was because residents who had not been involved respected what had been achieved.

(4) When asked whether residents involved in this scheme had gone on to become more politically involved in decision-making on the estate, she explained that although none had, to her knowledge, some community action had arisen from the project participants. She believed that a direct result of the project was a gaining in confidence. This had led to some of the residents petitioning the council about a footpath which had been in disrepair for a number of years. 'It made us more aware we don't have to put up with things as they are' (author's recording, 29 January 1999).

(5) When I asked the interviewee what learning she would pass on to others embarking on regeneration work her answer, simply, was to have 'more grassroots workers who speak our language who will come in and have a cup of tea, people who are approachable and don't sit in offices all day long'.

Analysis

(1) What we had achieved was later described in our strategy as 'groups/individuals can undergo a process of personal development, which in turn affects wider community resulting in positive change' (Groundwork Merthyr and Cynon, 1996). The example illustrates that by using physical environmental change as a vehicle, the process resulted in a small but sig-nificant, positive neighbourhood change.

(2) This was achieved by the approaches used. Once contact had been made and the intervention planned, the informality of the house meetings engendered not only a common aim but also a good working relationship. The process, even throughout the problems, resulted in working on the maintenance of the groups as well as the task in hand. It is important to note that 'familiar territory has a supportive and reassuring function for a group' (Brown, 1994, p. 43).

(3) The design of the scheme gave the feel that it was 'private' (author's recording, 29 January 1999) and not the standard, generic landscaping designs which residents often end up with on housing estates. This was due to the inclusion of the residents targeted from the outset, and to having a small but effective budget to play with. Residents owned the ideas from planning through to completion and have upheld their end of the bargain by maintaining their gardens to this day, thereby creating sustainability.

(4) The good working relationship engendered with the local authority was also an important factor in being able to achieve the goal. Some local authority practices do not allow for innovation and creativity and result in stifling change.

(5) The way in which the agreement had been made, both verbally and in writing, ensured that the residents valued the free plants and resources we were providing and did not see it as a hand-out. Succeeding in avoiding 'spoon-feeding' situations which can result in groups becoming dependent on any agency doing things for them, rather than with them, is a negative outcome of many projects I have encountered.

(6) Henderson and Thomas (1987) point out that workers need to know 'which streets go with which streets to form mini communities within the neighbourhood' (p. 72). It is obvious this part of the planning process was an area, which I had not paid enough attention. Knowing there was an ongoing feud between Row 1 and Row 2 may have led me to undertake some preparatory work with the groups regarding the pilot project. Planning is an important part of neighbourhood work, but I am not sure that anyone could have pre-empted the giving away of plants by Row 1, which arguably fuelled the ongoing arguments between the two factions.

(7) Although this is a good example of people becoming more

active and taking control of their power, none of the residents were involved in the decision-making structures of the existing Gurnos and Galon Uchaf Partnership. This was to have been the next stage, which I left as an unfinished piece of work to be carried out by another worker after I left the agency. However, there are a number of reasons why this may not have happened: (i) this was not the priority of the agency; (ii) this was not a priority of the worker; or (iii) the residents did not feel the need to engage with such a body unless they felt it would be relevant to them. I realize, in retrospect, that this would have been my agenda, my next priority – to work on this process intensively – and that this may have resulted in the residents moving from a micro- to a macro-perspective. I asked my interviewee if I had failed her in this but she could not answer me. Perhaps I will never know. My guess is that all three reasons stated had some part to play.

Conclusion

It is my belief that these small pieces of work are at the crux of regeneration strategies. There needs to be recognition that if resourced in a meaningful way we can make small steps towards achieving the larger vision. Agencies working in partnership may be able to mobilize significant resources but often lose sight of the grassroots work, which is needed to build up skills and knowledge within the community. Engaging with people on their terms, on issues which personally benefit them and their families, is a first step to creating stakeholders. This process is required in order to engender participation on a wider scale and to feed the whole regeneration dynamic.

Agencies often engage with existing, or set up new community organizations. However, community organizations do not necessarily have the capacity to be equal partners in complicated decision-making structures. This is not to say that they cannot, it is just that they often have not yet developed the multidisciplinary skills which are expected of them. These groups are often perceived by other members of the community as an elite group acting as a law unto themselves or colluding with those in power. Agencies can naively legitimize this in order to achieve their goals or output figures. This results in further disenfranchising those not involved and can often divide groups and allegiances, or create new feuds. Freire (1970) points out that those in power do not favour the community as a whole but rather selected leaders. This preserves a state of alienation that hinders the emergence of consciousness and critical intervention.

Unless we carry out the type of work with individuals and groups that enables change at the personal level, how do we expect to get real participation at the political level? It is obvious to me now that my next task would have been to work with the residents in becoming more politically involved. If both sides of the equation are not concentrated on it will be futile to expect widespread sustainable regeneration in today's social exclusion zones. If we truly believe in active citizenship then it is the personal-to-political process that we should be trying to nurture before we can succeed in engaging people critically in the more global issues which impact on their lives.

The emphasis within regeneration projects in the 1990s and into the new millennium concentrates on a 1980s middle-management phenomenon, evident in some of the newer regeneration pro-grammes recently devised (see Welsh Office, 1998b). This is not necessarily a negative shift, but these workers find themselves fulfilling their own role as well as the (by default) role of the grassroots worker, which is an impossible task. If we are going to make serious inroads into tackling poverty and injustice and believe in non-tokenistic participation, we have to be able to resource long-term, well-planned interventions at *all* levels. Other-wise we will end up with a situation where workers speak an alien language, cannot stop for a cup of tea, are unapproachable and 'sit in offices all day long'!

Health initiatives

Introduction to chapters 12 and 13

These chapters outline initiatives in the general sector of health. The first describes an initiative within and around a general medical practice in the Gwendraeth valley, and the other targets the New Public Health agenda towards increasing participation and sensitivity to local needs through the involvement of the community in the planning and decision-making processes. Both of these chapters highlight the significance of the problems faced by the established management when coming to terms with the demands of the local culture as they impact on the traditional 'medical model' of health.

It is very clear from the policies so far developed by the National Assembly for Wales that the engagement of community interests in the definition of health issues and the design and delivery of new-style services will require a heavy input of community development (National Assembly, 2000c). Without this, planning authorities will have no mechanism for reaching the people, mobilizing interest or developing their capacity for engagement. These two contributions illustrate this both from a social planning level and from locality development perspectives, and we can expect that in Wales community health development will emerge as a significant platform for the advancement of partnerships between the state and the community sector (Clarke, 2000; Labonté, 1999; Rothman, 1995; Thomas, D. N., 1995a). These two initiatives begin to point the way forward.

12   Prosiect Cymunedau Iach

MARIA FINNEMORE

Summary

In the Gwendraeth valley, three general practitioners decided to establish a holistic, and bilingual, approach to health issues in the community. The intention was to strengthen prevention, and the active participation of the local community in health matters was considered vital to this end. A pilot community development project, the Healthy Communities Project, was jointly funded by the Health Authority and Health Promotion Wales (National Assembly). Health issues are explored at the community level, using a village-appraisal approach. Interprofessional cooperation is essential, and so resources are deployed to ensure that the community development approach is understood and appreciated by all those working in the community. The bilingual approach is central, and the emphasis is on building alliances between professional and community organizations for the identification of health-related issues and seeking their solution. Community ownership of activities and planning is ensured through the widest possible involvement and creating mechanisms of joint initiatives. Local cultural activities and the raising of awareness of local history are enlisted in the capacity-building approach.

Rhagymadrodd

Amcan y Prosiect Cymunedau Iach yw datblygu strategaethau effeithiol i ddelio ag anghenion iechyd cymunedol a hybu cymunedau iach, deinamig drwy ystyried iechyd o safbwynt datblygiad cymunedol. Lleolir y prosiect ym mhractis meddygol Pen-y-groes ym mhen uchaf Cwm Gwendraeth, Sir Gaerfyrddin, ac mae'n gweithredu o fewn ffiniau tri phractis meddygol yn y cylch. Ar y cychwyn, cafodd ei ariannu ar y cyd am gyfnod o ddwy flynedd gan bractis meddygol Pen-y-groes/Crosshands (yn dal cronfa), Ymddiriedolaeth Gwasanaeth Iechyd Gwladol Llanelli/Dinefwr, Menter Cwm Gwendraeth a Hybu Iechyd Cymru. Lansiwyd ef ym 1997, a bu mewn bodolaeth hyd 2001.

Mae'r prosiect ar waith mewn ardal gyn-lofaol, rannol-wledig gyda chyfraddau uchel o ddiweithdra ac afiechyd/anabledd, gweithgaredd economaidd isel, a chyfleusterau ac isadeileddau annigonol. Nodwedd arbennig yr ardal yw cyfartaledd uchel y Cymry Cymraeg, gyda rhyw dri-chwarter o'r boblogaeth yn siarad Cymraeg fel iaith gyntaf neu fel iaith ddewisedig, ac mae'r rhwydwaith o weithgareddau ieithyddol a diwylliannol yn gryf.

Mae ymagweddu'n ddatblygol-gymunedol tuag at iechyd yn ein gorfodi i ystyried iechyd mewn dull mwy cyfannol, a chyfaddef ei fod yn cael ei effeithio gan ystod eang o ffactorau cymdeithasol, economaidd ac amgylcheddol, heb sôn am ffisioleg yr unigolyn. Mewn geiriau eraill, nid edrychir ar iechyd ar ei ben ei hun neu fel rhywbeth wedi'i ddiffinio'n gyfyng fel absenoldeb afiechyd, ond yn hytrach o fewn ei gefndir lleol ac yn nhermau lles a chysur cyffredinol.

Roedd newid y safbwynt fel hyn yn gofyn i ni archwilio dulliau eraill o ddelio ag anghenion unigol a chymunedol ac ystyried fframwaith y cefndir ehangach fel rhywbeth i gydweithio ag ef yn hytrach nag fel rhywbeth yr oeddem yn digwydd bod yn gweithio ynddo. Er mwyn sicrhau newid cadarnhaol i'r cyfeiriad hwn, mae'r prosiect yn amcanu at ddatblygu posibiliadau a strwythurau ar lefel asiantaeth a chymuned. Mae hyn yn golygu gweithio gydag amrywiaeth eang o unigolion a chynrychiolwyr o'r cyrff cyhoeddus a gwirfoddol sy'n effeithio'n uniongyrchol neu fel arall ar iechyd, yn ogystal â gweithio gyda'r gymuned. Mae hefyd yn cynnwys amrywiaeth eang o weithgareddau sy'n ymestyn o waith cysylltu a hybu hyd at waith cynllunio a chydlynu, i enwi ond rhai.

Hyd yn hyn, rhoddwyd arolwg bras o'r prosiect. Rhaid yn awr dangos sut mae'n gweithio. Er mwyn rhoi gwell syniad o'r hyn a olygir, edrychwn ar dair agwedd: cynllunio a chychwyn y prosiect; datblygu dulliau cydweithredol o asesu anghenion iechydol; a datblygu strategaethau ar gyfer iechyd a lles cymunedol.

Cynllunio a chychwyn y prosiect

Mae'r ffaith fod y Prosiect Cymunedau Iach yn rhoi'r pwyslais ar ddatblygu cymunedol, ac yr un pryd ei fod wedi'i leoli mewn practis meddygol, yn ei wneud yn fenter go anarferol. Oherwydd inni gychwyn y prosiect fel arbrawf, nid oedd gennym unrhyw fodel i gyfeirio ato ac, felly, agwedd bwysig ar y gwaith cychwynnol oedd cynllunio'r prosiect. Roedd hyn yn golygu ystyried yn ofalus a drafftio amcanion y prosiect er mwyn eu torri i lawr i weithgareddau a oedd yn berthnasol ac yn bosibl, fel proffilio, rhwydweithio, datblygu cysylltiadau rhwng asiantaethau, ac ati. Tanlinellodd hyn mor eang ei derfynau y gallai'r prosiect fod, a'r angen am ffocws. Gwnaeth hyn inni sylweddoli hefyd y gallai'r prosiect ddod yn fodel y gellid ei ddatblygu neu ei gymhwyso mewn cyd-destyn arall, yn ogystal â'r angen am ddatblygu peirianwaith i arolygu a recordio'r prosiect i'r perwyl hwn. Perthnasol i hyn oedd y ffaith ein bod yn sylweddoli pwysigrwydd hybu'r prosiect a'r angen am ddatblygu dulliau o wneud hynny ar nifer o lefelau.

Roeddem yn ymwybodol iawn o'r galwadau gwrthwynebol ar amser yn ystod y cyfnod hwn, yn enwedig o'r tensiwn rhwng yr angen i gynllunio a'r angen i ddelio â materion ymarferol. Roedd hyn yn tanlinellu mor bwysig oedd nodi'r blaenoriaethau yn ogystal â'r angen am gefnogaeth weinyddol ddigonol.

Wrth gynllunio'r prosiect, rydym yn cydnabod, fel yn achos unrhyw gyfundrefn arall, mai adeiladwaith ydyw, ac y gall strwythurau o'r fath fod yn ormesol a rhoi rhai pobl dan anfantais. Fodd bynnag, fel menter sy'n edrych ar iechyd o fewn cyd-destun y gymdeithas gyfan ac sydd hefyd yn cynnwys elfen gyfranogol yng ngwaith asesu anghenion, gan geisio datblygu potensial rhyngwynebau, gwnaethom ymdrech i ddatblygu adeiladwaith sy'n wrth-ormesol. Ymhellach, rydym yn ymwybodol o natur newidiol a deinamig yr amgylchedd, ac o'r angen am gyfaddasu strwythurau er mwyn sicrhau'r gallu ymateb.

Teimlwn hefyd mor bwysig yw fod yn ymwybodol o'r cyd-destun diwylliannol ehangach, ac yn sensitif iddo. Gan fod y prosiect ar waith mewn ardal lle mae'r mwyafrif yn siarad Cymraeg, un ffordd o ymateb oedd penodi cydlynwr dwyieithog, gyda'r gallu i gyfathrebu ag unigolion yn eu hiaith ddewisedig.

Fel prosiect datblygu cymunedol sydd wedi'i leoli mewn practis meddygol, rydym yn ymwybodol o'r gwahanol ymagweddau tuag at iechyd ym myd meddygaeth ar un llaw, a maes datblygu cymunedol ar y llaw arall. Yn fras, gellid disgrifio rhai o'r gwahaniaethau yn eu tro fel canolbwyntio ar yr unigolyn yn hytrach na'r gymuned neu'r amgylchedd ehangach; ar ddelio â'r symptomau yn hytrach nag â'r achosion; ar y duedd i adweithio yn hytrach na rhag-weld problemau; ac fel ffafrio ysgogiad o'r top i lawr yn hytrach nag o'r gwaelod i fyny. Mae'r prosiect yn mynd i'r afael â'r mater hwn drwy fabwysiadu ymagweddau ac arferion gweithredu newydd o fewn y cyd-destun hwn. Er enghraifft, y defnydd o ddulliau cyfranogol, ar ffurf holiaduron, er mwyn datblygu strategaethau sy'n ymateb i anghenion gwirioneddol. Yr ydym, fodd bynnag, yn cydnabod bod mabwysiadu dulliau neu ymagweddau newydd yn arwain at newid, ac mae hynny'n arwain yn ei dro at amrywiaeth gymhleth o brosesau, fel goresgyn y diffyg egni mewn strwythurau a chyfundrefnau sydd wedi ymsefydlogi dros gyfnod hir.

Rydym yn cydnabod hefyd mor bwysig yw'r gwaith hybu fel strategaeth i bontio rhwng y gwahanol ymagweddau tuag at y mater. Teimlwn ei bod yn bwysig esbonio amcanion ac ymagwedd-au'r prosiect i bobl broffesiynol yn y byd meddygol er mwyn ennyn mwy o ymwybyddiaeth a dealltwriaeth o'r prosiect a hefyd integr-eiddio'r gweithiwr i mewn i'r cyd-destun meddygol. Datblygwyd hefyd gysylltiadau â gweithwyr datblygu cymunedol eraill rhag ofn i'r gweithiwr yn y maes hwnnw deimlo unigedd proffesiynol yn y cyd-destun hwn.

Datblygu asesiadau cydweithrediadol ym maes anghenion iechyd

Un o agweddau allweddol y gwaith yw asesu anghenion iechyd y gymuned. Mae ymagwedd gydweithredol wedi'i datblygu sy'n golygu gweithio â nifer o gyrff a sefydliadau i ddatblygu hol-iaduron a ddosberthir ar lefel y gymuned.

Drwy fabwysiadu'r dull hwn o weithredu, ceisiwyd tynnu at ei gilydd wahanol gyrff mewn meysydd lle roedd eu diddordebau'n gyffredin neu'n gorgyffwrdd. Yr amcan oedd eu cael i gydweithio er mwyn nodi anghenion iechyd y gymuned gyda'r bwriad o ddatbygu strategaethau ymyraethol cydweithredol. Y tu mewn i'r math hwn o weithredu mae pob asiantaeth yn cyfrannu darn gwahanol i'r 'jigso' yn ôl ei gwybodaeth arbenigol, ei hadnoddau, sgiliau a rhwydweithiau. Canlyniad y gwaith yw'r holiaduron.

Mae cynllunio yn hanfodol os yw'r gweithgarwch i redeg yn esmwyth, oherwydd y bydd gan bob asiantaeth gyfraniad i'w roi ar wahanol adegau. Felly, os bydd un yn oedi, bydd hyn yn effeithio'n niweidiol ar waith eraill. Er mwyn osgoi problemau o'r fath, gwelsom fod angen peth 'llacrwydd' yn y cynllun. Gwaetha'r modd, nid oedd hyn yn bosibl bob amser oherwydd roedd gan rai o'r asiantaethau cyfranogol waith gosodedig na ellid mo'i ad-drefnu, ac roedd rhaid rhoi ystyriaeth i hyn wrth gynllunio'r gwaith. Ein profiad ni oedd ei bod yn bwysig sylweddoli a pharchu ymrwymiadau ehangach yr asiantaethau cyfranogol er mwyn i'r model weithio, yn ogystal â chydnabod gwerth eu cyfraniad.

Mae gweithio gyda gwahanol gyrff a sefydliadau yn golygu gweithio dros ystod o ddiwylliannau proffesiynol, cyfundrefnol ac adrannol, ac mae pob cyd-destun yn ymgorffori set arbennig o werthoedd, rhagfarn broffesiynol a blaenoriaethau. Yn ein barn ni mae'n bwysig bod yn ymwybodol o'r mater hwn wrth rwydweithio neu gychwyn prosiectau. Rhan o'r broses o ennill diddordeb ar y dechrau, ac o ennyn ymrwymiad i brosiectau unigol yn ddiweddarach, oedd defnyddio'r rhwydwaith er mwyn deffro ymwybyddiaeth a hybu'r prosiect, ei amcanion cyffredinol a'i ymagwedd tuag at y gwaith ymhlith pobl broffesiynol ac asiantaethau targed.

Hefyd rydym yn ymwybodol o'r ffaith fod cyfathrebu clir ac effeithiol yn hanfodol os yw'r prosiectau i weithio'n esmwyth. Gan fod y cyfranogwyr yn gweithio mewn gwahanol fannau a gwahanol broffesiynau mae perygl y gall camddeall a methiant mewn cyfathrebu godi. Cyfrifoldeb y gweithiwr sy'n hybu a chydgysylltu amrywiol agweddau'r prosiectau yw hyn; mae'n bwysig sicrhau bod y rhai sydd â rhan yn y gwaith yn ymroddedig i'r prosiect, a bod pob cyfranogwr yn deall ei gyfrifoldebau a'r hyn a ofynnir ganddo.

Rydym hefyd yn gwerthfawrogi bod iaith yn fwy nag offeryn cyfathrebu yn unig, a'i bod yn rhwym wrth ddychymyg, emosiwn, mynegiant, gwerthoedd, hunaniaeth a hanes. Gan ein bod yn deall hyn ac yn cydnabod bod rhai rannau o'r gymuned yn teimlo eu bod yn gallu mynegi eu meddyliau a'u teimladau yn well yn eu hiaith ddewisedig, roedd rheidrwydd arnom i gynnal asesiadau anghenion dwyieithog. Roedd i hyn, wrth gwrs, ymhlygiadau pellach, megis yr angen i ddod o hyd i arian ychwanegol i gyllido'r cyfieithu a'r gost ychwanegol ynglŷn ag argraffu'r holiaduron.

Datblygu strategaethau ar gyfer iechyd a lles y gymuned

Gan ein bod yn credu y dylid ystyried iechyd yn ei gyd-destun cymdeithasol, daethom yn ymwybodol o'r ystod eang o faterion sy'n cael effaith ar iechyd, megis diweithdra, unigedd, diffyg cyfundrefnau cefnogi, cludiant cyhoeddus gwael ac ati. Ar brydiau gall hyn fod yn llethol, oherwydd yr angen am ddelio ag amrywiaeth mawr o faterion yn ogystal â'r angen am flaenoriaethau a ffocws. Un ffordd o wneud hynny oedd gweithredu fel offeryn hwyluso drwy ddatblygu strategaethau y gallai cyrff eraill eu gweithredu. Mae'r strategaethau hyn yn mynd i'r afael â materion sy'n effeithio ar iechyd a lles y gymuned.

Wrth ddatblygu strategaethau cawsom fod sefyllfa'r sawl sy'n frodor o'r ardal leol o ddefnydd i ni, gan fod ei ddealltwriaeth a'i wybodaeth eang o'r ardal yn ein galluogi i ddatblygu strategaethau priodol a sensitif i ddiwylliant yr ardal honno. Mae tair ystyriaeth yn tanlinellu'r gwaith o ddatblygu strategaethau yn nhermau datblygu cymunedol; yn gyntaf, y syniad o alluogi; yn ail, pwysigrwydd creu cysylltiadau; ac yn drydydd, y mater o sicrhau parhad y gwaith. Rhagwelwn y bydd strategaethau fel meithrin perthynas agosach rhwng grwpiau yn y gymuned yn rhoi bod i strwythurau neu gysylltiadau newydd o fewn y gymuned. Bydd hyn yn rhoi iddynt lais cryfach, gan eu galluogi i achosi newid; a bydd strategaethau sy'n argymell hyfforddi gwirfoddolwyr neu gynghori pobl ifainc yn ateb y broblem o alluogi ac yn rhoi mwy o sicrwydd ynglŷn â pharhad.

Roeddem yn ymwybodol ei bod yn bwysig cael y gymuned i ymuno yn y broses gynllunio. Er mwyn hybu hyn, yn ogystal ag ennyn ymdeimlad fod ganddynt ran yn y strategaethau a ddatblygwyd, gwahoddwyd pob fforwm cymuned i wneud sylwadau ar y strategaethau cyn eu dosbarthu a'u lansio mewn cyfarfod cyhoeddus. Roedd ymrwymiad o'r fath yn help i sicrhau bod cynnydd yn ymwybyddiaeth pobl ac i godi hyder a meithrin dealltwriaeth, prosesau sydd fel arfer y tu hwnt i brofiad y gymuned leol.

Trefnwyd y strategaethau a ddatblygwyd fel eu bod yn ffitio i mewn i ffiniau amser priodol. Os oedd brwdfrydedd ac ymrwymiad y gymuned i barhau, roedd yn amlwg y byddai'n rhaid cynnwys yn y cynllun tymor-byr strategaethau y gellid eu gwireddu'n hawdd, er mwyn dangos bod pethau'n cael eu cyflawni, fel gosod hysbysfwrdd mewn pentref.

Un strategaeth effeithiol oedd cynnwys hanes byr yn y rhagarweiniad i adroddiadau arolwg cymunedol. Teimlwn fod hyn nid yn unig yn gosod yr adroddiadau yn eu cyd-destun econom-aidd-gymdeithasol a hanesyddol, ond hefyd yn help i ennyn balchder lleol a hunaniaeth. Roedd yn ennyn cryn dipyn o ymateb cadarnhaol, brwdfrydedd a diddordeb ymhlith pobl y gymuned, a gosodwyd copïau o'r adroddiadau mewn llyfrgelloedd a mannau allweddol eraill yn y pentref.

Gwyddom hefyd fod rhoi gwybodaeth i bobl am eu hanes lleol yn eu galluogi i adeiladu ar eu gorffennol. Er enghraifft, roedd darganfod bod system o gyd-gymorth yn gweithredu mewn cymuned leol yn ystod y ganrif ddiwethaf yn gallu bod yn ddylanwad ar agweddau pobl ac yn gwneud iddynt feddwl am rywbeth tebyg yn ein dyddiau ni. Mae'n ddiddorol nodi hefyd i lawer o'r traethodau hanesyddol cynnar gael eu hysgrifennu'n arbennig ar gyfer eisteddfodau lleol, a'u bod ar gael heddiw yn union oherwydd yr adeiladwaith diwylliannol a chymunedol hwn.

Gyda golwg ar fater iaith, datblygwyd strategaethau i alluogi unigolion i ddefnyddio eu hiaith ddewisedig mewn sefyllaoedd cyhoeddus, yn ogystal â strategaethau i hybu dwyieithrwydd, er mwyn sicrhau nad oedd neb yn cael ei gau allan ar sail iaith.

Casgliad

Mae creu agweddau datblygol tuag at iechyd wedi golygu gweithio'n agos â'r gymuned yn ogystal ag ystod eang o gyrff a sefydliadau. Darganfuom fod y dull hwn o weithio yn werthfawr, gan ei fod yn ein galluogi i ddelio ag amrywiaeth mawr o ffactorau sy'n cael effaith ar iechyd a lles yr unigolyn a'r gymuned. Ceisiwyd gweithredu arferion sensitif a deallus yn y broses o gynllunio a gweithredu drwy gynnwys syniadau fel galluogi, ymarfer wrth-ormesol, a phwysigrwydd a swyddogaeth proses. Fodd bynnag, rydym hefyd yn ymwybodol o'r galwadau sydd ar amser y gweithiwr, o'r angen am nodi blaenoriaethau ac o'r dewisiadau y mae'n rhaid wrthynt ym mater anghenion.

Mae swyddog datblygu cymunedol ar fin cael ei benodi, a bydd hyn yn ei gwneud yn bosibl i ni fynd i'r afael â'r materion hyn drwy ychwanegu at botensial y prosiect i ddatblygu mentrau iechyd cymunedol ar lefel y bobl. Bwriedir i'r datblygiad hwn roi hwb i'r gwaith o ddiffinio a gweithredu'r ymagwedd ddatblygol tuag at iechyd yn y gymuned.

Ôl-Nodyn

Penodwyd gweithiwr datblygu iechyd cymunedol ychydig cyn i'r adroddiad hwn fynd i'r wasg. Mae'r prosiect wedi newid ei enw: 'Cysylltiadau Iechyd Cymunedol' fydd y teitl o hyn ymlaen.

13 Datblygu cymunedol mewn cyd-destun hybu iechyd

HAYLEY THOMAS

Summary

This case study, based in Pembrokeshire, highlights the important role of community development in health improvement and the values and approaches that inform community development practice in a health promotion context. It is based on the personal views and experiences of a community development officer working in a health promotion unit of a health authority. A grassroots community health development project and the process for developing an inter-agency community development strategy for a county demonstrate the range of interdependent work required to facilitate effective community health development. A model outlining different elements of community development work provides a theoretical framework for reference (Health Promotion Wales, 1996). Developing an overview of work undertaken by community, voluntary, public and private organizations through the Local Alliance for Health will secure a strategic approach to facilitate community health development and to tackle inequalities in health. The role of the community development practitioner is

- to facilitate the involvement of all sectors to engage in inter-agency partnerships for health improvement;
- to act as a bridge between the range of interests at all appropriate levels: community, practitioner, management and strategic;
- to develop an overview of the process.

Community development practitioners can support the health service to integrate and embed appropriate community development practice as part of its core business and culture.

Mae cyd-destun polisi cryf eisoes ar gyfer cefnogi datblygu iechyd cymuned. Mae grymoedd gyriadol Cynulliad Cenedlaethol Cymru dros newid yn cynnwys, er enghraifft, 'Cymunedau yn Gyntaf – adfywio ein cymunedau mwyaf dan anfantais', 'Gwell Iechyd, Gwell Cymru' a datblygiad Cynghreiriau Iechyd Lleol i ddod â'r holl garfanau ynghyd i wella gweithredu partneriaeth er mwyn gwella iechyd. Mae cyfleoedd cyllido presennol a newydd megis Amcan Un, yn gofyn am bartneriaethau rhwng asiantaethau a chymunedau i gefnogi datblygu cymunedol. Mae'r amgylchedd cymdeithasol a gwleidyddol newidiol yng Nghymru, ac ar lefel polisi rhanbarthol, cenedlaethol a rhyngwladol, yn pwysleisio pwysigrwydd cefnogi datblygu cymunedol er mwyn adeiladu cymunedau iach a chryf a all ddelio ag anghydraddoldeb mewn iechyd a lles cymdeithasol. Mae tystiolaeth gref ar gael am effeithiolrwydd dulliau datblygu cymunedol a'u cyfraniad at dargedu angen iechyd a chymdeithasol, hybu iechyd a lles, mynd i'r afael ag anghydraddoldebau mewn iechyd, a hybu cynhwysiad cymdeithasol. Ar lefel leol, mae Cynghrair Sir Benfro dros Iechyd wedi sicrhau ymrwymiad cyrff lleol i weithio gyda'i gilydd er mwyn mynd i'r afael ag anghydraddoldebau mewn iechyd ac amlhau i'r eithaf weithgaredd gwella iechyd ar draws y sir.

Cafodd datblygu cymunedol, fel athroniaeth ac fel ffordd o weithio, ei gydnabod gan Adran Hybu Iechyd Sir Benfro, i fod yn agwedd bwysig o fewn strategaethau er hybu iechyd ac ar gyfer gwella penderfynyddion iechyd sylfaenol. Fe'm hapwyntiwyd gan Adran Hybu Iechyd Sir Benfro fel swyddog datblygu cymunedol ym mis Mai 1999 gyda chyfrifoldeb dros y sir. Cynigiodd y cyfle cyffrous hwn i hybu iechyd drwy ymarfer datblygu cymunedol sawl sialens bersonol a phroffesiynol. Roedd angen fframwaith i fod yn sail i ddatblygiad rhaglen waith, a rhoddwyd blaenoriaeth i weithio'n strategol i adeiladu ar waith presennol, ynghyd ag ymarfer, profiad ac arbenigedd da er mwyn amlhau i'r eithaf weithgaredd datblygu iechyd cymuned ar draws y sir.

Trwythir gwaith yr Adran Hybu Iechyd gan werthoedd sy'n cynnwys y gred sy'n rhan annatod o ddatblygu cymunedol – bod yna ymrwymiad i fynd i'r afael ag anghydraddoldeb ac anffafriaeth a chydnabod yr angen i alluogi pobl i gael mwy o rym dros eu bywydau er mwyn rheoli'r ffactorau sy'n effeithio ar eu hiechyd a'u lles. Mae datblygu cymunedol, wedi ei gysylltu â model iechyd cadarnhaol, cyfannol a chymdeithasol, yn chwarae rhan bwysig mewn hybu iechyd, yn enwedig yn y cymunedau mwyaf dan anfantais ac ar y cyrion, ac yn cyfrannu at ostyngiad mewn anghydraddoldebau. Ar ei orau, mae'n ysgogi cyfranogaeth; yn galluogi ac yn hybu hunan-barch a hyder unigolion a chymunedau drwy eu cefnogi i adnabod eu anghenion eu hunain; yn datblygu atebion i ddelio â'r anghenion hynny; yn cefnogi eu cyfranogaeth mewn sefydliadau cymunedol a rhwydweithiau; ac yn cynyddu eu dylanwad ar ddulliau gwneud penderfyniadau lleol sy'n effeithio ar eu bywydau. Mae'r broses o ddatblygu cymunedol cyn bwysiced â'r canlyniadau. Mae'r ffocws ar gydweithredu ac agenda a benwyd gan y gymuned. Targedwyd y gwaith i gynnwys pobl sy'n profi anghydraddoldebau a'r rheini dan y perygl mwyaf o ddatblygu afiechyd.

Dengys y ddwy enghraifft ganlynol o brosiectau gymhwysiad ymarferol gwerthoedd a ffyrdd o fynd ati. Er mwyn trafod a dadansoddi'r prosiectau hyn edrychir ar fodel damcaniaethol sy'n amlinellu'r pum elfen wahanol o waith cyd-ddibynnol y mae eu hangen er mwyn gwella gweithredu cymunedol dros iechyd (Health Promotion Wales, 1996). Dyma'r pum elfen:

(1) Gwaith cymunedol sylfaenol, sy'n cynnwys helpu pobl i ddod at ei gilydd a threfnu eu hunain er mwyn diffinio materion y maent yn eu hystyried yn bwysig. Canlyniad hyn fydd sefydlu grwpiau cymunedol; cryfhau grwpiau mewn bodolaeth; mwy o ddylanwad a chyfranogaeth mewn prosesau gwneud penderfyniadau lleol; a chynnydd mewn sgiliau a hyder unigolyddol a chymunedol sy'n arwain at fanteision iechyd cadarnhaol.

(2) Datblygu rhwydweithiau mewnol cymunedol, yn cynnwys helpu grwpiau a gweithwyr cymunedol i rwydweithio â'i gilydd, a chyfnewid gwybodaeth a chefnogaeth.

(3) Datblygu rhwydweithiau mewnol proffesiynol, a sicrhau bod adrannau, sefydliadau, rheolwyr ac ymarferwyr yn rhwyd-weithio â'i gilydd ac yn gallu gweithio mewn partneriaeth ag asiantaethau a chymunedau eraill. Y canlyniad yw fod yr effaith gyfun ar y gymuned yn fwy rhesymegol, ymatebol a chefnogol.

(4) Datblygiad sefydliadol sy'n anelu at wella effeithiolrwydd sefydliad drwy annog cyfranogaeth ac ymateb i anghenion a syniadau cymunedau lleol. Mae hyn yn berthnasol i'r holl

sefydliadau o fewn y gymuned, y sectorau gwirfoddol, cyhoeddus a phreifat.

(5) Arolwg, sy'n sicrhau cysylltiadau rhwng yr holl elfennau cyd-ddibynnol. Delir â'r rhain yn aml gan wahanol bobl, yn gweithio ar wahanol lefelau ac mewn sectorau gwahanol. Y canlyniad yw bydd syniadau ac anghenion lleol yn effeithio ar gynllunio, polisi ac ymarfer strategol ehangach.

Mae'r prosiect cyntaf yn enghraifft o waith cymunedol sylfaenol. Sefydlwyd grŵp o'r enw Iechyd a Datblygiad Cymunedol (IADC) yn Hakin a Hubberston ym mis Mehefin 1997 o ganlyniad i weithdy datblygu cymunedol undydd a gynhaliwyd yn y clwb rygbi lleol. Roedd yr Adran Hybu Iechyd yn cydnabod y gymuned hon fel ardal darged ar gyfer gweithredu oherwydd lefelau uchel o ddiffygion. Yn ogystal â hyn, mynegwyd diddordeb gan amrywiaeth o garfanau lleol mewn gweithio ar y cyd er mwyn gwella iechyd ac ansawdd bywyd pobl yn byw yn yr ardal. Tynnodd y gweithdy breswylwyr, grwpiau ac asiantaethau lleol at ei gilydd i weithio yn yr ardal.

O ganlyniad i'r gweithdy, sefydlwyd grŵp bychan i fwrw ymlaen â model datblygu cymunedol o weithio yn Hubberston a Hakin. Un o brif sialensiau'r grŵp oedd edrych ar sut gallai pobl leol gymryd rhan fwy bywiog mewn gwaith datblygu cymunedol. Er mwyn ceisio crynhoi cyfranogaeth gymuned, cynhaliwyd diwrnod agored cymunedol a diwrnod mabolgampau hwyl a sbri i godi proffil y grŵp, ac anogwyd aelodau o'r gymuned leol i gymryd rhan. Bu IADC hefyd yn gweithio gyda chanolfan iechyd Hakin i asesu anghenion iechyd poblogaeth y practis. Datblygwyd y darlun hwn o anghenion iechyd a chymdeithasol bellach gan holiadur iechyd a gynhyrchwyd gan Gymdeithas Cymuned Hubberston.

Dilynwyd hynt datblygiad y grŵp gan weithdy arall ynghyd â gweithgaredd y dyfodol a gynlluniwyd i gynnwys ennill cynrychiolaeth a chyfranogaeth ehangach y gymuned, yn enwedig pobl ifainc a phobl hŷn. Bu gweithgareddau cymunedol fel helfa drysor ar droed ac amryw o ddigwyddiadau hybu iechyd yn fodd i gynnal proffil y grŵp o fewn y gymuned.

Erbyn diwedd 2001, roedd y grŵp yn gorff sefydledig a arweinir gan y gymuned. Mae hyn yn ganlyniad cadarnhaol i waith datblygiadol yn ystod y blynyddoedd cyntaf. Ar hyd yr amser, mae aelodau cymunedol wedi dechrau codi pryderon mwy cymhleth ynglŷn â thlodi, tai, diweithdra ac iechyd. Y flaenoriaeth allweddol a gafodd ei chydnabod gan IADC oedd yr angen i sefydlu undeb gredyd i fynd i'r afael â phroblemau dyled a gwaharddiad ariannol yn yr ardal. Mae IADC ar hyn o bryd yn gweithio mewn partneriaeth â'r gymuned leol, sefydliadau gwirfoddol, cyhoeddus a phreifat ar draws Aberdaugleddau a Neyland i ddatblygu undeb gredyd. Gwireddwyd a chynlluniwyd y prosiect mewn cyfnod o ddeng mis a recriwtiwyd dros 20 o wirfoddolwyr i ymgymryd â rhaglen hyfforddi.

Yr allwedd i lwyddiant IADC oedd y gwaith sylfaenol cychwynnol a wnaed, gan weithio yn ôl cyflymder y gymuned a chefnogi pobl i wneud pethau drostynt hwy eu hunain. Mae'n eglur ddigon fod angen mwy o adnoddau i ddatblygu maint sefydliadol IADC er mwyn darparu atebion i gwrdd â'r anghenion a gafodd eu cydnabod gan y gymuned leol. Mae dadansoddiad o'r sefyllfa bresennol yn dangos bod agenda'r gymuned yn tyfu ar gyflymder na ellir mo'i ddiwallu'n unig gan adnoddau'r Adran Hybu Iechyd a phartneriaid eraill – bydd grym gyriadol a chyfranogaeth barhaol y gymuned yn hanfodol i sicrhau canlyniadau llwyddiannus.

Mae ymarferwyr yn wynebu sialens bersonol wrth barhau i gefnogi cymunedau yn y math hwn o waith, a hwythau'n cael eu siarsio i leihau eu cyfranogaeth er mwyn ymgymryd â gwaith newydd. Atgyfnertha hyn yr angen i fabwysiadu dull strategol tymor-hir wrth gyflawni gwaith datblygu cymunedol er mwyn amlhau i'r eithaf lefelau cefnogaeth ac adnoddau.

Mae'r prosiect hwn, yn debyg i fentrau cyffelyb eraill, yn peri tensiwn i'r ymarferwyr, rhwng atebolrwydd i'r gymuned ac i'r sefydliad sy'n eu cyflogi. Rhoir ar brawf yn aml y berthynas rhwng agendâu sefydliadol a rhai'r gymuned pan fydd ymrwymiad i ddilyn arweiniad pobl leol i gwrdd â'u blaenoriaethau eu hunain wedi'i wneud. Arddangosir y tensiwn hwn yn syml os, er enghraifft, bydd trefnwyr digwyddiadau cymunedol lleol am ganiatáu ysmygu ac yfed alcohol, sydd yn amlwg yn rhedeg yn groes i'r agenda hybu iechyd. Pan wynebir y math hwn o ddilema, y flaenoriaeth i'r gweithiwr datblygu cymunedol mewn hybu iechyd yw cynyddu cyfranogaeth gymaint â phosib mewn digwyddiadau lleol, a dros amser cynyddu ymwybyddiaeth aelodau'r gymuned o'u hiechyd eu hun. Nid ar ymddygiad niweidiol i iechyd yw eu ffocws yn y lle cyntaf.

Mae'r cyfraniad gwerthfawr a wneir gan wirfoddolwyr yn hanfodol i lwyddiant IADC, ond mae potensial y gall gwirfoddoli fod yn niweidiol i iechyd unigolion. Gall lefelau cynyddol o gyfrifoldeb, adnoddau gofal-plant annigonol, prinder costau teithio, hyfforddiant a chefnogaeth bersonol i gyd gyfrannu at lefelau cynyddol o straen. Mae hyn yn ddilema dro ar ôl tro i ymarferwyr datblygu cymunedol yng nghyd-destun hybu iechyd; maent yn dymuno annog gwirfoddoli ond yn ymwybodol o les yr unigolyn.

Yr ail enghraifft yw sefydlu Strategaeth Datblygu Cymunedol i'r sir. Mae hon yn flaenoriaeth a gafodd ei chydnabod gan Gynghrair Sir Benfro dros Iechyd ac mae ganddi gyfranogaeth aml-gorff. Mae'r broses o ddatblygu strategaeth o'r math hwn yn gyfle i gymhwyso pum elfen gyd-ddibynnol y model damcaniaethol a ddisgrifiwyd uchod. Mae hanes cryf o gydweithio a datblygu cymunedol yn Sir Benfro. Roedd yn glir y byddai'r strategaeth yn adeiladu ar ymarfer, profiad ac arbenigedd da cyfredol. Mae'r amrywiaeth eang o asiantaethau o fewn y sectorau cyhoeddus, gwirfoddol a chymunedol yn Sir Benfro yn defnyddio nifer o fodelau ymarfer datblygu cymunedol gwahanol, gan gynnwys sbectrwm o waith sy'n amrywio o ddatblygu grwpiau a phartner-iaethau i sefydliadau cymunedol a gweithredu gwleidyddol. Teimlwyd y byddai strategaeth yn atgyfnerthu gwaith rhyngasiant-aethol presennol ac yn y dyfodol.

Sefydlwyd is-grŵp o Gynghrair Sir Benfro dros Iechyd i ddatblygu'r gwaith hwn. Roedd yr is-grŵp yn cydnabod y byddai cynnydd yn y nifer o gymunedau a sefydliadau a fyddai'n gweithio mewn partneriaeth er mwyn gwella iechyd petai rhai materion allweddol arbennig yn cael eu hystyried. Roedd y rhain yn cynnwys: diffyg amlwg casgliad o egwyddorion a gwerthoedd craidd mewn partneriaethau rhyngasiantaethol; yr angen am rwydweithiau mewnol cryfach o fewn sefydliadau partner i gefnogi ymarfer, yn enwedig lle mae diffyg hyder, prinder sgiliau a phrinder cefnogaeth reoli ymysg staff wrth ddefnyddio dulliau datblygu cymunedol; diffyg hyfforddiant mewn datblygu cymunedol ar lefel gymunedol, lefel ymarferwyr, lefel reoli a lefel strategol. Wrth ddelio â'r materion allweddol hyn cydnabyddir y byddai'n rhaid i'r broses sicrhau cyfranogaeth a chefnogaeth partneriaid ar bob lefel.

Wrth weithio tuag at ddatblygu strategaeth, penderfynodd yr is-grŵp y byddai'r broses ei hun cyn bwysiced â'r ddogfen derfynol. Rhagwelwyd y byddai'r broses yn cynhyrchu'r canlyniadau canlynol:

(1) Diffiniad o ddatblygiad cymuned, gwerthoedd ac egwyddorion craidd y cytunwyd arnynt. Byddai hyn yn diffinio'r man cychwyn tuag at ddarparu gweledigaeth gyffredinol a chasgliad o ganlyniadau i weithio tuag atynt, gan alluogi pobl i fesur cynnydd cyffredinol ar drywydd nod ehangach o ddatblygu cymunedau iach a chynaliadwy.

(2) Eglurhad o rolau a chyfrifoldebau asiantaethau mewn perthynas â datblygu cymunedol.

(3) Ymrwymiad clir oddi wrth asiantaethau i ddatblygu partneriaethau cydradd.

(4) Bydd asiantaethau'n cyfuno ac yn gosod ymarfer datblygu cymunedol cymwys fel rhan o'u busnes a'u diwylliant craidd.

(5) Gwell dealltwriaeth ynglŷn â sut y gellir dygymod â mentrau 'o'r gwaelod i'r top' ac 'o'r top i'r gwaelod'.

(6) Cryfhau gweithio mewn partneriaeth.

Cytunodd yr is-grŵp ar broses o ddatblygu'r gwaith i ddelio â'r angen i ddatblygu dull cynhwysol o weithio er sicrhau cyfranogaeth cymunedau a sefydliadau ar bob lefel berthnasol. Cododd y syniad o gynhadledd i drafod yr angen am, a chynnwys, strategaeth, ynghyd â chynnig i ddatblygu rhwydwaith gweithwyr cymunedol. O ganlyniad i hyn, sefydlodd ymarferwyr o wahanol sefydliadau cymunedol, gwirfoddol a chyhoeddus grŵp llywio i ddatblygu'r rhwydwaith hwn er mwyn tynnu'r ymarfer-wyr ynghyd i weithio ar lefel sylfaenol. Cytunwyd y dylai'r is-grŵp gyd-drefnu'r gynhadledd i symbylu trafodaeth ynglŷn â strategaeth ac i lansio'r rhwydwaith, sef Datblygu Cymunedol Cymru.

Roedd sialensiau arbennig y gwaith hwn yn cynnwys cym-hlethdod y materion i'w trafod a'r rhychwant gwahanol iawn o ddiddordebau roedd rhaid eu hystyried os oedd y broses yn mynd i fod yn un gynhwysol. Mae'r broses hyd yn hyn wedi dibynnu'n drwm ar weithio mewn partneriaeth a datblygu parch, ym-ddiriedaeth a hyder y naill partner a'r llall. Yn y cyfnod cynnar hwn, beth bynnag, mae llawer o faterion i'w trafod a'u datrys o hyd, yn cynnwys sut mae'r broses yn mynd i fagu ymdeimlad o berchenogaeth yr holl bartneriaid ar bob lefel.

Rôl allweddol yr ymarferwyr datblygu cymunedol yn y cyd-destun hwn yw darparu gwybodaeth, adnoddau a chefnogaeth i alluogi pobl i gymryd rhan; hwyluso gweithio mewn partneriaeth rhwng yr holl sectorau; gweithredu fel pont rhwng y gwahanol garfanau; ac arolygu'r broses.

Bydd ymarferwyr yn manteisio'n bersonol ac yn broffesiynol ar rwydweithiau a strwythurau cefnogi ar lefel leol a chenedlaethol. Bydd hyn yn atgyfnerthu ac yn gwella gwybodaeth ac ymarferiad a bydd o'r pwys mwyaf i ddatblygu gwaith ar sail unigolion ac ar y cyd. Mae'n bosibl y gall strwythurau cefnogi gynnig atebion i arwahanrwydd, bylchau mewn gwybodaeth a dulliau o weithio newydd. Yn anad dim, mae Datblygu Cymunedol Cymru yn cynnig y cyfle i weithwyr ddefnyddio rhwydwaith genedlaethol, sy'n sensitif i anghenion arbennig Cymru ac a fydd yn cefnogi ac yn gwella ymarfer datblygu cymunedol ar draws ardaloedd gwledig a threfol.

Caiff rôl datblygu cymunedol ei chydnabod yn gyffredinol mewn gofal iechyd ataliol. Nid yw'n bosibl nac yn briodol cymryd y dull datblygu cymunedol ym mhob cyd-destun hybu iechyd ond dylid ei ystyried fel y dull allweddol mewn strategaethau a arweinir gan y gymuned dros hybu iechyd. Mae'n bwysig fod y gwasanaeth iechyd yn cael ei ddatblygu fel adnodd i gefnogi atebion 'o'r gwaelod i'r top' er mewn cwrdd ag anghenion iechyd a chymdeithasol a adnabuwyd yn lleol. Dywedodd Labonté (1999) fod yr adran iechyd yn rhan o'r gymuned a bod ganddi rôl bwysig i chwarae mewn datblygu cymunedol, gan ddod yn fwy ymatebol i anghenion cymunedau. Mae rôl yr ymarferwyr datblygu cymunedol yn hanfodol wrth gefnogi'r gwasanaeth iechyd i gyfuno a phlannu ymarfer datblygu cymunedol priodol fel rhan o'i fusnes a'i ddiwylliant craidd. Mae gwaith datblygu cymunedol yn galluogi pobl mewn cymunedau, a dangosir yn y cyd-destun hybu iechyd fod ganddo'r potensial i alluogi pobl i gymryd cyfrifoldeb am eu hanghenion iechyd eu hunain. Mae angen symudiad meddwl gwleidyddol er mwyn darparu'r gwasanaeth iechyd ag adnoddau digonol i fynd i'r afael â ac i ddatgloi potensial datblygu cymunedol.

14   Beyond a strong voice

PHIL COPE

Crynodeb

Mae 'Celfyddydau Cymunedol' yn dysgu arweinyddiaeth a sgiliau cymdeithasol eraill, sy'n ehangu cryfderau cymdeithasol unigolion. Yn ei dro,
mae hyn yn cryfhau'r diwylliant lleol, a'r gymuned yn sgîl hynny. Sbardunodd
tîm celfyddydau cymunedol 'Valley and Vale' gynlluniau a fanteisiodd ar
ddoniau ysgrifennu cudd, a chynhyrchodd ysgrifennu atgofus, uchel ei safon.
Mae profiadau lleol yn trosi'n naturiol i lenyddiaeth a barddoniaeth, a
rhoddodd gyfraniad y tîm sgiliau adeiladu-cymuned a oedd yn hwb i ffyniant
hunangymorth. Roedd y cynllun yn cael ei redeg o dan faner Ysgrifennu ar
gyfer Cynon, gyda'r profiad o fyw yn y Cymoedd yn elfen gyffredin i'r holl
waith. Tynnodd yr ysgrifennu ar ddigwyddiadau lleol a phrofiadau a
theimladau pobl a oedd yn ceisio gwneud synnwyr o ddigwyddiadau,
atgofion ac amgylchiadau cymdeithasol ac economaidd. Manteisiodd
menywod a phlant ysgol, yn arbennig, ar y gweithdai. Sicrhawyd arian
cyhoeddus i gynorthwyo gyda chyhoeddi'r gwaith, a dangosodd y fenter
gyfan i blant ac i eraill a gredai eu bod ar gyrion digwyddiadau'r brif ffrwd y
gallai eu cyfraniad hwy gael effaith sylweddol.

Community Arts is characterized by the objective to help provide
the facilities, the training and the support needed for communities
and individuals to develop *a strong voice*.

   This 'new' cultural direction – fought for from the 1960s
onwards – was, of course, not new at all. The movement was in
fact just a jolting reminder of where we had been, and a
readjustment of priorities. The participation of the majority of the
population in the activities of drama, song, dance, poetry and

storytelling underpins much of the history of our nation, defining much of what we think of as Wales and Welshness.

Culture here is seen as that which holds society together: its social heritage. The absence of social activity, in evidence in particular in the second part of the twentieth century, is the result of this breakdown of bonding activity, of communication between people, manifested most clearly in what we have come to know as 'social exclusion', and the soulless/artless nature of much of modern life for large numbers of people.

Culture, by contrast, is the process by which we understand our world and our place within it, and the meanings we make and the knowledge we hold shape our decisions and our actions, centrally determining the future development of our societies. Cultural activities give identity through membership and inclusion. In the apparently simple, though profound, words of Raymond Williams, 'the process of communication is in fact the process of community'.

It is ironic that at a time when we have 24-hour news on tap, an overload of information on offer through the Internet, and the opportunity soon to view up to 200 channels through digital television, the voices of 'ordinary people' are more silenced than ever, particularly the distinctive voices of the young.

I want to describe and illustrate four small, seemingly insignificant examples of writing projects from the south Wales valleys – the remembering series, and three of the workshops undertaken as part of the Write for Cynon project – to explore the importance and potential of this work for the development of confidence and identity and a foundation for radical and popular change:

In our own words

It's time to pull up the stool by the front door
and tell the story before the historians arrive.
Gabriel Garcia Marquez

I set up Valley and Vale in 1979, and coordinated this south-east-Wales-based community arts team for the following sixteen years. One of the media training areas for which I was responsible was creative writing and publications. A significant success in this area was the 'remembering' series, which dealt with notions of history and memory, and encouraged and supported acts of collective remembering and the rewriting of history.

Our culture persuades us that history is a country inhabited only by a privileged few, minimizing the role played in events by 'ordinary people'. We are the only experts in the stories of our own lives; not always perhaps in the dates and timings of what happened where – facts which progressively fade over time – but much more importantly in the feelings, the attitudes and the values which illustrate and underpin the changes that have occurred. Apparently insignificant memories – the personal triumphs, the tragedies, the moments of humour and of pain – can tell us more about the experience of living in a particular era or area than volumes of dry historical fact.

Writing about our lives and those of our family and friends, our village, town, city or country helps us understand and value our experiences, and gives us strength to celebrate and see more clearly our place within our private and public worlds.

Michel Foucault observed that 'if one controls people's memory, one controls their dynamism'. It's a sad irony that, with the near completion of the major reclamation work which will erase the last scars of intensive industrialization in the south Wales valleys, we are threatened at the same moment with the removal of all reminders of the reasons that people travelled from all over the world to live and work here less than one-and-a-half centuries ago. The south Wales valleys were populated to satisfy the needs of coal and iron extraction, changing in the process rural farming communities into major industrial sites almost overnight. And now that the pits have mostly gone, Valleys' people are having to find new reasons to stay, new strategies for survival. An understanding of the past, or more correctly the pasts, is an essential component of the foundations upon which to build that future.

The 'remembering' project offered a forum for expression to men and women, able-bodied and so-called 'disabled', gay and straight, old and young. The first book in the series was *They Made Light of their Darkness* (1994) by ex-headteacher Vernon Chilcott, a celebration of all that was good about life in the Garw and Ogmore valleys in the 1920s, 1930s and 1940s. *They Made Light* was followed by *Back to Blaengarw* by Grafton Radcliffe, who ploughed a similar furrow comparing the 'good old days' with the harsher realities of today. It would have been easy to continue in this direction, as most local history publications do, but we were intent upon providing a wider, more confused picture of life. Our aim was to offer space for different and discordant voices to be heard towards an unachievable, utopian vision of everyone in a community writing their own book, their version of the realities of living in their particular area, the sum of their conflicting, colliding, collective versions building to what could be seen as the only 'true' picture.

The third volume was by Arthur Wakefield and dealt with more uncomfortable realities of Valleys' life. *Little Boy Lost* explored the neglected histories of Protestant–Catholic conflict in the Maesteg area before the Second World War, and the overbearing and oppressive influences of church and chapel. On the day of his birth Arthur was forcibly taken from his mother, who was banished from his life by his Protestant grandparents because his father had been a Catholic. Arthur's 'search for identity', following these harrowing experiences, encompassed the arenas of nationality and sexuality in a passionately honest work.

In the next 'remembering' volume, Julie Rowlands, a woman categorized as 'learning disabled', made a plea for *An Ordinary Life*:

> When people use the word 'special' it usually means something nice and treasured. But when they use this word to describe us, it makes me feel just the same as when they call us 'mentally handicapped' or 'people with learning difficulties', or even when kids taunt us with 'Mong', 'Spastic' and Subnormal'. They're just different names or labels meaning exactly the same thing.

Write for Cynon

The Write for Cynon (W4C) project – supported between March 1997 and December 1998 by the Arts Council of Wales and Rhondda Cynon Taff and continuing into the new millennium in a limited and unfunded form – worked with nine groups of young people and adults. More than 200 people between the ages of 8 and 25 have participated actively in the sessions, most writing creatively for the very first time.

The W4C workers aimed to use creative writing workshop techniques to help young people in some of Britain's most deprived communities to voice their views, feelings and frustrations about living in their part of Wales at the end of the twentieth century.

Dreams and Nightmares

At 2 p.m. on Friday, 12 December 1997, Ann Clwyd MP launched the first publication by the Pen-y-waun Young Mothers' Writing Workshop (PYMWW). *Dreams and Nightmares* – a book of stories for children – is an important milestone for an area which only ever seems to get a bad press. The book was written by a group of local young women and has been beautifully illustrated by children from the Pen-y-waun Infants' and Junior Schools.

But *Dreams and Nightmares* is no ordinary children's story book. Its writers are mostly single mothers, none of whom had written, let alone been published, before. And the four stories they created reflect and deal head-on with the realities of life on estates like Pen-y-waun in a powerful and sometimes challenging way. 'Hit and Run' deals with the issues of joyriding and drink-driving, and the crippling consequences for a young child; 'A Dream Come True' charts the struggle of parents with a child with a terminal illness, and a callous theft; 'Christmas in February' is the tragic story of a house-fire which destroys the Christmas dreams of a young boy; and 'Lost' is a gripping tale of a young girl's experience, lost on the mountains surrounding Pen-y-waun.

While all of these stories are clearly based upon the darker realities of life on estates like Pen-y-waun, they all finally affirm the bonds of community life. They are encouragements to work together, ultimately positive pleas for cooperation and mutual care. The book is a testament to Pen-y-waun people's willingness and ability to understand and tackle head-on the problems that confront them. It is the good news that we rarely hear.

PYMWW offers the potential for women who have until now been excluded from local affairs to play a major social, educational and even economic role in their community. As a result of the scheme, two of the group have run writing workshops (funded by the Arts Council of Wales) in the evenings for young people on the estate.

The group has now completed their second publication, a 'collective autobiography' of one life made up of the experiences of them all. The book begins:

> My name is Penelope Wayne. I was born in 1969, 1971, 1971, 1975 and 1977. I live in a small estate called Penywaun.
>
> My earliest memory is of when I was five years old. But my mother's horror started on the day she gave birth . .
>
> Suddenly, the feeling of a knife sliced through her body. Reaching for the buzzer at the side of the bed, she hung on to it as hard as she could. The midwife came running into the room, cursing under her breath, obviously upset at having her peace shattered. 'What is it this time?' she asked.
>
> There was no reply from the woman on the bed. She was doubled over, straining and pushing.
>
> The midwife examined her and went running from the room. She quickly came back with a doctor following close behind. He explained there was nothing to worry about, but the baby was ready to put in an appearance. Unfortunately, it would be breech.
>
> After that everything was a blur to my mother. The room seemed to buzz with people. She was told not to push at all. The doctor wearing a jumper and trousers – as he hadn't had time to change into his gown and mask – gave orders to those around him. Suddenly into sight came a bottom. The doctor eased this out, closely followed by two legs and a body.
>
> All that was left was the head to be delivered. The baby resembled an ostrich with its head in the sand. After a few minutes, which felt like hours to my mother, the baby's head was finally delivered, a baby girl 5lb 13.5 ozs, born on Monday 10th March 1969 at 5.10 am.
>
> Bottom first and, according to my mother, arse backwards ever since.

Mixed Up Kids?

The Mixed Up Kids Writing Workshop – a title chosen by the participants themselves, aged between six and fourteen – met on a weekly basis at the Cana Centre on the Pen-y-waun estate near Aberdare. One of the early techniques I used with the group was the creation of 'collective poems', in which each child contributed a part of the final work. This process was intended both to remove the pressure to provide a complete work and to create a sense of cooperation and collaboration within the group.

What follows is a small extract from one of the early works on 'Our Earliest Memories', using this technique. It is significant that all of the memories are unhappy ones, posing the question of what experiences we are offering our young people on estates like Pen-y-waun upon which they can build a positive, constructive and caring future.

My first memory was
When I was about three.
I was at a fair
With my parents.
I won a goldfish.
I took it home
And named it Betty.
The next morning I woke up
And the fish was dead.

My first memory was
When I was one years old
And I drank a whole bottle
Of cough medicine.
The bottle was brown
And the colour of the medicine was pink.
I went to hospital.
I had to have my stomach pumped
And, as the pipe went down my throat,
I spewed all over the hospital bed.

When I was two
I was sitting on my settee
And my dog shit
All over my new dress
That my mother had bought for me.
It was red
And the flowers were pink.

One of the most compelling examples of the success of another technique used – the 'photos as stimuli' – came from a thirteen-year-old girl who used three images by Rolph Gobits, Cole Joseph and Paul Hill to explore her own experiences of an unhappy family life, thoughts of suicide and eventual resolution and strength:

Virgin is sitting on the edge
Of a cliff.
She thinks
Of all the hassle she is having.
Her father has turned
Into a pig.
Her mother is always
Ill with tonsillitis.
Virgin is thinking of jumping
Off the 300 foot cliff.
Below her
The long dark road
Winds beside the sea.
Her father was caught
Stealing flowers for
Her mother to make
Her feel better.
He was wild with rage
At being found out.
He struggled to break loose
From the shop manageress,
Who sprayed him
With pesticide.

He was knocked out
For 6 hours
And when he came round
He was startled by
The image in the mirror.
He had turned into a pig.
At home,
Her mother wears
A leopard skin
Belly dancer's costume.
Her pain is too much to bare.
She lights the fire eater's stick
And tries to burn
The pain away.
The house is in a mess.
The wall paper is peeling off
And the electric fire

Has been ripped
Out of the grate.
The father is ashamed to go home.
He believes his wife
Will divorce him
For looking like a pig.
Virgin has decided
To get off the cliff.
She goes home
And retires
To bed
For the night.

a bad name?

a bad name? – an important book of voices and photographs about life in the valleys, written by young women on the Fernhill estate – was launched on 1 February 1999. The seven members of the workshop who wrote all of the short stories and articles also staged the photographs, which powerfully portray life on the estate as they see it, including drug-taking and alcohol abuse, the lack of facilities, the dangers of the overhead pylons, graffiti, littering, theft, male aggression, sexism, the lack of places for children to play and facilities for all to meet, drink-driving, and the problems adolescents inevitably have with their parents and unemployment. It's a very long list!

The young women also typeset and designed the publication through training provided as part of the W4C project with the support of Save the Children (who also funded the printing costs) and the Arts Lottery Fund:

escaping Fernhill

One Monday afternoon, I wanted some peace and quiet because day in day out the people living next door blast their music.

I decided to go for a walk to the top of the mountain with my dog. It felt as if I wasn't in Fernhill anymore. It was silent from a few birds and it was so quiet. I could even hear the insects.

I know I could never stay up there forever, and it makes me feel empty thinking I have to return to Fernhill . . .

The W4C initiative is an essential part of a process which is successfully showing that young people have an important role to play in developing solutions for their future and the futures of their communities. *a bad name?* and works like it are challenges to politicians, policy-makers and all those with their hands on the reins of power to match the spirit shown by these young people in exploring without fear the problems which beset them.

Respite and diversion

But I am willing seriously to question whether projects like these really make any difference. Do they just give temporary respite and diversion from an unhappy life, possibly even making the condition worse by exploring its hopelessness?

The challenge for us now is to go beyond these strong voices – the explorations and celebrations of the extraordinary lives of ordinary people – to enable peoples' needs to be both expressed and met, to help communities translate their dreams into realities rather than, as is regrettably more often the case, to stage-manage their nightmares. The arts in this sense can be seen both as tools for change – the visual aids for the development of communities – and as the potential foundation for erasing the underlying causes of social exclusion.

Social exclusion is not the result of awkward people not wanting to join in our cosy game; it is a product of poor education, poor health, poverty, homelessness, unemployment. People who have little or no stake in society feel no compunction to abide by its rules. The real underlying issues are, as usual, economic.

Regrettably, perhaps, social exclusion will not be eliminated by the 'strong voice' option of cultural developments alone. If this were the case – given the investment in this area over the past two decades – we would not now need to discuss solutions to these ills which still plague us. The granting of Objective One status for the Valleys and west Wales is a great opportunity but at the same time a huge condemnation of the failure of our past programmes. If we are to be successful in future in tackling the real underlying causes of social exclusion, poverty and meaningless lives in Wales we will need to discover new, far-reaching and innovative policies, instead of trying to breathe life into the old dead ones. Culture, in the view of many, is the key!

The chief executive of Making Belfast Work, the government urban regeneration scheme, told a conference recently that if he was starting all over again now, he would begin with culture: it had proved to be the key transforming process in all that he had done . . . arts schemes open new doors and windows.

The disaffected young who would never go near youth clubs are easily enticed with music, art and drama. Art is exciting, it is status, it is inclusive, it is not do-goodery by others, nor does it proceed through quarrelsome committees. It has the power to transform anyone anywhere. (Polly Toynbee, *Guardian*, 2000)

Culture is today a driving force of our economy. It is the fastest growing sector in the UK, with direct creative employment rising by a massive 34 per cent between 1981 and 1991; it employs nearly 500,000 people (more than high-street banks and building societies combined, and twice the number working in the motor industry). The Wales Tourist Board identifies cultural tourism as *the* key growth area for the next decade, taking as examples the recent economic renaissances of Ireland and Catalonia which were both founded upon an almost exclusively cultural base.

Did the Millennium Stadium produce the new professional team or the team produce the Stadium? I'm not sure, but I'm convinced there was a connection.

The new Multicultural Arts Centre to be built in Cardiff will result in a huge revival in confidence and creativity of local groups, and this revival will be reflected in economic terms within those communities.

The Arts Factory in Ferndale runs five separate community businesses employing twenty-six people, making it the largest employer in the Upper Rhondda Fach. It offers training to a hundred people every day and 1997 saw a turnover of £320,000.

Valley and Vale's Ogwr Community Design (offered as a model in the report on Arts and Sport and Social Exclusion by the Department of Culture, Media and Sport, 1998) was a successful local business which spawned a range of new successful businesses and training opportunities for long-term unemployed and disabled people.

These and other embryonic developments offer real opportunities for the voices of the excluded to be rehearsed and heard; but, more importantly, they offer the possibilities – through community economic-development initiative in line with the knowledge-based and creative-industry future we are moving towards – to remove the conditions which create exclusion in the first place, to take the voices of communities more seriously, and to make the real change in peoples' lives beyond 'fiddling while Rhondda burns'.

15 How little things change: a salutary tale of the full circle of history

STEVE CLARKE

Crynodeb

Mae ymyriadau datblygu cymunedol yn arwain at drafferthion mewn gwleidyddiaeth leol, neu dyna sut mae'n ymddangos yma. Arweiniodd ddau ymyriad – un yng Nghasnewydd (Pillgwenlly) yn y 1970au cynnar a'r llall yn Abertawe (Bôn-y-maen) yng nghanol y 1990au – at adwaith cryf gan wleidyddion lleol. Yn y ddwy dref, cynorthwyodd gwleidyddion lleol y timau datblygu i gasglu gwybodaeth ac i gynllunio cyfeiriad a dulliau'r cynnig ar gyfer datblygu cymunedol. Galwodd canlyniad yr astudiaethau am brosiectau datblygu cymdogaethau. Yng Nghasnewydd, aeth y cynnig yn ei flaen, er gwaetha'r storm wleidyddol. Yn y pen draw, y gwleidyddion a gollodd gefnogaeth y cyngor a'r gymuned. Yn Abertawe, ar y llaw arall, daliodd y gwleidyddion afael ar eu hawdurdod i ganiatáu dim ond yr ymyriadau a gymeradwywyd yn eu hardal. Arweiniodd hyn at oedi wrth weithredu'r ymyriadau datblygu cymunedol, ynghyd â newid amlwg yn annibyniaeth yr ymyriadau oddi wrth reolaeth wleidyddol. Hwyrach fod yr angen am sgiliau diplomyddol yn flaenoriaeth i weithwyr cymunedol, ond yn sicr mae sensitifrwydd y cynghorwyr yn amharu ar yr elfen o ddewis sydd gan aelodau cyffredin y gymuned.

Introduction

> Those who cannot remember the past are condemned to repeat it.
>
> (George Santayana)

This study will examine two community development interventions in south Wales, separated in time by over twenty years. Both of these interventions were planned (in part) by the same person, and both experienced similar traumatic events around their launch.

The purpose of this analysis is to discover differences and similarities in the two examples of community development, and to suggest where some things might have been done differently. This can be done through looking at the basic design of the proposals and attempting to draw out any obvious defects. Secondly, the way in which the proposals were trailed through the political and administrative process might shed light on the rigidity of the barriers that presented themselves at the point when these projects became a reality. Looking at local government policies of the time, and at the professional culture, can throw some light on the way in which the plans for these projects might have been made. This might highlight gaps between the expectations of the parties involved, especially those in authority. Could it be a simple difference in the language used, or is there something more complex than that?

Each of these initiatives shared a similar fate, but there were considerable differences in the environment in which they were conceived. The first project came at a time when there was little experience in structural approaches to changing social issues. The second fell quite naturally within the expectations of central and local government in the field of overcoming marginalization and social exclusion. Over the intervening twenty years or so, the British experience of community development work had moved on considerably. By the time of the second scheme, a well-developed literature had emerged on the subject. There is, however, still a general lack of formal training for community development professionals and, as a subject area, it has slipped in priority. This has been marked within youth and community work training, and it has all but been eliminated from social work.

This lack of training is a strange feature, as there seems to be a wider acceptance of the discipline nowadays than there was in the 1960s. Professionals in the field are doing the job but, despite the apparent need, they appear not to have made the case properly for a formal education in their craft. For certain sectors of local governance, there is now government policy to ensure that cooperation with the community is effected as a precondition to obtaining funding. Words such as 'participation', 'consultation' and 'empowerment' are part of the everyday vocabulary of local and central government departments as divergent as planning, education, employment and personal social services. There are specialized 'units' serving social exclusion, poverty, urban regeneration, adult learning, etc., and all these tasks require that development takes place at community level. There are also expectations that staff will be better trained and prepared, and aware of the advantages and limitations of social intervention of this nature.

Council officers are now in their fourth decade of the 'corporate management' of local government (Benington, 1976; Cockburn, 1977), and local government is streamlined and modern. Its intelligence gathering and programme preparation procedures are now sophisticated, and its officials are aware of the need to consult and respond to community views of their work. Unfortunately, paid officials are only part of the story of local government. Politicians' sensitivities to anyone tampering with the 'democratic base' of their fiefdoms has been well analysed (Butcher et al., 1979), and politics, alas, seems not to have changed much at all.

1996 – City and County of Swansea

In 1996, the Council of the City and County of Swansea devoted the greater part of a full meeting of the Housing Committee to the rejection of a consultant's proposal for a community development project. The committee had commissioned a study of Bôn-y-maen, a high-profile, deprived area of the city. The recommendations, fully anticipated prior to the letting of the consultancy contract, were for the design of a project in which the council was to be an essential player. This surprise rejection followed an emotional and abrasive informal gathering of the full council, where the proposals were introduced by the consultant and then 'debated'. There had been considerable preparation for both meetings, and everyone concerned thought that it would be plain sailing. It was true that there had been some local political upsets, but the announcement of the project seemed like a good opportunity to regain the political initiative. What was to follow could not have been foreseen.

A working party of the Housing Committee and senior officials had overseen every step in the research and design of the final proposal (Clarke, 1996a). Local ward representatives had been briefed and kept in touch with the consultancy research, and preliminary findings were floated by them in advance. A meeting of all chief officers of the council had received a full preview of the consultant's report and presentation, and had unanimously approved it. When the public presentation of the proposal was made, however, the whole proposal was ignominiously thrown out. An emotional attack came from the ward councillors, and significant senior members of the majority political party added their opprobrium. Of the sponsoring committee chair, and the chief officers, nothing was heard.

The study had been originally commissioned in response to a localized outbreak of violence in this marginalized housing estate. A section of the younger population, together with the equally outspoken and unmanageable reaction to it by the adult community, had shattered the veil of official neglect and collusion which had prevailed over the area for far too long. One long, hot summer earlier, in 1995, the elected representatives, officials and police had been at their wits' end to find a solution to the eruption of anger and frustration of the residents of this troubled community. Public meetings had broken down as uncompromising views and veiled threats gave way to insults and discord. The council plainly had to do something, and appeasement would no longer wash. Despite the immediate political pressure, the housing department took the imaginative decision to seek long-term and proactive steps to tackle the issues.

There was considerable evidence of lawlessness among the young, especially the young men. Residents grew more and more apprehensive of thieves, vandals and street-corner gatherings of young people with nothing to do and a lot of energy besides. The local sport was to steal fast cars from other districts of the city, and race them around the home turf, to the admiration of assembled peers. Each ride culminated in a parts-stripping exercise and a triumphant immolation. The older faction would attempt to steal cars, successively working their way through the alphabet of brand names, while their younger brethren provided lookout and other support services. Police intervention was utterly foiled by the geography of the district, and the success of the early-warning systems. Vacant council-owned property was gutted by extremely young vandals, council workmen were threatened by thieves, and drug dealers began to operate with increasing boldness. The adult residents' response was to form a vociferous and extremely populist residents' association, which spearheaded a formal tormenting of the council and the vilification of the police at public meetings.

Despite the highly charged atmosphere, the council officers rightly judged that the situation was redeemable if the summer could be negotiated without any serious escalation of the trouble. Direct pressure was put on the young people through increased police activity, surveillance of public space and the closure of certain focal gathering points – one local public house was particularly notorious. This proved to be successful as a stopgap. In the longer term, however, solutions that tackled the underlying problems of the whole area needed urgent attention. The solution was seen to be a capacity-building partnership with the council and an increase in civic power and control over the social dimensions of life in the area. Community development, and the creation of a joint social planning mechanism with the community, was seen as the only way through.

A consultancy report into the area was commissioned without delay, and a proposal put forward for the shape and direction of a community development initiative. A research worker was sent to the district to obtain a round-the-clock profile of the community and its activities. Social statistics were compiled and the patterns of social and domestic life were chronicled. There was no attempt made to target economic activity, as other council initiatives had this under consideration. The focus for this initiative was the increase in the quality of social life in the area, and the capacity of the community to feel once again in control.

The final report contained the fruits of four months' full-time field research into the area: the nature of its community and the patterns of social organization. A comprehensive model for local community development, including preventive strategies to deal with the needs of young people, had been developed. Due to local 'sensitivities', publication was delayed until after a local by-election. Nevertheless, no doubt as a local reaction to the social outbursts of the previous summer, the local ruling-party candidate lost the seat to an 'independent', a prominent member of the residents' association. This was, perhaps, the symbolic writing on the wall for open government in the area, and the need for a scapegoat must have loomed large. In the event, at the informal meeting of the council before the Housing Committee meeting, the attack on the proposals was led both by the incumbent member of the majority party *and* by the newly elected, independent councillor. The project proposals were shelved indefinitely, but were finally revived, in much the same format some months later.

1972 – County Borough of Newport

A national voluntary organization approached the Newport County Borough Council in 1970 with the intention of opening a scheme which targeted young people and developed a strategy for integrating them into the service of the elderly and less fortunate. This scheme went ahead with the blessing of the council but, soon afterwards, the insights gained by the professional project team raised more fundamental questions than those that might be solved through the infusion of a few volunteers. Poverty and urban decline were the structural issues which most needed to be addressed. The council had adopted, and then shelved, a scheme for comprehensive redevelopment of one district of the town – Pillgwenlly, or 'Pill' as it was called locally. Its reintroduction was only a matter of time, and the social dimensions of this process had raised the interests of the voluntary project's team. A community development approach to combating urban blight was explored for this single district, and proposals were canvassed at length with Pill's ward representatives on the council, and the leaders of the party in power.

The district targeted for redevelopment was one in which there had been recent dramatic swings in political fortunes for the ruling political party. Intense local feelings about urban decline and housing blight had been harnessed by a populist political faction, and a number of Pill ward seats had been carried by them in the 1966 local elections. In the following years, however, most of these seats had been regained by the 'traditional' party of local leadership. There was now an air of optimism about the prospects for solving major urban and social problems in the years immediately ahead. In this atmosphere, support was given for the extension of the 'volunteer' scheme into the arena of community development, and a tailor-made project was designed for Pill. It opened in June 1971 under the name of Polypill.

Within months of the project opening (with two community development workers, and a part-time volunteer), the council erupted with attacks against the workers and the project. The whole concept was described, by one of the project's original sponsors within the council, as 'amateur' and as 'doing incalculable damage' to the local people (*South Wales Argus*, 26 July 1972). This had followed months of intrigue, consisting of covert intelligence gathering, an intense behind-the-scenes lobby and counter-strategy. It appeared that, on fundamentals, the project and the borough council were on irreconcilable paths. Irrespective of policy matters and the interpretation of statutory rights and obligations, ward politics were a matter of deep significance in the ensuing struggle. The issue of 'representation' would not go away, with both 'elected representatives' and residents' 'representative' groups claiming legitimacy from the very beginning.

In addition, from the start, there was total professional rejection of the project within the council's corps of chief officers, and there were calls for the subsidy to be withdrawn immediately. Their decision led to the council agreeing in 1972, to stop the grant to the project, and to replace it with a social services 'social work advice service' (*South Wales Argus*, 7 July 1972). This was to be staffed by 'highly trained professionals', whose task was to convince the residents of the 'benign intentions' of the council, and 'responsibly undertake a public relations function' (*South Wales Argus*, 17 July 1972). Battle lines began to harden between the 'community' and the council. Divisions cut across party loyalties and also some smaller political factions were drawn into the fray. Earlier, they had failed to make much impact on the redevelopment proposals but they now made their presence felt. This contributed to the general unmanageability of the district for the established political parties.

Locality and street organizations had been developed steadily by the project. They soon became powerful factors in local identity, as they generated purposeful agendas for planning their own environmental future. Residents wished to salvage something of their community, and their homes, from the council's 'comprehensive re-development plan'. Frustration at not being taken seriously soon gave rise to protest and resistance. In the short term, however, this would be of little consequence, as the council rejected the bid for funding the project. The community did not see a way forward for their agenda without professional assistance from the project. There followed a series of tactical battles, forays into 'higher' levels of governance (at the Welsh Office in London), and direct political confrontation, before the funding question was resolved in favour of the project and the residents' demands.

The initial role of the professional workers in this project was threefold: to gather information, both technical and social, on the area and the plans; to effect liaison between the community and the council; and to build local organizations within the community to digest the information and to respond to the plans. Early on, relations with officialdom deteriorated, especially with the planning department and social services. The former sought to defend comprehensive planning principles to a resistant community. Despite the Skeffington Report's stipulation that planning authorities consult their local population over all major planning proposals (Skeffington, 1969), those in authority over the process complained that they did not know how to do it! Newport Social Services rejected the whole idea of outside intervention, believing that one could not be 'professional' without the letters BASW (British Association of Social Workers) after your name. In 1972, many social workers (BASWs) had received no professional training whatsoever, since only a minority had completed the new CQSW (Certificate of Qualification in Social Work). There were a variety of 'training programmes' with their own diplomas, but some even operated on a letter of recognition issued by the Home Office.

A community newspaper was an early project (it ran for the next eleven years), and youth and social activities also featured high on the community-building agenda. The newspaper provides a comprehensive record of these activities (*Pill-box*, 1971–83). The professional workers gradually built a representative network of area committees, which were based upon the council's own redevelopment boundaries, and fused them together into a voice-piece and planning group for the whole district. In these early stages, only the initial, pioneering work had been done (about five local groups). There had been a dramatically successful summer festival, and the framework had been established for a parent-managed adventure playground. These methods would be fully consistent with Rothman's Models 'A' and 'B' – neighbourhood work and basic social planning interventions (Rothman, 1995; Henderson and Thomas, 1987; Clarke, 1996). Because of the area's history, and the collusive neglect by the council of the severe 'planning blight' which developed after the first redevelopment proposals in 1966, there was a high level of suspicion and anger at the state of local governance. Thus, the arrival of a community development team, 'independent' of the council, attracted many of those who had been active in the protests and political campaigns of the intervening years. The community development team, for its part, wanted to attract a 'following' so that it could justify its existence, but it was extremely circumspect about political alliances or 'extremist' views of any kind. Within the community camp, there were also calls for the project to be ignored as, at best, it would 'sell out' to the council, and, at worst, betray the residents to the authority.

The team was completely unprepared for the harsh reality of official opposition to what had originally been considered by the council to be the best possible solution to an embarrassing political situation. The team's strength lay in the rapidly growing number of residents who had had personal contact with the team. These had come to discuss their fears and aspirations for the district with the workers in the form of street and area committees. Residents found an openness and readiness to discuss and engage any reasonable issue, which was a dramatic change from bureaucratic indifference or hostility which ensued when the official, 'final solution' was queried. As opinions hardened, battle lines became drawn which were to outlast the early period of political upheaval. Luckily, one key senior councillor recognized that there was intrinsic value in the community development process, and this influence was sufficient to allow for some rehabilitation once the initial storm blew over (after another year).

Analysis

Early on in the Polypill (Newport) project, a community develop-ment worker received advice from a council social worker. 'Don't interfere with the elected representatives,' came the warning. 'We must not have any official contact with them about our work. They are the employers, and we are their servants. We recommend the same policy for you and the project team.' Things appear not to have changed too much, at least in Swansea. Social workers, at the interface between those who shape the policy and allocate the resources and those who are socially excluded – and vicariously sharing their life experiences on a daily basis – are warned not to trespass across the boundaries between public service and politics. No doubt it is convenient for both parties. But it cannot, and it does not, work!

Social work is a political act. It intervenes with the poor and attempts to enhance their lot. Despite the fact that they work for the local authority, social workers represent the whole power structure of society. They have to try to face both ways, and this role has to be understood. In the case of community development, as that branch of social work concerned with issues of citizenship, structural change and the brokerage of power, the profile of the political nature of the work is obvious. But has the track record of community development interventions, even in the 'extreme' cases of the Cardiff Hook Road and the Southern Link Road in Newport in the 1970s, or the conflicts of the CDP years, done any harm to local democracy? On the contrary, it is in areas where there are healthy community-building schemes that the very best relationships occur between the official and social dimensions of life. In the case of Newport, the leader of the council, and some of the new wave of chief officers who succeeded after the 1974 reforms, confided that democracy without tensions and frictions was not democracy at all. An informed and alert electorate was necessary to keep local government institutions up to their task. This was why the Polypill project was allowed to continue through six very turbulent years, and then to run for another six before being restructured.

Nevertheless, it is naive of community workers and senior council officials to think that they can ignore the baser interests of politicians. Councillors cannot do their job while simultaneously keeping abreast of community/ward culture and sustaining a political whip. They are extremely vulnerable to electoral pressure, especially of a populist and militant kind, but overarching political policies usually take preference when a vote has to be cast. Councillors rarely seek actually to generate change within their own wards in isolation from council or party policies. They have difficulty keeping up with the pace of change, and sustaining the quality of information which is necessary to be fully responsive to their constituency. They are mainly bound in to the policy decisions of their party, and they often get carried along on a wave of triumphalism when a new 'cure-all' policy breaks out from the secrecy of the political planning caucus. The professional, on the other hand, is best served through daily contact with the 'sharp end' of social developments, and by the quality of first-hand and personalized information so obtained. There is going to be imperfection on both sides, and community development workers are most likely to become personally identified with the work they are doing inside specific communities. Their investment in strategic and tactical activities becomes intense, and relationships within the community rest on a mutual dependency born out of their joint vision of the future. Objectivity is difficult to maintain but, nevertheless, the best form of support for local democracy must be for community development workers to become actively involved within the totality of this process on an objective and non-partisan basis (Hambleton and Hoggett, 1988). In other words, local representative democracy is also a part of the community development worker's brief.

The community development worker must develop the necessary mechanisms for sharing information and precise intentions throughout the planning stages of a new initiative. In addition, they must present the councillors with support mechanisms to assist them through the fast learning that will be required once community formations beginning to emerge and knock at the gates of the power-holders. A relationship of trust must not be taken for granted. It will take hard work and diplomacy to establish. But it will never happen if it has not been established from the very start. This was the essential learning in Newport back in the 1970s. But the lesson was not carried over into 1996. The fundamental reason for this was that, whilst there had been neglect in the 1970s, this was compounded in Bôn-y-maen. Modern time-constraints, detachment from the reality of governance through the consultancy process of project planning, and lack of sensitivity all contributed to the problems that arose. Elected representatives were to some extent taken for granted and also seen as a hostile and defensive force within the agenda for rapid change. Local political structures and systems are not altogether very flexible, either.

By the same token, political leaders must become aware of the nature of the process they are creating once the need for social change emerges and the actual planning of structural-change processes begins. They must look to the health of their democracy, and seek out ways of ensuring that they are able and willing to cope with the demands that an 'alert' electorate will present. The community development worker works to a pattern which, given the individual qualities and values of the individual worker, nevertheless produces predictable outcomes. Politicians must grasp the nettle of seeing local organizations spring into life, gain confidence and begin to challenge the status quo. This is the nature of the democratic, especially the 'developed' democratic, base of society. The professional worker is the key to this process, and should not blamed for the outcome.

We are reminded of the Shmoo which is freely adapted here. The Shmoo (invented by Al Capp, the prominent American strip cartoonist and creator of the L'il Abner strip) is a creature ten inches high and like a pear in shape. It has no arms, tiny feet, and big whiskers in its nose. The Shmoo has only one desire: to serve the needs of human beings, and it is well equipped to do so. It hunts out human needs and seeks ways of organizing public opinion so that everyone becomes aware of them. It assists people to respond to needs and gets them involved in their society at every level. It advises people on ways of getting the system to respond and, if it does not, then strategies for inducing social change are developed. Sometimes these strategies lead to conflict with those in power. 'Social change for the needy,' is their slogan. There are plenty of Shmoos for everybody.

Councils did not like the Shmoo. They ordered their inspectors to hunt them down, and kill them off. If the Shmoos organized the people, then there would be no authority left for the council – or such was their belief. This had to be stopped, and so the massacre was organized, with devastating effect on the Shmoos. Luckily, L'il Abner managed to save two Shmoos from the massacre – one male, the other female. He has secreted them away in a distant council estate, and there they remain hidden, breeding quietly, until it is safe for them to return. 'Folks ain't yet ready for the Shmoo,' sighs L'il Abner. But we all know that they are!!

16 The same old story: implications of current government policy for the involvement of residents in neighbourhood regeneration

MARTIN HOBAN

Crynodeb

Ym 1998, lansiodd Tony Blair bolisi Llafur Newydd ar fynd i'r afael â thlodi ac eithrio cymdeithasol mewn cymdogaethau tlawd. Dywedodd Blair fod 'gormod wedi ei orfodi oddi fry' ac argymhellodd dull newydd. Yn y bennod hon, mae'r awdur yn dadansoddi'r polisïau newydd hyn ac yn nodi nifer o fylchau sylweddol, cyfyngiadau a phroblemau. Mae'n dadlau mai ychydig iawn sy'n newydd am ddull Llafur Newydd – mae'n ei weld fel dim mwy nag ailbecynnu syniadau traddodiadol am bartneriaeth, cydlynu a hunangymorth. Mae hefyd yn dadlau y gall y rhaglenni newydd hyn gyfyngu ymhellach ar y posibiliadau i gynyddu cyfranogiad a grymuster yr union bobl y disgwylir iddynt eu helpu.

Mae'n cloi trwy alw am ddulliau newydd a ddatblygir o fewn a rhwng ardaloedd a grwpiau – dulliau sy'n pwysleisio cyfranogiad y bobl leol *eu hunain* wrth wella eu hamodau byw a'u cyfleoedd.

Introduction

Since the 1960s there have been a number of government initiatives in Britain designed to alleviate the problems of 'poor neighbourhoods'. From the Community Development Projects of the 1970s to the Single Regeneration Budget of the 1990s, poor people have been subjected to an array of interventions designed to alleviate the problems caused by poverty and exclusion. In 1984, Jeremy Seabrook posed the following question:

How is it possible that the kind of suffering to be found on any poor estate, in any city centre area, in any ghetto or poor district, seems to be beyond remedy? (p. 35)

Fifteen years later, very little appears to have changed as concentrations of poverty in particular geographical areas increase (Oppenheim, 1997; Power and Tunstall, 1995) and the gap between the rich and the poor widens (Social Exclusion Unit, 1998).

What then is the policy of New Labour in this area? What is their response to poverty, neighbourhood decline and social exclusion? What are their proposals and what roles do they foresee for local people in tackling these problems? In this chapter I will critically examine current government policy as outlined in the policy report *Bringing Britain Together: A National Strategy for Neighbourhood Renewal* (Social Exclusion Unit, 1998). I will conclude this analysis by considering the implications for community work practice in Wales.

Bringing Britain Together

In September 1998, Prime Minister Tony Blair launched the above report and outlined the policy framework to tackle social exclusion on the 'worst estates'. In the preface to the report the prime minister clearly states the problem from his perspective:

Over the last two decades the gap between the 'worst estates' and the rest of the country has grown. It has left us with a situation that no civilised country should tolerate. It is simply not acceptable that so many children go to school hungry, or not at all, that so many teenagers grow up with no real prospect of a job and that so many pensioners are afraid to go out of their homes. It shames us as a nation, it wastes lives and we all have to pay the costs of dependency and social division. (p. 7)

With reference to previous initiatives he states that: 'Too much has been imposed from above, when experience shows that success depends on communities themselves having the power and taking the responsibility to make things better' (p. 7). It is proposed that government policy will consist of three strands. One strand comprises New Deals for the unemployed, lone parents and the disabled, with action on education, crime and health. The second strand will try to ensure that national government policies are coordinated across a range of departments, which will impact on the neighbourhood and add up to a 'coherent strategy'. The final strand will comprise new funding programmes targeted at 'poor neighbourhoods', with £800 million being provided to develop and implement local area plans covering matters such as jobs, crime and health. 'Dynamic local leaders' will be given the power and resources to 'turn their community around' (p. 10).

In Wales in 1998, and in line with government policy, the Welsh Office launched its own programme to tackle social exclusion (Welsh Office, 1998b). This programme is called 'People in Communities' and its overall aim is to 'demonstrate that community based co-ordination can effectively tackle social exclusion through targeted action' (ibid.). In the first year, eight demonstration projects were selected throughout Wales with a total financial allocation of £750,000. Local authorities are expected to play a leading role in the programme, designating a 'social exclusion champion' and employing a development coordinator for each area. Social audits will be undertaken, gaps identified and strategic action plans developed. Funding will then be sought from various sources. Action plans are expected to last for three to five years. Partnership boards will be made up of local authorities, voluntary and private sector representatives, and 'local people from a cross section of the community'. It is anticipated that the boards will be chaired by 'independent' people.

What's new?

How then does the latest major initiative from the new government compare with previous government policies in this area? The main difference appears to be that while previous government initiatives had a purely area-based approach to problems of regeneration (Department of the Environment, 1992), the Labour government is attempting to tackle social exclusion through a series of social planning initiatives at a number of levels. In other words, regeneration policy will seek to integrate area-based programmes into the polices of central government (Nevin and Shiner, 1995).

However, a close examination of these policies indicates that there is really nothing new or radical about this approach. It appears to be a case of old policies dressed up as new, with mainly the same kinds of people, applying the same old formulas, within the same institutional arrangements. The strategy of regenerating neighbourhoods through the mechanism of 'partnership' runs clearly through new government policy as it does through Conservative policies since the late 1980s. While the philosophy may differ slightly, the mechanism for delivering regeneration is basically the same. McArthur (1995) states that:

> The theme of coordination, where agencies cooperate in a consensus based approach to develop and deliver regeneration strategy, is a long established tradition within British urban policy . . . Community Partnership can be located as a contemporary example of the coordinated approach, revised and recast to suit the context of the 1990s. (p. 63)

Implications for practice

It appears that while there are no radical shifts on the policy front, we are going to have more 'joined-up thinking', 'better coordination' and 'neighbourhood management'. While I am sure we would all welcome more of the above, what does it actually mean on the ground and what are the implications for practice?

Localized partnerships can mean low levels of resident involvement

Firstly, the notion of partnership, coordination and local targeting will continue to underpin the model of neighbourhood renewal. Used in this context, the term 'partnership' will be expected to embrace the government, local authorities and the private and voluntary sectors. Partnership is based on the notion of consensus over principles, aims and priorities and delivered through mechanisms of 'action plans' and 'programmes'. This approach is based on the notion that each partner has a stake in the regeneration process and that 'the best policies work through genuine partnerships' (Social Exclusion Unit, 1998, p. 34).

However, new structures and processes of this nature may not result in the active participation of local residents. The agenda for implementation will still be largely determined by the external perceptions of those who neither live in these areas nor experience poverty at first hand. This means that residents will still mainly be reacting to an external agenda. This approach may weaken local involvement rather than strengthen it. One of the basic principles of community work is that people who live in an area must be the starting point in any process of change (Frazer, 1996). It is the ownership of the action that increases involvement. Dudley (1993) distinguishes between the process of participation involving residents and the process as initiated by an external agent:

> Community participation in our [agency] decision-making process is a false horizon – it is a necessary step but it is not a goal in itself – we must advance our thinking beyond it. Community participation in our process is only important in so far as it can help us to improve the quality of our intervention in *their* process. It is *their* process which matters. (p. 164; my italics)

Disempowerment

Secondly, the emphasis on partnership ignores the fundamental issues of the unequal power relations between residents and agency representatives (Stewart and Taylor, 1995; Colenutt and Cutten, 1994). This form of intervention may further disempower the very people such initiatives are expected to help. Many people in these communities feel powerless to begin with (Frazer, 1996). People are already experiencing feelings of dependency because they rely on the local and national states for the basics of life. Far from being empowered by this process, they may experience it as another form of external intervention that seeks to determine *their* roles, limit *their* involvement and stifle *their* ways of tackling problems in *their* neighbourhood. The unequal power relationship between residents and professionals (Cruikshank, 1994) needs to be addressed as part of any regeneration initiative.

New roles and responsibilities for activists

Thirdly, partnership structures and managerial planning may determine the roles of local activists within the regeneration process. Activists may also be expected to take on increased responsibilities associated with the various stages of the 'action plan'. These roles may involve a great deal of unpaid voluntary effort. Small groups of activists will be expected to help with diagnosing problems, planning projects, implementing solutions and setting up and managing programmes (Stewart and Taylor, 1995). Those who have played the important roles of 'campaigners' in the past may now find themselves recast as 'voluntary service providers' (Conway and Green, 1996). The language of new government policy refers to terms such as 'community self-help' and 'volunteerism'. Such terms indicate passive and depoliticized roles for residents that may result in low forms of involvement and ownership.

This burden of responsibility in some of the 'poorest neighbourhoods' often falls on the shoulders of women (Campbell, 1993). Some of these women often have to juggle the main responsibility of housework, childcare and sometimes part-time employment. They often have unsupportive partners who actively discourage their involvement. Having to take on additional unpaid voluntary responsibility will do nothing to address these underlying issues and, for some, will merely add to their burdens.

Co-options and conflicts

Fourthly, the proposed model of community partnership may have the effect of co-opting individual activists into existing power relations (Stewart and Taylor, 1995) and away from grassroots and small-scale initiatives:

> The pursuit of the mega-initiative and of a consensus approach can swamp the foundations of local activity and suck community leaders out of their constituency and into a process that is not of their making. (p. 72)

Conversely, the process of regeneration has the potential for conflict to operate at a number of levels (Conway and Green, 1996). To begin with, it can begin at the vertical level between residents and agencies. Different cultures, class and power relations will exist between the partners. In addition, there will be different goals, expectations, interests, priorities and benefits within the regeneration process. Indeed, it could be argued that, within a structure of this nature, the more the residents are empowered to raise their agendas within the partnership, the more potential there is for conflict.

There is also potential for conflict at the horizontal level between the residents who are involved in the partnership and the wider community. Their participation within official structures will often mean they are involved in unpopular decisions such as demolition programmes or the allocation of scarce resources among competing interests. Residents will find themselves caught between the expectations of other partners and the many demands of residents in the locality. There are therefore real dangers, as R. Atkinson (1999) explains:

> There is a strong possibility that community representatives will find themselves committed to a view of 'best interests' not shared by significant sections of the community, opening up the very real possibility of a 'gap' developing between the representative and the represented. (p. 69)

Finally there is a potential for conflict between community groups within the neighbourhood. Some groups may choose to participate in the partnership while others will not. This means that there is potential for tension between 'in groups' and 'out groups'. Decisions made within the partnership may clash with the priorities and interests of groups outside. It could be argued that regeneration strategies of this nature have the effect of dividing activists and groups and thus weaken the long-term potential of local groups to develop their own forms of empowerment.

Management rather than empowerment

Fifthly, the process of management rather than empowerment may dominate the partnership approach. The effect of this new policy is clearly visible in Wales. As part of the 'People in Communities' initiative, local authorities such as Swansea, Caerphilly and Rhondda Cynon Taff County Borough Councils advertised for community development coordinators to develop and implement community plans for the first phase of the programme. In effect, a new form of community work role is being developed – a type of local 'manager' which combines some aspects of the traditional community work role with a clear coordination and management function (Rhondda Cynon Taff County Borough Council, 1999). While this role has been around for some time in various regeneration initiatives in Britain, it has now become official state policy.

While a traditional model of neighbourhood community work allowed the worker to adopt a wide variety of roles depending on the circumstances and the needs of the neighbourhood at any particular time (Henderson and Thomas, 1987), new policy constraints limit the role of the community worker. In effect, this shift reflects the increased co-option by the state of the practice of community work as a vehicle for social intervention in 'poor neighbourhoods'. This approach may see an increased emphasis on the strategic management of local area strategies, rather than the empowerment of local residents or wider area participation (Rothman cited in Henderson and Thomas, 1987). One of the effects of this approach may not only weaken the potential impact of the residents within the partnership process but also limit the development of small-scale initiatives that starts the empowerment process in the first place (Stewart and Taylor, 1995). The traditional role of the community worker as a full-time informal educator/enabler/facilitator who works to develop the widest possible empowerment and involvement within the neighbourhood may be no more.

'Capacity-building' will become a method of delivering sessional-based training with the aim of improving the participation of individual residents on the partnership boards. There is a danger that residents will be 'trained up' to be 'good partners'. There may be an emphasis on the 'how' of management rather than enabling residents to explore the wider social and economic issues that impinge on their areas. After all, training is not a neutral process (Freire, 1976).

Excluding the excluded

Finally, will this new partnership model actually improve the opportunities to include the 'voice' of the most excluded groups in the neighbourhood? On the basis of my working experience with colleagues in two major regeneration initiatives (Scotswood, Newcastle upon Tyne; and Perthcelyn, Cynon valley, south Wales), I can only say that trying to obtain resources for, and give a hearing to, issues relating to just one specific group, namely young people, has been a constant battle.

Issues such as gender are rarely addressed within these initiatives (Green and Chapman, 1992), despite the fact that it is women who often lead the process of action in many neighbourhoods and who suffer most because of blatant sexism and violence (Campbell, 1993). Minority ethnic groups are also often ignored or excluded within this partnership process despite the fact that racism is a major issue in our society (Joseph Rowntree Foundation, 1998).

Conclusion

Despite many attempts since the 1960s to alleviate the problems of 'poor neighbourhoods', there is a great deal of evidence to suggest that the situation is getting worse rather than better. The new Labour government has opted for a safe and traditional model based on partnership, coordination and targeting. Within this model of regeneration, it is likely that the involvement and participation of local people will remain on the periphery of the decision-making process.

There is also evidence to suggest that the traditional community work role will be weakened by the further development of new managerial approaches to local strategic planning. One effect of this development will be to further limit the already narrow base for educational and participative working at neighbourhood level. It is also questionable to what extent these strategic structures will challenge various forms of oppressions such as racism and sexism.

There is now a real need within the community and voluntary sectors to develop effective responses to such policies and to be able to argue for increased involvement and participation at neighbourhood level. For those of us who are committed to challenging poverty and exclusion, we must not forget that the notion of 'partnership' is merely a strategy and not an end in itself. It must be evaluated to establish the extent to which it responds to the agenda of local people. Local projects in Wales are likely to come under pressure as state and institutional funding programmes become increasingly incorporated within this approach. It is vital that projects in Wales seek to maintain their independence and assert their own agendas within this model. We need an empowerment process that seeks to change the nature of the relationship between the participants involved (Beresford and Croft, 1993). Crickley (1996) concludes an analysis of partnership working in the Republic of Ireland over the past ten years by stating:

> Partnerships I suggest can only be really engaged in by a well resourced and independent voluntary and community sector which can operate as

an advocate as well as a service provider in collective as opposed to only individual ways. (p. 30)

In addition, we need to be able to adopt and argue for alternative strategies when necessary. It is imperative that activists and workers who are uncomfortable with this approach and who are committed to working *with* people rather than *for* them or *on* their behalf (Freire, 1976), should seek to expose the contradictions and the limitations of these regeneration policies. Most importantly, we must explore new models and opportunities. It could be argued that the real dialogue first needs to take place within the neighbourhood itself, between the people who live there. A starting point must be to meet, share and learn from our successes and failures. Most importantly, we need to ensure that the people who live in these localities are central to the process of shaping and owning *their own* strategies to improve *their* living conditions and opportunities.

17 Conclusions: the choices that have to be made

STEVE CLARKE, ANTONINA MENDOLA BYATT, MARTIN HOBAN
and DERITH POWELL

Crynodeb

Mae gwahaniaethau arwyddocaol rhwng dulliau a lleoliadau deunydd yr astudiaethau achos yma, a lleoliadau hanesyddol datblygu cymunedol yn ne Cymru. Heddiw, mae tystiolaeth bod mwy o reolaeth ganolog, mae absenoldeb gwrthdaro, a sianelir mynediad gweithwyr i arian cyhoeddus drwy raglenni sydd â'u ffiniau wedi'u gosod ymlaen llaw. Ceir gostyngiad mewn mentrau cynlluniau cymdeithasol a mwy o ganolbwyntio ar ddatblygiad lleol. O fewn y cynlluniau hyn, mae dylanwadau ffeministiaeth a Paulo Freire yn amlwg, gan wneud argraff sylweddol. Mae mudiadau'r Gymraeg wedi amlinellu dull arbennig o ymdrin ag ymyriad sydd â'i ffocws ar y gymuned, ac mae gwersi i'w dysgu yma gan ymarferwyr yn gyffredinol ar sut i ddelio â mecanwaith ariannu. Mae datblygu cymunedol yn parhau yn weithgaredd byd-eang ac yno, yn y cyd-destunau mwyaf amrywiol, y ceir y modelau, gwerthoedd a fframweithiau ar gyfer ymarfer a all gynnig arweiniad blaengar i ni ar sut i weithredu.

At the beginning of the end

We hope in this concluding chapter to examine some of the lessons that have emerged from the theoretical and historical context, and from the specific studies of contemporary practice. It is quite easy to identify what the main issues are, but finding solutions to them may be another matter altogether. We will discuss the themes that have emerged, and we will consider what lessons for the future of community development can be drawn from this exercise. We have acknowledged at the beginning that our study is incomplete, as the field is too vast and complicated to cover in one attempt. Nevertheless, we believe that we have covered enough of the picture to make a fair analysis of how this complex and varied subject is being treated today, and how it emerged over the last thirty years or so.

We now know something of the special social and political factors that contributed to the making of community development in Wales. We can now discover what impact, if any, our history makes on what is happening today, or whether things start anew. The importance we are seeking to elicit from the past is firstly that it provides a political and economic backdrop for today's activities. It allows us to try to understand how the professional culture may have changed: values, outlook, employment patterns, technology, socio-political forces and so on. We can put the past in a new light, as we put the values and expectations of yesterday alongside those of today. From these, we can begin to construct a framework for understanding our own work, and we can begin to assess what is significant and what distinguishing features to look for. How have the forces from the past helped to create the strengths in our practice, and how have they helped to set up the predicaments in which we find ourselves?

There are also practical things to learn from these discussions. Strategic and tactical mistakes stand out starkly when there is distance between us and the excitement of the events. We hope that we can use this investigation to plan for more beneficial outcomes in the future and to gain clearer insight into how the pressures of the work can be tamed by building stronger ethical guidelines and frameworks for practice.

The focus for today

We begin by concentrating in detail on the messages that emerge from our current examples. The most obvious theme is the high concentration of work around locality development. This is emphasized by the relative shallowness of the planning processes done on the spot; in the locality so to speak. It appears that the funding agencies (predominantly local authorities and government institutions) play a pre-emptive and determining role in setting the scene for much of our material. This is not to say that our sample is representative (as we acknowledge in our introduction), but it is important to recognize the form in which the pressure from government institutions influences our examples. It is evident that there is a great deal of activity funded explicitly to implement strategic priorities that originate in government policy documents. Linkages with 'partnership' schemes, 'regeneration programmes' and strategic development initiatives abound (chapters 8, 10, 11 and 16). The money that funds this work is made available expressly to achieve the objectives set out by local and/or central government. The agencies that implement these strategies may be drawn from the voluntary, community and local government sectors, but they all go about their work in very similar ways.

We find that practitioners on the ground have few freedoms to select targets for intervention, and even fewer degrees of freedom over the choice of sector in which they are to work. This is despite the polyphony of exhortations from those who frame policy that residents/communities/stakeholders/citizens must exercise the maximum of choice over the areas for involvement. Nevertheless, the heavy hand of the funder is everywhere to be found. This reflects the tensions between the historical culture of community development and new approaches to 'joined-up government'. The current language of officialdom implies a new form of 'social contract' for citizens in their communities. In order that we attain certain social objectives, about which there is supposedly broad agreement in principle at official level, must there now also be conformity (or near conformity) of intervention methods? What are the implications in this for the sensitive and fragile methods of community development practice? What is the role of the practitioner in all of this? The worker alone carries the responsibility for convincing the citizen that the effort and self-sacrifice of a public commitment is worthwhile. The citizen has to be persuaded, and then convinced through some valued pay-off that the participants' best interests will be met through compliance and cooperation. Is this compliance with policy the price that must be paid in order that we may collectively strive for commonly desired outcomes? Are these priorities actually meeting the long-term needs of the people, or will disillusionment set in? Who sets the agenda for assessing the priority needs of the community? These are some of the questions that arise forcefully from our case studies. We are saying that 'partnerships' create tensions of principle for the practitioner because of the tension between 'top-down' policies having to be implemented through 'bottom-up' practices.

Partnership without equity?

We are concerned with the shape of the structures that emerge from partnership agreements, and agency service-agreements (chapter 7). Despite the claims of inter-agency cooperation, and policy documents that call for demarcation lines to be dissolved in the name of rational problem-solving, we find that actual practice comes out looking very different. Those with power (and money) forge relationships with the agencies from which participation and consultation is required. Then the 'community' is identified and a detailed initiative planned. There are preconceptions about desirable 'outcomes'. There is a sense that the quantity and quality of these outcomes has been fixed in advance. The obstacles or resistance that may be found on the ground, in the community, are the real problems to be solved. The citizen is being bound into the contract culture between the authority with the money and the agency that needs it to survive. Not much community self-determination here!

In these plans, there is usually no presumption that a 'community sector' will be developed, and there is no expectation of any devolution of power or funding to the grassroots. Partnership agreements rarely extend to the creation of a pot of resources that allows the 'partnership' to decide in what direction it wants to go or how to spend it. Detailed plans are laid well in advance, and the world of welfare, community enhancement, regeneration, health and so on is sliced vertically with one powerful and unsharing determining agency in charge of each (and the many) 'slices'. The reality for citizens is that they need horizontal as well as vertical relationships in a planning and capacity-building process. Real situations need to draw on all the available resources, and this means making organizational and working relationships with agencies and people from all different quarters in society. The strengths of all need to be pooled, and the most appropriate leadership must be selected on merit. People and agencies now need to receive a different kind of training for changed circumstances. Only in this way can the human resources be made available in a significant way to cope with the complexities of community development and for the processes that will emerge to change the social, physical and economic fabric of the community. Failure to achieve this will result in the failure of the programme, and the waste of public and personal resources. At the same time, however, the worker is in direct and continuous contact with the funders, or those who responsible for the funding contract. It would hardly be surprising if the pressures of goal attainment did not make a significant impact on the outlook of the practitioner and on the way in which this investment of skilled professional resources is deployed. This is one of the major forces that hold the structure firmly in the 'vertical' mode.

In these 'vertical' relationships, we sense an air of isolation among the workers. The essential element of community power (and we mean the ability to take meaningful responsibility, as much as anything else) is the need to forge alliances and to increase experience of and leverage over social and political processes. Workers have a duty to ensure that the efforts of their communities are not dissipated on fragile and petty activities, especially when greater potential could be realized through adopting broader horizons and more ambitious methods. This could cut across communities and agencies, and across the sectors of care, welfare and socio-economic concern. Being isolated within a micro-project is the best way of achieving introspection – 'small goals for small people' – and limited change for entrapped communities.

A step towards more sensitive insight

Four of our examples explore the dynamics of consciousness-raising, using feminist ideas and inspiration from the Zimbabwean training manuals *Training for Transformation* (Hope and Timmel, 1984) – chapters 4, 5, 6 and 14. From this standpoint, professionals seek first to engage citizens on the basis of personal orientations towards the community. Gradually their confidence and competence is developed to embrace, and then challenge, the structural issues that surround them. This approach has great strengths. It builds personal independence and self-awareness within a context of mutual support and sensitivity. It 'starts where the client is at' in every sense, and it allows for the take-up of new skills and perceptions from the relative security of a supportive environment. The 'whole person' is the subject and the object of the process. The worker has to develop a great deal of trust with the citizens, both individually, and as a group, if this method is going to make any headway. Once this achieved, however, then the ongoing support of the practitioner can be relied upon when situations push out beyond the customary boundaries of social existence, and into new organizational forms.

We can see the benefit of this method, especially in the context of basic agreement between the funding authority and the citizens' perceptions where they want to go. These transformation manuals were developed in Zimbabwe, where the national reconstruction programme sought to harness the goodwill and energies of all citizens towards achieving the post-colonial agenda. Within a philosophy of national agreement on the direction of change, and boosted by the spirit of liberation in the process, it is easy to see how morale and citizen energies can be harnessed and focused for common cause. Then the state's agenda changed dramatically to restructure the economy in line with World Bank and International Monetary Fund expectations. This saw economic and social conditions decline rapidly; they met head on with the people's rising expectations, and there was consternation in the community development training camp (Lennock, 1994; Balleis, 1993; MacGarry, 1993; Berridge, 1993).

When Training for Transformation methods are introduced in this country, into the time-strapped nature of funding and operational control which are the hallmark of partnership agreements and the like, we are not sure how they will hold up. Can there be enough input through our new policies to sustain citizens as they move into a state of fresh consciousness, confidence and purpose? They must achieve new levels of consciousness if they are to confront fully the structural and power interests within their present environments. We have very scarce resources and cannot afford to invest in outcomes that waste the real potential of the community. Nevertheless, the people may find comfort, despite the obstacles and restraints that we describe, in relatively unambitious projects. They may find more individual security within the cosiness of more 'domestic' and non-political activities, especially those that conform to the expectations of funders. How is a transformation to political awareness achieved? How are people enabled to take on the logic of the technical planning processes and the arena of political decision-making when their own perception of 'project' or organization is based upon a consensual view of community development? When we consider the implications of partnership and the processes envisaged by *Communities First* (National Assembly, 2000e), for example, considerable investment is being made, and the good burghers of Cardiff Bay will expect a solid outcome for their money. But if they guard against the possible liberation of the population, then they will lose most of the energy that could be released into the community for its own benefit.

Despite these cautionary notes, it is necessary that the identity of local community development work reflects the outlook and nature of the local community. As we highlight below, this process of transformation may have to be radically reinterpreted. It is most often the women in their localities who recognize the need to support community life, because childcare and other social needs impinge on them forcefully every day. They are the ones who can present those in authority with a meaningful description of local needs. We need their lead to find a way out of the dilemmas that this example reveals. In an age where there is a general abandonment of ideology, the common cause of women's ideas might prove to be the vehicle for community regeneration. Perhaps transformational groups can forge women's solidarity because of their special perceptions of local life. We suspect that they are aware of the need for more far-reaching transformation than pre-school play groups, tupperware parties and 'Avon-Calling'.

A departure from this is the study on poetry and community arts projects (chapter 14). There is a link here with the Welsh-language concentration on culture, and the capacity of the Welsh communities to draw on their rich heritage to produce community-forming, humanizing, spiritual upliftment from the most hard-pressed circumstances. People need to find expression for their powers to communicate, especially about the most personal aspects of their lives. In the struggles against oppression, community development often forgets how people can mobilize themselves for a multitude of reasons, and through a wide array of processes. In the end, common cause is what community development is all about. The example from the Rhondda and Cynon valleys is one in a long line of similar initiatives that have harnessed people's histories (for instance, an earlier Valley and Vale initiative with veterans of the Spanish Civil War and the Garw valley) with their desire to share the poetry of their lives with others around the world.

Reviewing the past

This picture of south Wales practice today, whatever its limitations, allows us to consider differences and similarities from our history. In many respects, they are worlds apart. In the 1970s, there was a wide divergence of intervention. The early days were marked by a dynamic tension that transmitted itself to the corridors of power. Workers appeared to have autonomy, or relative autonomy, over their target issues, and there was a presumption that citizens were free to use public moneys and to seek solutions to the problems that imposed on their communities. Class was an issue to stir the heart, and the feet, of great segments of the population. There was a stridency about the whole process. Organizations were seemingly prepared to argue and protest their rights and needs in the face of government opposition. There was also the presence, in the midst of community activity, of many activists who were not organic to those communities. They were those who were drawn from the professions and from academic life, and they sought a particular kind of social change and the convergence of society towards ideological goals. There was a unifying theme about these early activities, which appears to be absent today. There was a sense of striving towards belonging to or becoming a 'social movement' of some sort. The desire was to create linkages across social and economic divides for the attainment of socially valued objectives. These were focused, mainly, upon class issues, hostility to authoritarian government, resistance to victimization by landlords and activities aimed at taming centralized objectives like social engineering and planning (such as road schemes, redevelopment, 'consultation' exercises, etc.).

Today's activities, by contrast, are more aware of gender, race and other social oppressions. The personal welfare of all citizens is very much to the fore, and the linkage with the formal welfare and health service delivery systems is manifest. Today there is almost a complete absence of ideology in the way activities are presented. This would have been problematic in the 1970s and 1980s. Then, ideological labels were worn as uniforms in the worldwide struggle for the overthrow of international capitalism, the conservative government or the like. Today, practitioners appear to take a pragmatic approach to tackling social issues. There is an air of concentration on the presenting welfare needs of the participants, within a localized context. In the previous era, the focus was more on the overall situation, and the forces that set it up. Local 'struggles' merely identified the issues for local people and illustrated the general predicament of the poor and disadvantaged. It is interesting to speculate whether this trend is a reflection of a more widespread disaffection with common belief systems or with all dogma in particular, or whether this marks a genuine step forward towards dealing with today's problems today? Nowadays, class divisions have become blurred, except that everyone wants to avoid being in, or near to, the underclass.

Essential linkages

Two themes emerge that also distinguish modern practice, and they are closely connected to each other. The one is the emergence of the Afro-Freirean school of individual consciousness-raising (Training for Transformation – see above pp. 236–8; also the liberation of pedagogy – Paulo Freire, 1972). The other is the impact of feminist values and approaches to the individual in the community. Both require intensive relationship and dependency regimes. Through them, individuals can often make the journey to sensitization and awareness in relative safety, and can take up the challenges of confronting new understandings about the oppressive situations within which they live.

The introduction into post-industrial, post-Marxist, post-trade union Valleys life of a 'group-feely' approach to self-realization seems more like a candidate for an alternative religion than a route towards meaningful social change. Hard-bitten veterans of the 1970s might baulk at these. Nevertheless, as an approach to the development of communal solidarity, it does work to a limited extent, although it is a light year away from earlier approaches. Some benefits of this new method are obvious (we have discussed this in chapter 3, above); it recognizes that the bulk of community activists are women, that social issues concerning childcare, poverty, safety in the community and 'catch-up' employability are essentially women's issues and should feature centre stage in any 'regeneration' or capacity-building exercise. Instead of building on the presumed strengths of class solidarity and historical and traditional connections of place and ancestry, these fresh approaches draw upon the reality of communal life. They deal with the complexity of needs, the diversity of background, trans-generational unemployment, run-down residential environments, consumerism and instant-gratification value-systems that under-mine family life and contradict the experience of people in excluded communities. It roots its activities in the realities of everyday life of the participants.

The *Welsh* perspective

The issues surrounding the Welsh language suggest that there may be different principles in operation in issues where the Welsh language is the salient feature (chapter 12). It appears that the cultural ties that set Welsh-language schemes apart from the rest make their own impact on the process. These projects are prominent as mainly rural initiatives that gain their strength from national ideological considerations as well as local initiatives. Those driving these schemes manage to achieve priorities set outside the central themes of policy. Instead, they concentrate on the presenting issues in the community, with a heavy emphasis on cultural events. They then work backwards to the philosophy of centralized policy considerations, if there is space, if there is sufficient need and if it is thought politically necessary. It could be suggested that the champions of the Welsh-language cultural movement present a more assertive and determined case in implementing their own agenda than do the more 'secular' urban programmes. There is also obviously more involvement by formal agencies and authorities in the latter than in the Welsh-language schemes. What the Welsh-language projects have in common with these is a concern with capacity-building in the community. The main difference appears to be that, in the more general local authority–voluntary organization partnership, there is much closer control from the main funders. It appears, therefore, that there is greater freedom for manoeuvre in 'language' projects than in other lines of work.

The end of the beginning of the end

As local authorities line up with centralist policies for the regeneration of local communities, they are lending their support to the establishment of high-profile schemes. What remains in doubt, and there is not much evidence from our examples, is what real commitment there is to community development interventions over the long term. There is still no real evidence of serious evaluation of the projects we have described in this volume. It appears that the resources allocated to social programmes are sufficient only to the daily needs of the work, and nothing is set aside to confirm or deny its viability. There are strains here of the lack of official learning that was a feature of the Urban Programme back in the 1970s and 1980s.

These shifts in the ideology, and in the presentation of community development, reflect significant changes all around. In turn, they spark off some obvious questions regarding the fundamental nature of the people involved today and the purpose of the activity. Is the day of the eccentric, iconoclastic 'trouble-stirrer' now *passé*? Does the 'death of socialism' mean that community development workers are no longer to be the radical vanguard of the forces for democratic and beneficial change? It would be timely for a survey similar to that of Francis et al. (1984) to be undertaken in Wales. This might ask all the questions that are of relevance today, especially as there is a greater body of knowledge about the nature and purpose of community development than there was back in the early 1980s.

It is now time to return to some of the general lessons that can be gleaned from the whole span of this study. The early chapters dealt in depth with a more abstracted discussion of history and values. Now that we have discussed specific lessons that can be drawn from today's practice, it is fitting that we broaden the discussion again onto a more theoretical plane.

The individual worker: characteristics and preparation

The exercise of studying the history of community development in south Wales is a very rewarding one. The area has witnessed a rich tapestry of intervention, projects and social change experiences, which cut across all layers of life. Within the complexities of contending political structures, the aspirations, the personal feelings and motives of workers and the agenda of the employer, there exists an exciting mix of choice and opportunity. It is a potential minefield. Clarity of purpose and an ability to focus on objectives will be, and are, essential qualities for any that venture into the field. It is apparent that, despite varying complexities of management and stated frameworks and purpose, it is the worker on the ground that must take the most significant decisions on a daily basis. To do this, a path must be steered through the maze of conflicting pressures. In the end, it is the practitioner who is responsible for keeping the show on the road at all times. As many of the 'stakeholders' as possible must be kept happy for as much of the time as possible, in order to sustain the momentum and credibility of the project. Not many of the texts spell out what complex procedures might be involved, and sometimes experience has to be bought dearly (Clarke, 2000).

A community development worker has to be a versatile person, prepared and able to deliver a sophisticated service to diverse interests, simultaneously. The shape and direction of professional training for this person must be designed to provide for the varied needs that are presented. This image is in conflict with the commonly held idea that truly authentic community workers must be chosen from their own communities. Home-grown representation of this kind is seen to be the most able in expressing the needs of the local people, and to be able to communicate within their own communities with complete understanding. There is a definite problem of interpretation involved in this position. We must try to distinguish between a 'community activist' and a development worker. The one is suited to lead and represent the community. The other specializes in preparing activists, and all other members of the community, to represent themselves. At the outset, let us state that in the history of community development professionals there has been a fair quota of feckless, opportunist, inadequate and badly prepared 'professionals' who have not come anywhere need the standards required for this exacting role. By the same token, the roll-call of 'community activists' who have entered the development 'industry' contains a large number of breakdowns, co-options, defections and agendas packed with self-serving priorities.

There are in fact considerable difficulties facing an activist or community leader who tries to negotiate relationships across the line between the home base and the more formal institutions of governance and officialdom. Political parties are always seeking new recruits with potential, and community activists are a ready target for co-option and incorporation. Citizens are wary of 'representative' leadership, and are even more wary of their own kind appearing to cross the divide between 'local' and 'official' status. The halls of influence are already host to previous generations of 'local heroes' who have successfully made the break. Activists are already beset with the problems of survival within their own circumstances. They have few surplus resources to help them live a double life – to move within the corridors of power without joining, and at the same time sustain credibility on their own streets. They also have little previous experience of the standards and protocols of legal and policy structures. Very often these are false creations of those in power, and are erected in order to deny access or understanding to outsiders (Cumella, 1983; Zald, 1975). Nevertheless, these barriers are there, and wishing them away is not going to make it happen. We would not like to suggest that it is not possible to make this transition, but we fear that it is going to be extremely rare and difficult to accomplish successfully. Local people are extremely difficult to sack when they let you down because, politically, they bring their own constituency with them. Similarly, 'professional' development workers cannot truly aspire to this organic political relationship with the communities in which they work.

This raises the question of recruitment and training. Access to this form of education has been addressed seriously but, as yet, not on any large scale. In the past two or three years, some colleges (for instance, Newport College of Further Education) and universities have begun to provide progressive and incremental training in community work. This is, at the time of writing, awaiting accreditation, but there has already been the establishment of National Vocational Qualification (NVQ) certificate frameworks for NVQ 2 and 3. The University of Glamorgan offers a small modular programme as part of a certificate programme in community work, and the University of Wales College, Newport, has a first degree in Community Studies that includes a small community development component.

At the University of Wales Swansea social work students for the Masters degree in Applied Social Studies must all do at least one module in community development (they may do up to three modules). All must do a composite skills programme that gives equal weighting to community organizational skills alongside individual and group-work skills. Community development is included in the curriculum for the Masters degree in Public Administration, which started in October 2000. This university also boasts an undergraduate honours programme in Development Studies, and various Masters degrees aimed mainly at work in developing economies. There is also a community work package being offered by Swansea College, which is aimed mainly at access students looking for mature entry to higher education.

We can see from this that there are possibly between sixty and seventy students coming into the market each year with a range of insight and competence in community development. Most of these never have the opportunity to put their skills to the test, as mainstream local authority departments have not yet grasped the proactive, preventative nettle when it comes to social welfare. There is no career structure, outside the youth work sector of local education departments, and the main sources of work appear to be those advertised in the back pages of the *Big Issue*.

We have traced the sorry history of community work within social services departments, but there is hope that the National Assembly for Wales will breathe new life into the profession through its focus on preventative health initiatives. If this is the case, then efforts must be made to standardize training and educational inputs. There is a need, also, for the value of this activity to be formally recognized, and some regulation brought in. In the past, 'community work' was a job given to whoever was available, on a self-selecting basis. This did produce a corps of people with considerable flair, as well as integrity. However, this approach is totally unprofessional, and it will result in employers failing to come to terms with just what is required of the role. It will ensure that the special skills and values of development remain outside the pale of institutional respectability, and this will limit the influence that community workers will have in influencing the planning and implementation of social change strategies. The role of rectifying this situation may be one immediate task for Community Development Cymru (see p. 252 below) and, it is to be hoped, for the National Assembly for Wales. There has been a recent secondment from the University of Wales Swansea to the

National Assembly Ministry for Health and Social Services in community development. On the agenda is the training for health and social welfare professionals and the way in which public bodies take advantage of the opportunities generated through community development approaches to their responsibilities.

Selecting a framework and understanding the values

Stabilizing a purposeful, interventionist activity like community development is going to take time, given its rather maverick and untamed history. Meanwhile, the activity goes on, and people are being deployed whatever the career structure or field objectives may be. This highlights yet another significant question. So much depends on the model of intervention that is selected initially, and the degree to which all those concerned are aware of the factors needed for a successful outcome.

Community development operates at the locality level, or at the planning/problem-solving level, or at both, simultaneously. Just when you are sure that you have the level and the potential impact of a programme analysed and packaged, you discover that it has had knock-on effects in another quarter and the plans have to be redrawn. Someone has to take responsibility for the accommodation of new facts and fresh pressures. This is, finally, a responsibility of management, but, as we have seen, management is a relative concept in community development. All the 'stakeholders' have a legitimate right to exercise their influence, and failure to recognize this will result in frustration, conflict, and the failure of the scheme. The professional workers on the ground have the crucial role and responsibility here. Unless they know what they are doing, how far their responsibilities extend, and have the support of the other parties in the equation, then the result will be confusion. When a mismatch of expectations arises out of a change situation, it is the worker that must support the whole structure and assist it to make a soft landing. This is a social planning skill par excellence, but it is not one which is often anticipated when recruiting staff for locality-based projects.

We have discussed the question of values at great length. In fact, any meaningful discussion about community development is really about values. Depending on the level of sophistication of the planning process, and the height of any expectations of penetration and change within a given social/economic situation, so the relationships between contending priorities and moral judgements become more complex too. Another attendant difficulty comes with the perceptions and interests of the different parties involved. At grassroots level, and in the beginning, it may appear that simple organizational changes are needed. The human potential is there, the heart is willing, and the impetus is given. From outside, and with funding considerations in mind, the same initiative may be planned with the idea that, soon, the resource input can be allowed to wither away. The resources of the newly motivated 'consumers' must be manipulated and manoeuvred to take the strain, once the activity is up and running. We wish to emphasize again that this is a vulnerable position, and it reflects the fact that those who fund community development do not understand its key role in community life and continuous social change.

Simultaneously, the agenda of other stakeholders may require the same original development for different reasons. They may require that the planned organizations be formed to provide a focus for citizens. This will then provide a platform from which the first steps in conscientization, or critical awareness, can be taken. For them, this leads towards political as well as institutional adjustments in community life. The intention is not just to enhance the status quo, but to engineer fundamental changes in the order of decision-making and power relationships. Political will is required in this situation to ensure that any changes that do take place do so in the preordained direction, and that not too much is left to chance.

Both starting points share the same problems. When you start out to manipulate people, they do not behave according to plan. As soon as things begin to take shape, everyone's perceptions begin to change, people become more experienced and knowledgeable, frictions arise and participants begin to take stock of each other. Interpersonal politics and interorganizational politics rear their heads, and there is no real time to review this process. There is an initiative under way, and it must go forward, and properly. The worker has to perform a balancing act, engage in dynamic diplomacy and still maintain standards of output that have been programmed in the original strategy. Pleasing all of the stakeholders, all of the time, is likely to be an exacting task. There is a job at stake, after all! It can readily be seen that, 'If you don't like my principles, I have others.'

Among grassroots workers, the paramount concern is to ensure the greatest feasible level of participation, the widest choice for those participating, and the entrenchment of their collective will over the forces of change. They must also, somehow, safeguard the interests of individuals and minorities who may be potentially damaged by any changes in social forces that result. In the texts on development work for the developing economies, the whole emphasis is on the involvement of the whole 'community', using participatory evaluation, empowerment, conscious and reflective practice. In our post-modern, post-industrial and market-oriented social situation, this is never going to be a possibility. Nevertheless, this still remains the ideal, and the need for practitioners to seek out relevance of purpose for their work is always before them.

None of the studies of current practice has been set up on a conflict model. This is a significant feature of British community development, and we have seen how the trend has moved through the years. Originally, there was a strong possibility that citizens might be empowered directly through placing at their disposal the resources of a community project through, say, the Urban Programme. This created relatively unaccountable projects, workers who were more or less free to become accountable to their citizen clients, and the potential to engage in directly confrontational tactics with the local authority or other funding agency. Sometimes, as in the case of the Community Development Project, it was the workers themselves who set the criteria for success and the agenda for action and conflict.

There is also an apocryphal case of the schools' volunteering scheme in the English Potteries, where the project workers disguised their real activities from their (distant) employer. They worked on their own agenda for almost a full year until circumstances revealed themselves. At that point, the press announced conflict between the local council and a newly formed local tenants' association. This was the outcome of months of undercover work (Craig, 1974). The Welsh connection here is that one of the staff of this project was later sent (by the same employer) to do the feasibility study for what is today Voluntary Action Cardiff! Another irony of this case was that the Potteries council was so impressed by the bid for resources by the London-based agency (the 'distant' employer, above), that they took the grant-in-aid away from another local voluntary organization to give it to them. The displaced worker from that project then moved to the Welsh Office, where he rose rapidly into a very prominent position in social services.

To theorize, or not to theorize?

There is no adequate theory for community development (Midgley, 1995). Economic theories concerned with multiplier effects and markets may suffice under some circumstances; in others, the dynamics may be governed by theories concerned with groups, leadership and systems theory (Clarke, 2000, pp. 27–32). Certainly, in programmes governed by consumerist values, liberal theories about value for money and the power of the plan to deliver the required outcomes, then cost–benefit analysis and quantifiable outcome evaluation may serve as the best gauge for judging progress. 'How to' books all stress the *process* of engaging the community in the selection of their own agenda, and the essential valuing of every human input above all other aspects of the change process (Feuerstein, 1986; Pretty et al., 1995; Mikkelsen, 1995). For example, where do the Barnardos' support workers in Ely, Cardiff, stand in relation to the community's credit union? Are they helping to support a people's bank, a fully-fledged business enterprise, with hundreds of the local residents as shareholders, or are they involved in a sharing-caring relationship? To do both would exhaust the resources of most people.

The idea of community, or community self-help, or capacity-building may sound well around a policy committee meeting, but the practical implications may not be fully understood. How can a firm structure be conceptualized in advance and then implemented with any hope of certainty? We have explored how small projects impact on the sensitivities of politicians and senior officials. We have seen how the ambitions of citizen-clients are raised through exposure to the developmental processes, and how expectations can be thwarted if the potentials of change processes are not achieved. Much depends on the scope of the planning done before a community initiative is started, and much depends, also, on how the boundaries and focus are allowed to change throughout the process. Adjustments to aims, activities, values and objectives may require varying the basic premises upon which an initiative is based. It is difficult to work flexibly if the need for it is not anticipated from the very beginning of the scheme.

We have investigated the need for practitioners, planners, policy-makers and funders all to become aware of the way in which methods and roles can change dramatically if the concept of an intervention varies. Policy-making and planning require very different skills, perspectives, and even personalities, from those who have to implement them. Each level of intervention will require different qualities and skills. This is true for all the players in a process, and at all levels. Planners and funders must ask themselves what they hope to achieve by initiating activity at a local level without considering the impact (or lack of impact) on structural issues which assail any given community. This was the lesson from the CDP, and we have seen how the funders of that 'experiment' shied away from the consequences of their actions.

We can see from the history and from the current studies that much of the work is being done on a project basis. The scope and limitations of this approach must be recognized, as these will always be hostage to circumstances, timing and the specific qualities of individual workers and community feelings at a particular time (Chanan, 1992; Thomas, 1995b). Nevertheless, projects have some advantages. The essential trade-off in this form of practice must be between the level of direction and control exercised by the practitioner, and the range of choice and freedom of action experienced by the citizen-clients. If boundaries are fixed too rigidly, and the autonomy of the worker and the local participants is restricted, then the life will be taken out of the social change process. The management of community development, at fieldwork level, has to incorporate a very high degree of trust, and the accompanying level of risk must be accepted.

The climate under (New) Labour

We have attempted to trace the path of community development in south Wales since its limited beginnings, and to detect how patterns may have been formed which dictated the fashion for practice. We believe that there have been some dramatic changes in the way in which the activity has been perceived and implemented. None of these has been so dramatic as since the election of a Labour government in 1997. The previous Conservative government always liked the idea of community and self-help, but they did very little to sponsor it. Labour, on the other hand, has been until recently the champion of the collective, but on a universal or macro-scale. Localized activity and the pooling of personal resources towards local political ends was always seen as the manifestation of privilege and elitism. That tide of socialist thinking has now been radically reversed. The Tory idea of 'citizens' charters' and the passing of judgement has not been abandoned despite the decision of the National Assembly not to continue with 'league tables' in education. Additionally, in parallel to this, there has been the focused and targeted introduction of resources into those crucial sectors of community life that stimulate citizen effort and enhance capacity. Community development, of a sort, is the direct beneficiary of those resources. *Better Wales* (National Assembly for Wales, 2000c) must stand as a beacon for all who wish to take comfort that their waiting has not been in vain.

If we are to accept that this fresh approach by Labour is worthy of our cooperation – and the scores of people who are taking up employment in the field are testimony to this trend – then we might like to find a focus for our interest. This may take the form of a 'natural' source of employment, such as a 'home' in one local authority department or another. Community development workers have always been 'employees' in Britain, whereas, elsewhere, personal autonomy is fostered through self-employment and consultancies. Within a post-modern, New Labour regime, perhaps community development can 'get out from under' and prosper as an independent profession. Alternatively, consolidation of the workers' collective aspirations may take the form of a national association of professionals that takes responsibility for negotiating with employers on such matters as career prospects, self-employment, regulation and accreditation of training and professional status. Some of these may be easier to deal with than others.

It was the question of professionalization that divided the field back in the 1970s. When it came to a head in 1972, it forced the split with social work, which has continued up to and until today. That split may have been the correct one for some reasons, but it forced community development off the agenda of employer institutions across the nation. It also deprived professionals of a voice inside the corridors of power for more than thirty years. It denied activists, and others seeking a natural reference point for their activities, an institutional focus. It had the effect of reducing the status of a legitimate and complex activity at a time when other activities were gaining recognition and establishing organized bodies to defend their interests (for instance, youth work). There was evidence of this in the discussion and debate in the inaugural meeting of Community Development Cymru (CDC) in April, 2000. There is also evidence that CDC is destined to become the vehicle for grassroots workers and local activists, rather than the voice-piece for a professional group that extends from the grass-roots upwards into the echelons of management and policy-planning.

If the managers and the planners of community-level inter-ventions are not identifying with the workers on the ground, then the schisms of the past will be kept alive. There is no benefit from perpetuating a class divide at a time when the future looks encouraging. A way must be found to bridge the gap in order to establish a contained dialogue about the nature, purpose and framework for community development within a Welsh context. The wounding experiences of the early days of ideological differ-ences and the fragmentation of resources can be avoided if factions and levels within the profession can be brought together.

Theory, ideology, and the 'secret agenda'

Community development is a crossover activity, and an extremely flexible one at that. We have explored how it can and is being employed to further government strategies, sectarian interests and also to address the needs of oppressed and minority groups. Is community development possible in one country, or does it address global issues at the local level, for the relief of localized suffering?

Most of our case-study material illustrates how the agency that controls the purse strings also controls the direction and planned outcomes of the development activities. Is there something special about community development practice in Wales, or in some specific class or geographical setting, that can transcend this restraint? Is it time for a new dimension of ideology to be developed from within the community development movement that can promote a definitive, desired agenda for this kind of social intervention? Somehow, the mechanisms must be created to examine new models of development, and new and equitable approaches to the distribution of the benefits of change and 'progress'. The emergence of CDC and the rich experience of work in this country must certainly provide a basis for some serious work to be done on this issue. The presumptions of development as planned change, the expectations of government that their wishes be met to justify funding, and the detachment of individual workers from meaningful contact with fellow citizens because of the death of ideology, traditional social ties, and the solidarity of class can and, we contend, must be challenged.

People do not want to feel that they are being manipulated, that outsiders are prying into their lives (and their life chances), but they also readily acknowledge that, without the special assistance that community development workers provide, they would not have been able to organize around their specific needs. If community development does contribute a unique and irreplaceable ingredient into their progress towards meeting these needs, should this work be required to declare its implicit value and or ideological purpose? Does this 'secret agenda' have special significance for Wales and for the shape of our society's future?

Looking for an ethical framework

We have demonstrated that there is no code of ethics, no statement of values, no common framework or frame of reference which is universally accepted by the body of workers in community development. This means that employers and employees alike are free to undertake any activity, on whatever basis they consider fit, without any fear of sanction, criticism or moral regulation by anyone. Employers will always be in the driving seat in this situation. If workers could agree a common approach to what they are doing and be prepared to stand up for certain principles, then they could impose limits on employers and the shape of developmental initiatives in which they participate. Solidarity and unity of purpose has not proved to be a strong point in the past, but perhaps this is the time to launch a new attempt to bring all levels of the profession together through CDC.

CDC has produced a statement about the nature and purpose of community development. It reflects the limiting role within which most community development practitioners cast themselves. The CDC statement is all about the maximum feasible amount of participation and choice that citizens can presume to have, as of right, in a developmental process. The statement reflects the inability of workers ever to visualize that their 'clients' could really participate fully in the real arenas of the power system: the planning and decision-making processes. Part of this is because there is a basic distrust of the planning and decision-making process by the practitioners, and they have no desire to witness 'their' citizens taking any part in these 'corrupt' and controlling processes. Many community workers are very cynical about the representational political system and the power interests of officialdom. They have mixed feelings about fully involving community-based organizations in its processes (Cumella, 1983). In the current low-status position of the profession, workers have themselves become dependants of centralized planning systems, where, as employees, they exercise little influence over the structures of decision-making. Thus, they cannot visualize the role any more, nor see beyond their own situation in order to promote their client communities into a dynamic relationship with their employers.

The skill of the consummate community development workers is to function as effectively at the sharp end of organizing participation at the grassroots level of development, as they do within the corridors of power and influence. The citizen-clients of community development must expect to be members of the power systems, with the rights and the capacities to choose how they prefer their own futures to be planned and changed. Drawing in the power and the experience of citizens – organized and prepared citizens – to the decision-making process on merit is the function of the professional developmental role (Clarke, 2000). If the managers were absent from the inaugural meeting of CDC then it was as much because of this limiting perspective that most field workers have about themselves, as any other. There was 'nothing in it for them'. They could expect that there would be antagonism from 'below', and they recognize that the workers at the grassroots level lack any substantial power. This situation will continue until the citizens, rather than the professional developers of the citizens, demand their own place around the decision-making table. What do you do? You are a professional, with the training, the insight and the ability to plan ahead and foresee the shape of the future in social, political and economic terms. Then you are faced with the need to act to take advantage of a 'window' of opportunity for making your role significant within the official scheme of things. Do you set this aside until the citizen-client is in a position to exercise control personally/collectively? How does one choose when faced with two or more moral choices or ways forward that are of equal moral worth? Someone has to make a decision, and that, in the final analysis, is the professional. To do less would be to deny the special skill and preparation upon which the role is founded.

The situation is complex; even when there is a relatively uncomplicated relationship between the worker and the community. This can become much more complicated when institutional forces become involved. There are many who call into question the role of organized or entrenched 'organizers', who dominate the voluntary sector and who establish powerful positions as intercessory agents – those that control the process of access. They not only stand between the funders/planners/policy-makers and the citizens, but they also exercise executive authority over the resources that pass thorough their hands. In some situations, they appear to be the source of all good things themselves. Unless challenged, they may never have to divulge that they are not really in ultimate control (Midgley, 1981; Chambers, 1983; Fowler, 1997; Green and Mattias, 1997; Guijt and Shah, 1998; Edwards and Hulme, 1995; Goulet, 1995; Hulme and Edwards, 1997).

We have already commented on the question of 'working yourself out of a job'. The conflict of ethics is very apparent in a situation where there is no career structure in community develop-ment, and this forces workers to 'move on'. At the same time, if they do stay, they become compendiums of local knowledge, sources of instant access to the community (and to the networks of power outside the community). They can broker 'deals' based upon their own 'good offices', and they can speak with great authority on behalf of 'their' communities. From the point of view of the community, it must appear greatly disadvantageous that their resource workers are removed (and often not replaced) at the time when they become most productive. If they are replaced with new, cheaper, short-contract staff, then citizens can foresee more movement and instability in the future (Cumella, 1983; Clarke, 2000). From the point of view of a funder or a local authority, a long-term key worker can be seen as a malleable instrument with direct influence over the direction of the intervention. The more vulnerable the worker is to outside pressure of this kind, the more vulnerable the community becomes to getting less than a truly impartial service. Workers must be able to understand, evaluate and publicly acknowledge these tensions, and to establish an ethical framework for dealing with personal, community and political pressures.

What degree of sophistication are we looking for in the community practitioner? Can we expect our communities to expect less than the best? Is community development an ecological activity? If it is, then who sets the boundaries for understanding or organizing? We have looked at models of intervention that can embrace life and change at all levels and about all matters. Alternatively, community development can be a limited and confined activity. It can set or be set boundaries of change where needs are seen to be local and immediate, accepting the wider social, political and economic order and not looking to change any of it. Some of us will say that, in practice, the boundaries are set by the employer and so the worker must just get on with the job. Others are driven by a world-view, and wish to make the links at all levels and across all boundaries. Some perceive that they have the freedom to choose one or the other; others believe that they have very limited freedom. Yet another group has never thought about it.

The role of the coordinator

In our discussions, we have considered how the new Community Development Cymru can influence the future directions of community development in Wales. We have done this as a response to a new phenomenon, but we are mindful of the role over the years that has been delivered by coordinating organizations – the Wales Council for Voluntary Action (WCVA), and the counties' Councils for Voluntary Service (CVS). The WCVA has been a supporter of community development since the very earliest days of community activism in the 1970s. In those days, the organization was dominated by the caucus of traditional voluntary organizations, most of whom had never considered anything but a charitable approach to welfare outside the state services. They also saw their whole sector as being completely distinct from state services, funded largely by bequests and fund-raising, unlike today's heavy dependence on contracts and partnerships. With the advent of the Urban Programme and the Skeffington Report on planning, came an increased interest by the Welsh Office in the funding and extension of citizen activity down to the grassroots. Her Majesty's Inspectorate of Education (the HMIs), and the new Social Services Inspectorate played an important role in promoting the Urban Programme and its take-up by the voluntary sector and, in particular, by small-scale community groups. A number of established agencies (three funded by the Young Volunteer Force Foundation (YVFF) and Cardiff's CVS) actively sought out community initiatives in adventure play and project-based work. WCVA acted as a broker for the Welsh Office, whose officials could not be seen directly to sponsor local activities. Together with workers from YVFF and the Welsh Office, a guide for applying for Urban Programme funding was published and a network for mutual support established. Through this mechanism, the Welsh Office was able to obtain intelligence about the feelings at the grassroots, and this assisted them in prioritizing the bids for Urban Aid as they arrived from the local authorities. It was not unknown for the Welsh Office to overturn an individual local authority's priorities, and to favour community and developmental applications instead of straight, centrally controlled service schemes (an example of this is the Newport project described in chapter 15).

WCVA has continued to support community development. It has a much more substantial role in Welsh affairs since moving from those cramped quarters on Cathedral Road. It has provided resources for the coordination and development of community work training accreditation. It has sustained the momentum of the Community Work Training Group, the Welsh arm of the Federation of Community Work Training Groups. In recent years, it has managed Jigso, the community-level capacity-building agency and, until the advent of CDC, it sustained the Standing Conference for

Community Development in Wales. In 2000, it moved from Caer-philly to premises only a stone's throw from the National Assembly in Cardiff Bay. This physical proximity will reinforce the relation-ship forged over the successfully negotiated Compact between the Voluntary Sector and the National Assembly that highlighted community development as a special protocol (National Assembly/ Wales Council for Voluntary Action, 2000).

This item has not been included as a propaganda vehicle for WCVA, and there are obvious limitations for national institutions when confronted by local needs. What this section serves to promote, however, is the function of centralized planning and coordination within a profession that does not shine much in this respect. At the local level, counties (all twenty-two!) have their own coordinating organization. Since the latest reorganization of local government and the assumption of the National Assembly, it has been deemed necessary to establish coordinating agencies on the same pattern as local government. This was, apparently, the case before but, in the famous case of Swansea, during the 1980s, the West Glamorgan Voluntary Service Council coexisted in its major population centre with the Swansea Council of Voluntary Service. Negotiating separate domains proved to be a ticklish experience for all concerned, which could not be resolved until they merged.

The lessons here are about power, centralization, the function and impact of planning agencies and the problems associated with coordination and liaison. New formations are now emerging, this time in the sphere of health (Clarke, 1998). The Health Alliances are a direct response to the National Assembly's need for inter-agency, and interdisciplinary cooperation. As these alliances will coordinate all non-NHS aspects of public health, they will make a huge impact on developmental strategies, particular at the local level. It will be more difficult than ever for workers on the ground to set their own objectives, as there will be unremitting pressure for local effort to be included in coordinated initiatives.

A future in the new Wales

The introduction of government policies in the community arena still falls short of a formal recognition of a 'community sector'. These new programmes carry with them a powerful element of centralist control, and start with the premise that local policy emanates from the centre. At the end of 1999, the then secretary for economic development of the National Assembly for Wales issued a consultation document outlining the establishment of a Local Regeneration Fund. It invited comment on the move to consolidate the Strategic Development Scheme (SDS) funds into the local authorities' normal budget, and to create a new fund, the Local Regeneration Fund. The voluntary sector will be allowed a measured percentage of this new fund, and the consolidation of the SDS will mean more local control over the allocation of spending in this area.

In another 'initiative', the National Assembly has announced a 'new concept in community regeneration' – *Communities First* (National Assembly, 2000a, p. 5). This document recognizes that, 'Throughout Wales there are examples of self-starting, community based projects which exist to tackle social disadvantage and recreate communities where people are pleased to live' (p. 3). This document does mention community development, but it does so as if 'participation and sustainability' (p. 7) just materialize. Apparently, these 'self-starting' community efforts are able to burst spontaneously into life. This document demonstrates how little those in high places know about the process of community development. In their follow-up document *Communities First – The Way Forward* (National Assembly for Wales, 2000e), the questions are asked: what is participation, and how is it achieved? The tenor of this consultative document demonstrates just how far away are the capabilities to build the capacity of the communities that are in the greatest need (http://www.wales.gov.uk/polinfo/housing/consultationpapers/cf2/CF2main_e.htm – accessed 8 January 2001). There is such an air of unreality about this. Restructured economies, fragmented communities, a national philosophy of survivalism, individualism and opportunism do not add up to spontaneous community regeneration. The essential ingredient is missing – the community development worker. The challenge for the National Assembly is how properly to resource the communities so that they can create the space and the capacity to accept new collective responsibilities, over and above the challenge of survival in a competitive environment.

In a supranational context, we might have drawn some succour from the prime minister before and after the last general election.

It was alleged that Mr Blair is a disciple of communitarianism (*The Times*, 25 March 1995). This is the American, middle-class community-building movement championed by the sociologist Amitai Etzioni. From the public announcements of the National Assembly, it appears that the depressed communities of the Valleys in Wales are to be urged to emulate the efforts of middle-class communities in the United States. These are heavily into becoming self-stimulating, self-resourcing, community-building social systems (Etzioni, 1993, 1995a and 1995b; Atkinson, 1995; Sacks, 1995). These American communities are the bastions of the 'American Dream', where the virtues of the neighbourhood school and the two-parent family set the tone for the stable society. Actually, this approach also reflects the core idea of professionalization. But in the American context, it is the well-resourced, well-educated community that musters all the necessary skills and resources from within itself. How this process can be resourced from the communities in south Wales is another matter entirely.

Final statement

In this study, we have drawn on the experiences of local workers, and yet we have found that we must refer far and wide to find the theory and models for action. Only in this way can we best inform ourselves how to analyse our own history. Community development is a global discipline, adapting itself to suit local conditions and cultures (Midgley, 1997). Nevertheless, moving along parallel lines, we have found common cause in the most disparate circumstances. The influences of the global economic market impact every bit as strongly in Wales as they do in Scotland, Africa or the Far East, albeit that the British safety net is better constructed and the poor better protected. Allowing for the widely different social settings of the work, the issues being faced are remarkably similar. The human potential and capacity to organize for common cause is one of the sustaining rewards for workers everywhere. Even where workers are bound by restrictive controls, and are harried by political interference to the point of corruption (Marris and Rein, 1967; Edwards and Hulme, 1995; Hulme and Edwards, 1997; Porter et al., 1991; Rondinelli, 1993), the same aims keep coming through: maximum feasible participation; build organizations for power;

plan, execute, reflect and plan, then act again. Not only have we been able to draw on the work being done in the Celtic fringe, Wales's cultural and geographical neighbours, but we can draw great strength from the fact that work here in Wales mirrors the experience and standards found anywhere else. Thus, workers in Wales can draw support from the lessons of others. Similarly, they have a contribution to make internationally towards the achievement of objectives of the profession as a whole. The enduring responsibility we have is to be mindful of the work of others, and to ensure that we are making them mindful of ours.

Endpiece

The most significant questions that have emerged from this exercise are:

- Who defines 'community', and to what extent does this determine the actual power relationship between citizens, worker and funders/authority?
- Who sets the boundaries of the organization, and the target action area?
- Will the citizens ever be given the authority to determine the agenda for the 'experts' that they employ to serve them?
- Will the masses ever be trusted with self-determination, and be allowed to 'squander' their own resources on 'mistakes'?
- What is the role of government in the generation of community-based development, and can truly 'bottom-up' planning and decision-making systems be established?
- Are the interests of professionalism truly committed to sharing the 'secrets' of power creation? We have still to discover how far down the trail to citizen emancipation professional community development practitioners want to go.
- Can community organizations create the space for themselves to break down the barriers of parochialism, and join in wider coalitions for power and influence?
- Can we remain forever open to the values, ideas and models for practice from around the world?

254 S. CLARKE, A. MENDOLA BYATT, M. HOBAN, D. POWELL

Whatever the answers to these questions are, we are still committed to the philosophy of a higher authority:

> Whatever fortune brings,
> Don't be afraid of doing things
>
> A.A. Milne

Bibliography

Abel-Smith, B. and P. Townsend (1965). *The Poor and the Poorest*, London, Bell.

Adams, B. (1993). Sustainable development and the greening of development theory, in F. J. Schuurman (ed.), *Beyond the Impasse: New Directions in Development Theory*, London, Zed Books.

Adams, R. (1996). *Social Work and Empowerment* (2nd edn), London, Macmillan.

Alinsky, S. D. (1969). *Reveille for Radicals*, New York, Vintage Books.

Alinsky, S. D. (1972). *Rules for Radicals: A Programmatic Primer for Realistic Radicals*, New York, Vintage Books.

Anderson, M. B. (1999). Understanding difference and building diversity: a challenge to development initiatives, in M. B. Anderson, *Development and Social Diversity*, Oxford, Oxfam, pp. 7–15.

Antrobus, P. (1991). Women in development, in T. Wallace and C. March (eds), *Changing Perceptions: Writings on Gender and Development*, Oxford, Oxfam, pp. 311–17.

Archbishop of Canterbury's Commission on Urban Priority Areas (1985). *Faith in the City: A Call for Action by the Church and Nation*, London, Church House Publishing.

Ardener, S. and S. Burman (eds) (1995). *Money-go-Rounds: The Importance of Rotating Savings and Credit Associations for Women*, Oxford, Berg.

Ardrey, R. (1966). *The Territorial Imperative: A Personal Inquiry into the Animal Origins of Property and Nations*, New York, Kodansha International.

Arnstein, S. (1969). A ladder of citizen participation, *Journal of the American Institute of Planners*, Vol. 35, No. 4, pp. 216–24.

Association of Community Workers (1981). *The Community Worker's Skills Manual* (2nd edn), London, Association of Community Workers.

Atkinson, D. (1995). *The Common Sense of Community*, London, Demos.

Atkinson, R (1999). Discourses of partnership and empowerment in contemporary British urban regeneration, *Urban Studies*, Vol. 36, No. 1, pp. 59–72.

Bailey Jnr., R. (1974). *Radicals in Urban Politics: The Alinsky Approach*, Chicago, University of Chicago.

Baldock, P. (1974). *Community Work and Social Work*, London, Routledge and Kegan Paul.

Baldock, P. (1977). Why community action? The historical origins of the radical trend in British community work, *Community Development Journal*, Vol. 12, No. 2, pp. 68–74.

Baldock, P. (1983). Community development and community care, *Community Development Journal*, Vol. 18, No. 3, pp. 231–7.

Ball, C., M. Ball and M. Dungate (eds) (1980). *Community Works 1: Aspects of Three Innovatory Projects*, London, Community Projects Foundation.

Ballard, P. (1985). A theology of church-based community work, in W. Godfrey (ed.), *Down to Earth: Stories of Chuch-based Community Work*, London, British Council of Churches, pp. 79–87.

Ballard, P. (ed.) (1990). *Issues in Church-related Community Work*, Cardiff, Collegiate Faculty of Theology, University of Wales Cardiff.

Balleis, P., SJ. (1993). *ESAP and Theology*, Gweru, Silveira House/Mambo Press.

Banks, S. (1995). *Ethics and Values in Social Work*, London, Macmillan.

Barclay, P. M. (chair) (1982). *Social Workers: Their Role and Their Tasks*, London, Bedford Square Press/NISW.

Barr, A. (1991). *Practising Community Development: Experience in Strathclyde*, London, Community Development Foundation.

Barr, A. (1996). *Practising Community Development* (revised edn), London, Community Development Foundation.

Barr, A., S. Hashagen and R. Purcell (1996a). *Monitoring and Evaluation of Community Development in Northern Ireland*, Belfast, Voluntary Activity Unit/Department of Health and Social Services.

Barr, A., S. Hashagen and R. Purcell (1996b). *Measuring Community Development in Northern Ireland: A Handbook for Practitioners*, Belfast, Voluntary Activity Unit/Department of Health and Social Services.

Baruah, M. (1997). *Making Voices Heard: Access to Services by Black and Ethnic Minority Women*, Swansea, City and County of Swansea.

Batten, T. R. (1957). *Communities and their Development*, London, Oxford University Press.

Batten, T. R. (1962). *Training for Community Development: A Critical Study of Method*, London, Oxford University Press.

Batten, T. R. (with collaboration of Madge Batten) (1965). *The Human Factor in Community Work*, London, Oxford University Press.

Batten, T. R. (with collaboration of Madge Batten). (1967). *The Non-Directive Approach in Group and Community Work*, London, Oxford University Press.

Benington, J. (1970). Community development project, *Social Work Today*, August, pp 5–17.

Benington, J. (1976). *Local Government Becomes Big Business* (2nd edn), London, CDP Information and Intelligence Unit.

Benn, C. and J. Fairley (1986). *Challenging the MSC on Jobs, Education and Training*, London, Pluto Press.

Beresford, P. and S. Croft (1993). *Citizen Involvement: A Practical Guide for Change*, London, Methuen.

Berridge, A., SJ. (1993). *ESAP and Education for the Poor*, Gweru, Silveira House/Mambo Press.

Berthoud, R. and Hinton, T. (1989). *Credit Unions in the United Kingdom*, London, Policy Studies Institute.

Biddle, W. and L. Biddle (1965). *The Community Development Process: The Rediscovery of Local Initiative*, New York, Holt, Rinehart and Winston.

Blaustein, A. I. and G. Faux (1972). *The Star-Spangled Hustle: White Power and Black Capitalism*, Garden City NY, Doubleday.

Bobo, K., J. Kendall and S. Max (1996). *Organizing for Social Change: A Manual for Activists in the 1990s* (2nd edn), Santa Ana CA., Seven Locks Press.

Bolger, P. (1977). *The Irish Co-operative Movement: Its History and Development*, Dublin, Institute of Public Administration.

Bolger, S., P. Corrigan, J. Docking and N. Frost (1981). *Towards Socialist Welfare Work*, London, Macmillan.

Booth, D. (1994). Rethinking social development: an overview, in D. Booth (ed.), *Rethinking Social Development: Theory, Research and Practice*, Harlow, Longman, pp. 3–41.

Boyte, H. C. (1984). *Community is Possible*, New York, Harper and Row.

Brabrook, E. W. (1898). *Provident Societies and Industrial Welfare*, London, Blackie and Son.

Brager, G. and Holloway, S. (1978). *Changing Human Service Organizations: Politics and Practice*, New York NY, The Free Press.

Brager, G. and H. Specht (1969). *Community Organizing*, New York, University of Columbia Press.

Braye, S. and D. Preston-Shoot (1995). *Empowering Practice in Social Care*, Buckingham, Open University Press.

Brohman, J. (1996). *Popular Development: Rethinking the Theory and Practice of Development*, Oxford, Blackwell.

Brotherhood, J. and A. Thurley (1998). An assessment of the social economy in the Highlands, *Scottish Journal of Community Work and Development*, Vol. 3, pp. 31–42.

Brown, A. (1994). *Groupwork* (3rd edn), Aldershot, Arena.

Bryant, B. and R. Bryant (1982). *Change and Conflict: A Study of Community Work in Glasgow*, Aberdeen, Aberdeen University Press.

Burghardt, S. (1982). *The Other Side Of Organizing: Resolving the Personal Dilemmas and Political Demands of Daily Practice*, Cambridge MA, Schenkman.

Burns D. (1991). Ladders of Participation, *Going Local*, No. 18, pp. 14–15.

Butcher, H., J. Pearce and I. Cole, with A. Glen (1979). *Community Participation and Poverty: The Final Report of Cumbria CDP*, York, Department of Social Administration and Social Work, University of York.

Butterworth, E., R. Lees and P. Arnold (1981). *The Challenge of Community Work: The Final Report of Batley CDP*, York, University of York.

Byrne, P. (1997). *Social Movements in Britain*, London, Routledge.

Calouste Gulbenkian Foundation (1968). *Community Work and Social Change: A Report on Training*, London, Longman.

Calouste Gulbenkian Foundation (1973). *Current Issues in Community Work: A Study by the Community Work Group*, London, Longman.

Calouste Gulbenkian Foundation. (1981). *Whose Business is Business: A Report*. London, Calouste Gulbenkian Foundation.

Calouste Gulbenkian Foundation. (1982). *Community Business Works: A Report*. London, Calouste Gulbenkian Foundation.

Campbell, B. (1993). *Goliath: Britain's Dangerous Places*, London, Methuen.

Case Con Manifesto (1975), in R. Bailey and M. Brake, *Radical Social Work*, London, Arnold, pp. 144–7.

Castells, M. (1977). *The Urban Question: A Marxist Approach*, London, Edward Arnold.

Castro, J. (1986). Co-Chomunn Bharraidh (Bara Community Co-operative), in J. Nelson et.al. (eds), *Communities in Business: A Report*, London, CEI/Community Initiatives Research Trust, pp. 89–96.

Centre for Contemporary Cultural Studies (1982). *The Empire Strikes Back: Race and Racism in the 1970s*, London, Hutchinson/CCCS University of Birmingham.

Chambers, R. (1983). *Rural Development: Putting the Last First*, Harlow, Longman.

Chambers, R. (1992). Spreading and self-improving: a strategy for scaling up, in M. Edwards and D. Hulme (eds), *Making a Difference: NGOs and Development in a Chnaging World*, London, Earthscan, pp. 40–8.

Chambers, R. (1993). *Challenging the Professions: Frontiers for Rural Development*, London, Intermediate Technology.

Chambers, R. (1997). *Whose Reality Counts? Putting the Last First*, London, Intermediate Technology.

Chambers, R. (1998). Foreword, in I. Guijt and M. K. Shah (eds), *The Myth of Community: Gender Issues in Participatory Development*, London, Intermediate Technology.

Chanan, G. (1992). *Out of the Shadows: Local Community Action and the European Community*, Shankill, IE, Loughlinstown House.

Cheetham, J., W. James, M. Loney, M. Mayor and W. Prescott (eds) (1981). *Social and Community Work in a Multiracial Society*, London, Harper and Row.

Church in Wales Board of Mission (1988a). *Faith in Wales: Part 1: A Challenge to Faith*, Cardiff, Church in Wales.

Church in Wales Board of Mission: Division for Social Responsibility (1988b). *Faith in Wales: Part 2: An Atlas of Disadvantage*, Penarth, Church in Wales.

Church in Wales Board of Mission: Division for Social Responsibility (1988c). *Faith in Wales: Part 3: An Atlas of Advantage*, Penarth, Church in Wales.

Church in Wales Board of Mission: Rural Commission (1992). *The Church in the Welsh Countryside: A Programme for Action by the Church in Wales*, Penarth, Church in Wales.

Clarke, S. (1998). Community Development and Health Professionals, in A. Symonds and A. Kelly (eds), *The Social Construction of Community Care*, London, Macmillan, pp. 125–34.

Clarke, S. (2000). *Social Work as Community Development: A Management Model for Change* (2nd edn), Aldershot, Avebury.

Clarke, S. J. G. (1996). *Bon-y-maen: The Community Development Options*, Swansea, Department of Applied Social Studies, University of Wales Swansea.

Coalfields Task Force (CTF) (1998). *Making a Difference: Empowering Communities to Make Their Own Sustainable New Starts*, London, Department of Environment, Transport and the Regions.

Cockburn, C. (1977). *The Local State: Management of Cities and People*, London, Pluto Press.

Colenutt, B. and A. Cutten (1994). Community empowerment in vogue or in vain?, *Local Economy*, Vol. 9, No. 3, pp. 236–50.

Collins, P. H. (1990). *Black Feminist Thought: Knowledge, Consciousness and the Politics of Empowerment*, New York NY, Routledge.

Colonial Office: Advisory Committee on Education in the Colonies (1943). *Mass Education in African Society*, London, HMSO.

Colonial Office (1958). *Community Development: A Handbook*, London, HMSO.

Community Action (1972–1983), London.

Community Development Project Working Group (1974). The British National Community Development Project, *Community Development Journal*, Vol. 9, No. 3, pp 162–86.

Communities that Care (1997). *Communities that Care: A New Kind of Prevention Programme*, London, Communities that Care.

Conway, E. and J. Green (1996). *The Story of the Scotswood Area Strategy*, Newcastle upon Tyne, Social Welfare Research Unit, University of Northumbria.

Cooper, M. (1981). The Normanton Patch System, in L. Smith and D. Jones (eds), *Deprivation, Participation and Community Action*, London, Routledge and Kegan Paul, pp. 168–80.

Corbridge, S. (1993). Ethics in development studies: the example of debt, in F. J. Schuurman (ed.), *Beyond the Impasse: New Directions in Development Theory*, London, Zed Books, pp. 123–39.

Cornia, G. A. (1987). Adjustment policies 1980–1985: effects on child welfare, in G. A. Cornia, R. Jolly and F. Stewart, *Adjustment with a Human Face: Protecting the Vulnerable and Protecting Growth*, Oxford, Clarendon Press, pp. 48–73.

Corrigan, P. (1975). Community work and political struggle: the possibilities of working on the contradiction, in P. Leonard (ed.), *The Sociology of Community Action*, Keele, Sociological Review Monograph, University of Keele, pp. 5–20.

Corrigan, P. and P. Leonard (1978). *Social Work Practice under Capitalism: A Marxist Approach*, London, Macmillan.

Coulshed, V. and J. Orme (1998). *Social Work Practice: An Introduction*, London, Macmillan.

Cox, D. J. and N. J. Derricourt (1975). The de-professionalisation of community work, in D. Jones and M. Mayo (eds), *Community Work Two*, Routledge and Kegan Paul, London, pp. 75–89.

Craig, G. (1974). How not to encourage independence, in G. Craig, *Community Work Case Studies*, London, Association of Community Workers, pp. 6–9.

Crickley, A (1996). The role of community development: the development of partnerships, in Community Workers' Co-operative, *Partnerships in Action: The Role of Community Development and Partnership in Ireland*, Galway, Community Workers' Co-operative, pp. 19–30.

Croft, S. and P. Beresford (1992). *Citizen Involvement: A Practical Guide for Change*, London, Macmillan.

Cruikshank, J. (1994). The consequences of our actions: a value issue in community development, *Community Development Journal*, Vol. 29, No. 1, pp. 75–89.

Crummy, H. (1992). *Let the People Sing: The Story of Craigmillar*, Newcraighall, Helen Crummy.

Cullingworth, J. B. (chair) (1967). *The Needs of New Communities: A Report on Social Provision in New and Expanding Communities*, London, Ministry of Housing and Welsh Office, HMSO.

Cumella, M. (1983). The changing face of British community work: the Polypill community project in south Wales, *COMM*, Vol. 19, pp. 224–44.

Curno, A., A. Lamming, L. Leach, J. Stiles, V. Ward and T. Ziff (eds) (1982). *Women in Collective Action*, London, Association of Community Workers in the UK.

Dalla Costa, M. and S. James (1972). *The Power of Women and the Subversion of the Community*, Bristol, Falling Wall Press.

Dasgupta, S. (1961). *A Poet and a Plan: Tagore's Experiments in Rural Reform*, Calcutta, Thacker Spink.

Davies, J. (1939). *The Chartist Movement in Monmouthshire*, Newport, Newport Chartist Centenary Committee.

Davies, M. (1985). *The Essential Social Worker: A Guide to Positive Practice*, Aldershot, Wildwood House.

Day, G., E. Morris and P. Knight (1998). *Where do we go from here? A Review of Community Participation Methods*, Aberystwyth, Jigso.

Delgado, G. (1986). *Organizing the Movement: The Roots and Growth of ACORN*, Philadelphia, Temple University Press.

Department of Education and Science (1967). *Children and their Primary Schools* (Chair: Lady Plowden), London, HMSO.

Department of the Environment (1990). *Community Business: Good Practice in Urban Regeneration*, London, HMSO.

Department of the Environment (1992). *City Challenge: Working Partnerships, Implementing Agencies – An Advisory Note*, London, Victor Hauser and Associates/Department of the Environment.

Departments of Health, Social Security, Wales and Scotland (1989). *Caring for People: Community Care in the Next Decade and Beyond*, London, HMSO, Cm 849.

Departments of Health and Social Services – Northern Ireland (1999). Baseline study of community development approaches to health and social well being, by Coopers and Lybrand, in *Mainstreaming Community Development in the Health and Personal Social Services*, Belfast, Community Development Working Group, p. 1 of Report Section.

Dolci, D. (1959). *To Feed the Hungry: Enquiry in Palermo*, London, MacGibbon and Kee.

Dominelli, L. (1990). *Women and Community Action*, London, Venture Press.

Drakeford, M. (1996). Social Movements and their Supporters: The Case of the Kippo and Green Shirt Movement for Social Credit, University of Wales Swansea, unpublished Ph.D. thesis.

Dudley, E. (1993). *Critical Villager: Beyond Community Participation*, London, Routledge.

du Sautoy, P. (1962). *The Organisation of a Community Development Programme*, London, Oxford University Press.

Eade, D. (1997). *Capacity-Building: An Approach to People-Centred Development*, Oxford, Oxfam.

Eade, D. and S. Williams (1995). *The Oxfam Handbook for Development and Relief*, Oxford, Oxfam.

Edwards, M. (1989). The irrelevance of development studies, *Third World Quarterly*, Vol. 11, No. 1, pp. 116–36.

Edwards, M. (1993). How relevant is development studies?, in F. J. Schuurman (ed.), *Beyond the Impasse: New Directions in Development Theory*, London, Zed Books, pp. 77–92.

Edwards, M. and D. Hulme (eds) (1995). *Non-Governmental Organisations – Performance and Accountability: Beyond the Magic Bullet*, London, Earthscan.

Ellis, J. (1989). *Breaking New Ground: Community Development with Asian Communities*, London, Community Projects Foundation/Bedford Square Press.

Etzioni, A. (1993). *The Spirit of Community: The Reinvention of American Society*, New York, Simon Schuster.

Etzioni, A. (1995a). Responsibility, in D. Atkinson (ed.), *Cities of Pride: Rebuilding Community, Refocusing Government*, London, Cassell, pp. 33–6.

Etzioni, A. (1995b). Nation in need of community values, *The Times*, 20 February, p. 9.

Fagan, H. (1979). *Empowerment: Skills for Parish Social Action*, New York, Paulist Press.

Fanon, F. (1967). *The Wretched of the Earth*, London, Penguin.

Fanon, F. (1970). *A Dying Colonialism*, London, Penguin.

Federation of Community Work Training Groups. (1992). *Setting up a Community Work Skills Course*, Sheffield, Federation of Community Work Training Groups.

Feuerstein, M. T. (1986). *Partners in Evaluation: Evaluating Development and Community Programmes with Participants*, New Delhi, Sage.

Fish, J. H. (1973). *Black Power/White Control: The Struggle of the Woodlawn Organization in Chicago*, Princeton NJ, Princeton University Press.

Fisher, R. (1994). *Let the People Decide: Neighbourhood Organizing in America*, New York, Twane.

Fleetwood, M. and J. Lambert (1982). Bringing socialism home: theory and practice for radical community action, in G. Craig, N. Derricourt and M. Loney (eds), *Community Work and the State: Towards a Radical Practice*, London, Routledge and Kegan Paul, pp. 48–58.

Foweraker, J. (1995). *Theorizing Social Movements*, London, Pluto Press.

Fowler, A (1997). *Striking a Balance: A Guide to Enhancing the Effectiveness of Non-Governmental Organisations in International Development*, London, Earthscan.

Francis, D., P. Henderson and D. N. Thomas (1984). *A Survey of Community Workers in the United Kingdom*, London, National Institute of Social Workers.

Frazer, H. (ed.) (1981). *Community Work in a Divided Society*, Belfast, Farset Co-operative Press.

Frazer, H. (ed.) (1990). *Community Work in Ireland: Trends in the 1980s, Options for the 1990s*, Dublin, Combat Poverty Agency, Community Workers' Co-operative and St Patrick's College.

Frazer, H. (1996). The role of community development on local development, in Community Workers' Co-operative, *Partnership in Action: The Role of Community Development and Partnership in Ireland*, Galway, Community Workers' Co-operative, pp. 37–56.

Freeman, J. (1975). *The Tyranny of Structurelessness*, London, Anarchist Workers Association.

Freire, P. (1970). *Cultural Action for Freedom*, London, Penguin.

Freire, P. (1972). *Pedagogy of the Oppressed*, London, Penguin.

Freire, P. (1976). *Education: The Practice of Freedom*, London, Writers' and Readers' Publishing Cooperative.

Friedmann, J. (1992). *Empowerment: The Politics of Alternative Development*, Cambridge MA, Blackwell.

Fryer, P (1984). *Staying Power: The History of Black People in Britain*, London, Pluto Press.

Gallagher, A. (1977). Women and community work, in M. Mayo (ed.), *Women in the Community*, London, Routledge and Kegan Paul, pp. 121–41.

Gandhi, M. K. (1951). *Non-violent Resistance*, New York, Schoken.

Gilroy, P. (1987). *There Ain't No Black in the Union Jack: The Cultural Politics of Race and Nation*, London, Hutchinson.

Gittell, R. and Vidal, A. (1998). *Community Organizing: Building Social Capital as a Development Strategy*, Thousand Oaks CA, Sage.

Goetschius G. W. (1969). *Working with Community Groups*, London, Routledge and Kegan Paul.

Gortz, A. (1977). The reproduction of labour power: the model of consumption, in J. Cowley, A. Kaye, M. Mayo and M. Thompson (eds), *Community or Class Struggle?*, London, Stage 1, pp. 22–39.

Goulet, D. (1995). *Development Ethics: A Guide to Theory and Practice*, London, Zed Books.

Gramsci, A. (trans. Q. Hoare and G. Nowell Smith) (1971). *Antonio Gramsci: Selections from the Prison Notebooks*, London, Lawrence and Wishart.

Green, A. and A. Mattias (1997). *Non-Governmental Organisations and Health in Developing Countries*, London, Macmillan.

Green, J. and A. Chapman (1992). The British Community Development Projects: lessons for today, *Community Development Journal*, Vol. 27, No. 3, pp. 242–59.

Griffiths, Sir R. (1988). *Community Care: Agenda for Action*, London, HMSO.

Groundwork Foundation (1993). *Marks and Spencer Groundwork Youth Environmnet Project Phase II – South Wales and South East England*, Birmingham, Groundwork Foundation.

Groundwork Merthyr and Cynon (1995). *New Gurnos Environmental Improvements SDS Bid 1994/5*, Merthyr Tydfil, Groundwork Foundation.

Groundwork Merthyr and Cynon (1996). *New Gurnos Environmental Strategy*, Merthyr Tydfil, Groundwork Foundation.

Groundwork Merthyr and Cynon (1996). *Ten-year Review and Annual Report*, Merthyr Tydfil, Groundwork Foundation.

Guijt, I. and M. K. Shah (1998). General introduction: waking up to power, process and conflict, in I. Guijt and M. K. Shah, *The Myth of Community: Gender Issues in Participatory Development*, London, Intermediate Technology.

Hambleton, R. and P. Hoggett (1988). Beyond bureaucratic paternalism, in P. Hoggett and R. Hambleton (eds), *Decentralisation of Democracy: Localising Public Services*, Bristol, School for Advanced Urban Studies, pp. 9–28.

Harper, M. (1998). *Profit for the Poor: Cases in Micro-Finance*, London, Intermediate Technology.

Hart, R. (1992). *Children's Participation: From Tokenism to Citizenship*, New York, , UNICEF.

Hasler, J. (1990). Community organising – an offer you might refuse, in P. Ballard (ed.), *Issues in Church-related Community Work*, Cardiff, Collegiate Faculty of Theology, University of Wales Cardiff, pp. 99–102.

Hayes, L. (1990). *Working for Change: A Study of Three Women's Community Projects*, Dublin, Combat Poverty Agency.

Hayton, K. (1984). *What Business in the Port: The Development of a Community Company in Port Glasgow*, Glasgow, Strathclyde Community Business Ltd.

Health Promotion Wales (1996). *A Community Approach to Primary Care*, Cardiff, Health Promotion Wales.

Henderson, P. and H. Salmon (1995). *Community Organizing: The UK Context*, London, Community Development Foundation.

Henderson, P. and D. N. Thomas (1987). *Skills in Neighbourhood Work* (2nd edn), London, Allen and Unwin.

Higgins, J., N. Deakin, J. Edwards and M. Wicks (1983). *Government and Urban Policy: Inside the Policy-making Process*, Oxford, Basil Blackwell.

Highlands and Islands Development Board (1982). *The Highlands and Islands: A Contemporary Account*, Inverness, Highlands and Islands Development Board.

Holcombe, S. (1995). *Managing to Empower: The Grameen Bank's Experience in Poverty Alleviation*, Dhaka, University Press Ltd.

Holman, B. (1998). *Faith in the Poor*, Oxford, Lion.

Holman, B. (1997). *Fare Dealing: Neighbourhood Involvement in a Housing Scheme*, London, Community Development Foundation Publications.

Home Office (1999). *Report of the Policy Action Team on Community Self-help*, London, Active Community Unit.

Hope, A. and S. Timmel (with C. Hodze) (1984). *Training for Transformation: A Handbook for Community Workers*, Gweru Zimbabwe, Mambo Press.

Hughes, J. and P. Carmichael (1998). Building partnerships in urban regeneration: a case study from Belfast, *Community Development Journal*, Vol. 33, No. 3, pp. 205–25.

Hulme, D. and M. Edwards (eds) (1997). *NGOs, States and Donors: Too Close for Comfort?*, London, Macmillan.

Hurley, D. (1990). *Income Generation Schemes for the Urban Poor*, Oxford, Oxfam.

Irish League of Credit Unions (2000). *The Irish League of Credit Unions*, Dublin, Irish League of Credit Unions.

Jack, R. (1995). Empowerment in community care, in R. Jack (ed.), *Empowerment in Community Care*, London, Chapman and Hall, pp. 11–42.

Jameson, N. (1988). *Organising for a Change*, Birmingham, Citizen Organising Foundation.

Jones, C. (1983). *State Social Work and the Working Class*, London, Macmillan.

Joseph Rowntree Foundation (1998). *Findings 0108: Inclusive Strategies for Race and Gender in Urban Regeneration*, York, Joseph Rowntree Foundation.

Kelleher, P. and M. Whelan (1988). *Dublin Communities in Action: A Study of Six Projects*, Dublin, Community Action Network/Combat Poverty Agency.

Kelly, A. and S. Sewell (1988). *With Head, Heart and Hand: Dimensions of Community Building*, Brisbane, Boolarong Publications.

Kemmis, S. and R. McTaggart (eds) (1988). *The Action Research Planner*, Victoria, Deakin University Press.

Kennedy, R. S. S. (chair) (1980). *Final Report: Pilot Schemes to Combat Poverty in Ireland 1974–1980*, Dublin, National Committee on Pilot Schemes to Combat Poverty.

Key, M., P. Hudson and J. Armstrong (1976). *Evaluation Theory and Community Work by YVFF Workers in Stoke-on-Trent*, London, Young Volunteer Force.

Kindred, M. (1991). *Once upon a Group* (revised edn), Nottingham, Southwell Diocesan Education Committee.

Labonté, R. (1999). *Developing Community Health in Wales: A Community Development Approach to Health Promotion*, Cardiff, Health Promotion Wales.

Landry, C., D. Morley, R. Southwood and P. Wright (1985). *What a Way to Run a Railroad: An Analysis of Radical Failure*, London, Comedia Publishing Group.

Lapping, A. (ed.) (1970). *Community Action*, London, Fabian Society, Fabian Tract 400.

LEAP (1984). *The Last LEAP Year: Final Report of the Local Enterprise Project*, Glasgow, Strathclyde Community Business Ltd.

Leaper, R. A. B. (1968). *Community Work*, London, National Council of Social Service.

Leaper, R. A. B. (1971). *Community Work* (revised edn), London, National Council of Social Service.

Lees, R. and G. Smith (eds) (1975). *Action Research in Community Development*, London, Routledge and Kegan Paul.

Lees, R. and M. Mayo (1984). *Community Action for Change*, London, Routledge and Kegan Paul.

Lennock, J. (1994). *Paying for Health: Poverty and Structural Adjustment in Zimbabwe*, Oxford, Oxfam.

Leonard, P. (1975). Towards a paradigm for radical practice, in R. Bailey and M. Brake (eds), *Radical Social Work*, London, Edward Arnold, pp. 46–61.

Loney, M. (1983). *Community Against Government: The British Community Development Project, 1968–1978*, London, Heinemann.

London Edinburgh Weekend Return Group (1979). *In and Against the State*, London, Pluto Press.

Longworth, N. and W. Davies (1996). *Lifelong Learning: New Visions, New Implications, New Roles for People, Organisations, Nations and Communities in the Twenty-first Century*, London, Kogan Page.

Lopes, C. (1994). *Enough is Enough! For an Alternative Diagnosis of the African Crisis*, Uppsala, Nordiska Afrikainstitutet.

Lovett, T., N. Gillespie and D. Gunn (1995). *Community Development, Education and Community Relations*, Belfast, University of Ulster, Community Research and Development Centre.

Lucia-Hoagland, S. and J. Penelope (eds) (1988). *For Lesbians Only: A Separatist Anthology*, London, Onlywomen Press Ltd.

McArthur, A. (1984). *Local Economic Regeneration: Community Level Effects in Clydeside*, Glasgow, Centre for Urban and Regional Research.

McArthur, A. (1995). The active involvement of local residents in strategic community partnerships, *Policy and Politics*, Vol. 23, No. 1, pp. 61–71.

MacGarry, B., SJ. (1993). *Growth without Equity?*, Gweru, Silveira House/Mambo Press.

MacInnes, J. (1987). *Thatcherism at Work: Industrial Relations and Economic Change*, Milton Keynes, Open University Press.

Mackintosh, M. and H. Wainwright (eds) (1987). *A Taste of Power: The Politics of Local Economics*, London, Verso.

McMichael, P., B. Lynch and D. Wight (1988). *Building Bridges into Work: The Role of the Community Worker*, Edinburgh, Moray House College.

Mama, A. (1989). *The Hidden Struggle: Statutory and Voluntary Responses to Violence against Black Women in the Home*, London, London Race and Housing Research Unit.

Marris, P. and M. Rein (1967). *Dilemmas of Social Reform: Poverty and Community Action in the United States*, London, Routledge and Kegan Paul.

May, J. (1994). *Reference Wales*, Cardiff, University of Wales Press.

Mayo, M. (1975). Community development: a radical alternative?, in R. Bailey and M. Brake (eds), *Radical Social Work*, London, Edward Arnold, pp. 129–43.

Mayo, M. (ed.) (1977). *Women in the Community*, London, Routledge and Kegan Paul.

Mayo, M. (1979). Radical politics and community action, in M. Loney and M. Allen (eds), *The Crisis of the Inner City*, London, Macmillan, pp. 139–48.

Mayo, M. (1994). *Communities and Caring*, London, Macmillan.

Midgley, J. (1981). *Professional Imperialism: Social Work in the Third World*, London, Heinemann.

Midgley, J. (1986). Community participation: history, concepts and controversies, in J. Midgley, A. Hall, M. Hardiman and D. Narine (eds), *Community Participation, Social Development and the State*, London, Methuen, pp. 13–44.

Midgley, J. (1995). *Social Development: The Developmental Perspective in Social Welfare*, London, Sage.

Midgley, J. (1997). *Social Welfare in a Global Context*, Thousand Oaks CA, Sage.

Mikkelsen, B. (1995). *Methods for Development Work and Research: A Guide for Practitioners*, New Delhi, Sage.

Miller, J. (1982). *Situation Vacant: The Social Consequences of Unemployment in a Welsh Town*, London, Community Projects Foundation.

Miller, M. (1987). Organizing: a map for explorers, *Christianity in Crisis*, Vol. 47, No. 1, pp. 3–9.

Mondros, J. B. and S. M. Wilson (1994). *Organizing for Power and Empowerment*, New York, Columbia University Press.

Morgan, Derek Llwyd (trans. Dyfnallt Morgan) (1988). *The Great Awakening in Wales*, London, Epworth Press.

Moser, C. O. N. (1993). *Gender Planning and Development: Theory, Practice and Training*, London, Routledge.

Murray, C. (1990). *The Emerging British Underclass*, IEA Health and Welfare Unit, London.

Murray, C. (1994). *Underclass: The Crisis Deepens*, IEA Health and Welfare Unit/Sunday Times, London.

Naples, N. A. (ed.) (1998a). *Community Activism and Feminist Politics*, New York NY, Routledge.

Naples, N. A. (1998b). *Grassroots Warriors: Activist Mothering, Community Work and the War on Poverty*, London, Routledge.

National Assembly for Wales/Wales Council for Voluntary Action (2000). *Compact between the Government and the Voluntary Sector in Wales: Community Development*, Cardiff, Urban and Rural Division, National Assembly for Wales.

National Assembly for Wales (1999). *Developing Local Health Alliances*, Cardiff, National Assembly for Wales.

National Assembly for Wales (2000a). *Communities First: Regenerating Our Most Disadvantaged Communities – A Consultation Paper*, Cardiff, National Assembly for Wales, April.

National Assembly for Wales (2000b). *Objective One: Single Programming Document for West Wales and the Valleys*, Cardiff, National Assembly for Wales.

National Assembly for Wales (2000c). *Better Wales*, Cardiff, National Assembly for Wales.

National Assembly for Wales (2000d). *The Health Potential of the Objective One Programme for West Wales and the Valleys*, Cardiff National Assembly for Wales.

National Assembly for Wales (2000e). *Communities First: The Way Forward – Second Consultation Paper*, Cardiff, National Assembly for Wales, December.

Naylor, B. (1986). *Quakers in the Rhondda, 1926–1986*, Chepstow, Maes-yr-haf Educational Trust.

Nelson, N. and S. Wright (1995). *Power and Participatory Development: Theory and Practice*, London, Intermediate Technology.

Nevin, B. and P. Shiner (1995). The left, urban policy and community empowerment, *Local Economy*, Vol. 10., No. 3, pp. 204–17.

Oakley, P. et al. (1991). *Projects with People: The Practice of Participation in Rural Development*, Geneva, International Labour Organization.

Ocean Area Recreation Union (1931). *After Ten Years: A Report of Miners' Welfare Work in the South Wales Coalfield*, Treorchy, OARU Ocean Collieries.

O'Cearbhaill, D. and M. S. O'Cinneide (1986). Community development in the west of Ireland: a case study of the Kilalla area, *Community Development Journal*, Vol. 21, pp. 195–207.

O'Donohue, K. (1990). Rural development and community work, in H. Frazer (ed.), *Community Work in Ireland: Trends in the 1980s, Options for the 1990s*, Dublin, Combat Poverty Agency et al., pp. 133–42.

Ohri, A., D. Manning and P. Curno (eds) (1982). *Community Work and Racism*, London, Routledge and Kegan Paul.

O'Malley, J. (1977). *The Politics of Community Action: A Decade of Struggle in Notting Hill*, Nottingham, Spokesman.

Oppenheim, C. (1997). The growth of poverty and inequality, in A. Walker and C. Walker, *Britain Divided: The Growth of Social Exclusion in the 1980s and 1990s*, London, Child Poverty Action Group, pp. 17–31.

Overseas Development Administration (1995). *A Guide to Social Analysis for Projects in Developing Countries*, London, HMSO.

Patton, M. Q. (1997). *Utilization-focused Evaluation: The New Century Text* (3rd edn), Thousand Oaks CA, Sage.

Penn, R. and J. Alden (1977). *Upper Afan CDP Final Report to Sponsors: Joint Report by Action Team and Research Team Directors*, Cardiff, University of Wales, Institute of Science and Technology.

Perlman, R. and A. Gurin (1972). *Community Organization and Social Planning*, New York, John Wiley and Son/Council for Social Work Education.

Pinder, C. (1995). *Community Start Up: How To Start a Community Group and Keep It Going*, Cambridge, National Extension College/ Community Matters.

Pitt, J., and M. Keane (1984). *Community Organising? You've Never Really Tried It!: The Challenge to Britain from the USA*, Birmingham, J. & P. Consultancy.

Popple, K. (1995). *Analysing Community Work: Its Theory and Practice*, Buckingham, Open University Press.

Popplestone, G. (1971). The ideology of professional community workers, *British Journal of Social Work*, Vol. 1, No. 1, pp. 85–104.

Porter, D., B. Allen and G. Thompson (1991). *Development in Practice: Paved with Good Intentions*, London, Routledge.

Power, A. and R. Tunstall (1995). *Swimming Against the Tide:*

Polarisation or Progress on Twenty Unpopular Housing Estates, York, Joseph Rowntree Foundation.

Pretty, J. N., I. Guijt, J. Thompson and I. Scoones (1995). *Participatory Learning and Action: A Trainer's Guide*, London, International Institute for Environment and Development.

Rahman, Md. A. (1993). *People's Self-Development: Perspectives on Participatory Action Research*, London, Zed Books.

Rahnema, M. (1993). Participation, in W. Sachs (ed.), *The Development Dictionary: A Guide to Knowledge and Power*, Johannesburg, University of the Witwatersrand Press, pp. 116–31.

Rhondda Cynon Taff Borough Council (1999). *Job Description: Community Development Co-ordinator*, Tonypandy, Chief Executive's Department, Rhondda Cynon Taff Borough Council.

Rhondda Cynon Taff Borough County Council (2001). *Credit Union Training Pack*, Pontypridd, Rhondda Cynon Taff County Council.

Riley, N. (1967). Muintir Na Tire (Ireland), *Community Development Journal*, Vol. 7, pp. 22–7.

Ritzer, G. (2000). *The McDonaldization of Society* (New Century edn), Thousand Oaks CA, Pine Forge Press.

Rogers, A. (1992). *Adults Learning for Development*, London, Cassell.

Rogers, M. B. (1990). *Cold Anger: A Story of Faith and Power Politics*, Denton TX, University of North Texas Press.

Rondinelli, D. A. (1993). *Development Projects as Policy Experiments: An Adaptive Approach to Development Administration* (2nd edn), London, Routledge.

Ross, M. G. (1955). *Community Organization: Theory and Principles*, New York, Harper and Brothers.

Rostow, W. W. (1964). *The Stages of Economic Growth: A Non-Communist Manifesto*, Cambridge, Cambridge University Press.

Rothman, J. (1995). Approaches to community intervention, in J. Rothman, J. Erlich and J. E. Tropman (1995), *Strategies of Community Intervention* (3rd edn), Itasca IL, F. E. Peacock, pp. 26–63.

Rowlands, J. (1997). *Questioning Empowerment: Working with Women in Honduras*, Oxford, Oxfam.

Roy, R. (1993). Swadhyaha: values and message, in P. Wignaraja (ed.), *New Social Movements in the South*, London, Zed Books, pp. 183–94.

Rubin, F. (1995). *A Basic Guide to Evaluation for Development Workers*, Oxford, Oxfam.

Rubin, H. J. and I. S. Rubin (1992). *Community Organizing and Development* (2nd edn), Boston, Allyn and Bacon.

Sacks, J. (1995). *Faith in the Future*, London, Darton, Longman and Todd.

Schuurman, F. J. (1993). Introduction: development theory in the 1990s, in F. J. Schuurman (ed.), *Beyond the Impasse: New Directions in Development Theory*, London, Zed Books, pp.1–48.

Seabrook, J. (1984). *The Idea of Neighbourhood: What Local Politics Should Be About*, London, Pluto.

Secretary of State for Wales (1998). *Compact between the Government and the Voluntary Sector in Wales*, Cardiff, Welsh Office, Cm 4107.

Seebohm, F. (chair) (1968). *Report of the Committee on Local Authority and Allied Personal Social Services*, London, Home Department et al., HMSO.

Segal, L. (1979). A local experience, in S. Rowbotham, L. Segal and H. Wainwright (eds), *Beyond the Fragments: Feminism and the Making of Socialism*, London, Merlin Press, pp. 157–210.

Selby, B. (1985). The story of Community House, in W. Godfrey (ed.), *Down to Earth: Stories of Church-based Community Work*, London, British Council of Churches, pp. 23–34.

Skeffington, A. M. (chair of working group) (1969). *People and Planning*, London, HMSO.

Skinner, S. (1997). *Building Community Strengths: A Resource Book on Capacity-building*, London, Community Development Foundation.

Smale, G., G. Tuson, M. Cooper, M. Wardle and D. Crosbie (1988). *Community Social Work: A Paradigm for Change*, London, National Institute for Social Work.

Smith, J. (1978). Hard lines and soft options: a criticism of some Left attitudes to community work, in P. Curno (ed.), *Political Issues and Community Work*, London, Routledge and Kegan Paul, pp. 17–35.

Smith, J. (1981). Possibilities for a socialist community work practice, in P. Henderson and D. N. Thomas (eds), *Readings in Community Work*, London, George Allen and Unwin, pp. 55–60.

Smith, T. (1980). Community work: profession or social movement?, in P. Henderson, D. Jones and D. N. Thomas (eds), *The Boundaries of Change in Community Work*, London, National Institute for Social Work/George Allen and Unwin, pp. 212–27.

Social Exclusion Unit (1998). *Bringing Britain Together: A National Strategy for Neighbourhood Renewal*, London, Stationery Office.

Solanas, V. (1983). *The SCUM Manifesto*, London, Matriarchy Study Group.

Southall Black Sisters (1990). *Against the Grain: A Celebration of Survival and Struggle, 1979–1989*, Southall, Southall Black Sisters Collective.

South Wales Tenants' Association (1982). Coming alive hurts, in A. Curno et al. (eds), *Women in Collective Action*, London, Association of Community Workers.

Specht, H. (1975). *Community Development in the UK: An Assessment and Recommendation for Change*, London, Association of Community Workers.

Specht, H. (1976). *The Community Development Project: National and Local Strategies for Improving the Delivery of Services*, London, National Institute for Social Work.

Standing Conference for Community Development (SCCD) (1995). New challenges in community development, *SCCD News*, Sheffield, Vol. 12, p. 1.

Stayton, R. A. (1986). *Back of the Yards: The Making of a Local Democracy*, Chicago, University of Chicago Press.

Stevenson, O. and P. Parsloe (1993). *Community Care and Empowerment*, York, Joseph Rowntree Foundation.

Stewart, M. and M. Taylor (1995). *Empowerment and Estate Regeneration: A Critical Review*, Bristol, Polity/University of Bristol.

Stokes, R. R. (1955). Local government in the Republic of Ireland, *Journal of African Administration*, Vol. 7, pp. 27–32.

Swain, J., V. Finkelstein, S. French and M. Oliver (eds) (1993). *Disabling Barriers – Enabling Environments*, London, Sage.

Swedner, H. (1982). A white island in a black sea, in H. Swedner (ed.), *Human Welfare and Action Research in Urban Settings*, Stockholm, Delegation for Social Research/Swedish Council for Building Research. pp. 7–41.

Taoiseach, Office of the (2000). *Programme for Prosperity and Fairness*, Dublin, Stationery Office.

Taylor, M. (1980). *Street Level: Two Resource Centres and Their Users*, London, Community Projects Foundation.

Taylor, M. (1983). *Resource Centres for Community Groups*, London, Community Projects Foundation.

Thomas, A. (1999). *The Cynon Valley Project: Investing in the Future*, The Hague, Bernard van Leer Foundation.

Thomas, A. (2000). What makes good development management?, in T. Wallace (ed.), *Development and Management: Selected Essays from Development in Practice*, Oxford, Oxfam/Open University. pp. 40–52.

Thomas, D. N. (1983). *The Making of Community Work*, London, George Allen and Unwin.

Thomas, D. N. (1995a). *Helping Communities to Better Health: The Community Development Approach*, Cardiff, Health Promotion Wales.

Thomas, D. N. (1995b). *Community Development at Work: A Case of Obscurity in Accomplishment*, London, Community Development Foundation.

Thomas, D. N. (1996). *Uses and Abuses in Community Development: Essays from the Work of the Community Development Foundation*, London, Community Development Foundation.

Tobin, P. (1990). Women in community work, in H. Frazer (ed.), *Community Work in Ireland: Trends in the 1980s, Options for the 1990s*, Dublin, Combat Poverty Agency et. al., pp. 235–47.

Todd, H. (ed.) (1996). *Cloning the Grameen Bank: Replicating a Poverty Reduction Model in India, Nepal and Vietnam*, London, Intermediate Technology.

Topping, P. and G. Smith (1977). *Government against Poverty? Liverpool Community Development Project, 1970–1975*, Oxford, Social Evaluation Unit.

Toye, J. (1993). *Dilemmas of Development: Reflections on the Counter-revolution in Development Economics* (2nd edn), Oxford, Basil Blackwell.

Trotman, C. and S. Morris (1996). *Communities in Transition: The Role of Continuing Education*, Swansea, University of Wales Swansea, Department of Adult and Continuing Education.

United Kingdom Central Council for Nursing, Midwifery and Health Visiting (UKCC) (1998). *Standards for Specialist Education and Practice*, London, UKCC.

United Nations: Bureau of Social Affairs (1955). *Social Progress through Community Development*, New York, UN Bureau of Social Affairs.

UN Secretary-General (1961). *Community Development in Urban Areas*, New York, UN Department of Economic and Social Affairs.

Vincent, K. and T. Davison (eds) (1984). *Unemployment Strategies: A Search for a New Way Forward*, Edinburgh, AEGIS.

Walsh, J., S. Craig and D. McCaffety (1998). *Local Partnerships for Social Inclusion?*, Dublin, Oak Tree Press.

WEA (undated). Workers' Education Association Centre for Unemployed, Application for grant aid, Torfaen, WEA.

Wearmouth, R. F. (1945). *Methodism and the Common People in the Eighteenth Century*, London, Epworth Press.

Welsh Office (1998a). *Better Health, Better Wales*, London, The Stationery Office.

Welsh Office (1998b). *Circular 24/98: People in Communities: A Programme To Tackle Social Exclusion in Wales*, London, Stationery Office.

Wilson, A. (1978). *Finding a Voice: Asian Women in Britain*, London, Virago.

Wilson, E. (1980). Feminism and social work, in M. Brake and R. Bailey (eds), *Radical Social Work and Practice*, London, Edward Arnold, pp. 26–42.

Wolfe, M. (1996). *Elusive Development*, London, Zed Books.

Wooley, T. (1970). 'The Politics of Community Action' (unpublished version), Motherwell, Scotland.

Younghusband, E. L. (1959). *Report of the Working Party on Social Workers in Local Authority Health and Welfare Services*, London, HMSO.

Zald, M. N. (1975). Organizations as politics: an analysis of community organization agencies, in R. M. Kramer and H. Sprecht (eds), *Readings in Community Organizations* (2nd edn), Englewood Cliffs NJ, Prentice Hall, pp. 87–96.

Index